OCR
A LEVEL

D0416513

1

ECONOMICS
FOR A LEVEL YEAR 1 AND AS

Peter Smith

**HODDER
EDUCATION**
AN HACHETTE UK COMPANY

Orders
Bookpoint Ltd, 130 Milton Park, Abingdon, Oxfordshire OX14 4SB
tel: 01235 827827
fax: 01235 400401
e-mail: education@bookpoint.co.uk
Lines are open 9.00 a.m.–5.00 p.m., Monday to Saturday, with a 24-hour message
answering service. You can also order through the Hodder Education website:
www.hoddereducation.co.uk

ISBN 978-1-4718-2989-5

Hodder Education,
Carmelite House,
50 Victoria Embankment,
London EC4Y 0DZ

Impression number	8	7	6	5
Year	2020	2019	2018	2017

The publishers would like to thank the following for permission to reproduce photographs:

Cover Oleksiy Mark/Fotolia; **Section 1** Images/Alamy; **Section 2** Gavin Hellier/Alamy;
p5 Fototrm12/Fotolia; **p10** DPA Picture Alliance/Alamy; **p15** Renate W/Fotolia; **p19** Jochen
Tack/Alamy; **p22** Ian M Butterfield (Concepts)/Alamy; **p25** PhotoEdit/Alamy; **p28** KC
Hunter/Alamy; **p33** Glowonconcept/Fotolia; **p37** Gyula Gyukli/Fotolia; **p40** Costin79/
Fotolia; **p44** Ingram; **p47** Ullsteinbild/TopFoto; **p48** Antje Lindert-Rottke/Fotolia;
p52 Anjelagr/Fotolia; **p56** Steve Vidler/Alamy; **p59** British Retail Photography/Alamy;
p68 Galina Barskaya/Fotolia; **p72** Danicek/Fotolia; **p79** Sean Gladwell/Fotolia; **p85** Dmitry
Naumov/Fotolia; **p89** Riccardo Arata/Fotolia; **p95** BE&W Agencja Fotograficzna Sp. z o.o./
Alamy; **p97** David Pearson/Alamy; **p101** JEP News/Alamy; **p105** Pressmaster/Fotolia;
p107 Nabok Volodymyr/Fotolia; **p122** 06photo/Fotolia; **p129** Desmond Kwande/Stringer;
p134 Geoffrey Robinson/Alamy; **p136** Kevin Britland/Alamy; **p142** RAM/Fotolia;
p145 NLPhotos/Fotolia; **p152** ImageBroker/Alamy; **p158** TopFoto; **p161** Justin Kase
Zninez/Alamy; **p167** Keith Morris/Alamy; **p173** LianeM/Fotolia; **p181** TopFoto; **p184**
AFP/Pool; **p187** JY Cessay/Fotolia; **p195** Michael Langley/Fotolia; **p199** Artwell/Fotolia;
p201 Konstantinos Moraiti/Fotolia; **p215** Hulton Archive/Stringer; **p220** Xinhua/Alamy;
p223 Fotolia

Typeset by Integra Software Services Pvt., Pondicherry, India.
Printed in Dubai.

Hachette UK's policy is to use papers that are natural, renewable and recyclable products
and made from wood grown in sustainable forests. The logging and manufacturing
processes are expected to conform to the environmental regulations of the country of origin.

Get the most from this book

This textbook provides an introduction to economics. It has been tailored explicitly to cover the content of the OCR specification for the AS qualification and for the first year of the A Level course. The book is divided into sections, each covering one of the components that make up the OCR programme of study.

The text provides the foundation for studying OCR Economics, but you will no doubt wish to keep up to date by referring to additional topical sources of information about economic events. This can be done by reading the serious newspapers, visiting key sites on the internet, and reading such magazines as *Economic Review*.

Special features

Learning objectives
A statement of the intended learning objectives for each chapter.

Key terms
Clear, concise definitions of essential key terms where they first appear and a list at the end of each section.

Study tips
Short pieces of advice to help you present your ideas effectively and avoid potential pitfalls.

Extension material
Extension points to stretch your understanding.

Summaries
Bulleted summaries of each topic that can be used as a revision tool.

Case studies
Case studies to show economic concepts applied to real-world situations.

Exercises and questions
Exercises to provide active engagement with economic analysis and practice questions at the end of each section to check your knowledge and understanding.

Quantitative skills
Worked examples of quantitative skills that you will need to develop.

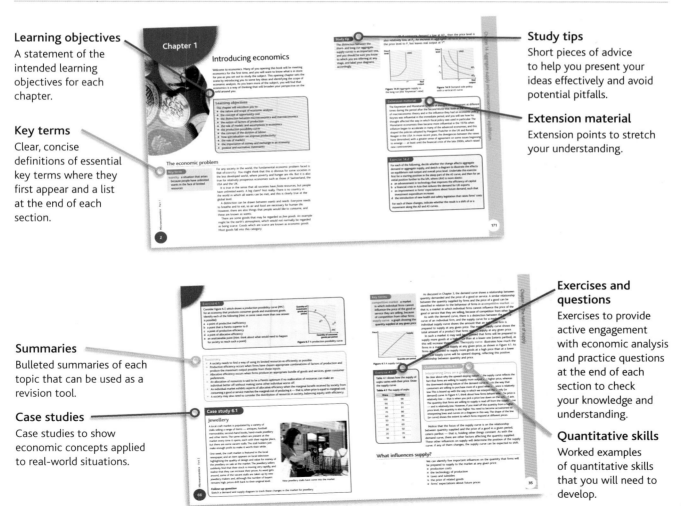

Contents

Section 2 Macroeconomics

Introduction

Prior learning, knowledge and progression

Most students who choose to study AS or A Level Economics are meeting economics for the first time, and no prior learning or knowledge of economics is required. The study of economics complements a range of other AS and A Level subjects such as history, geography, business, mathematics and the sciences, and the way of thinking that you will develop as you study economics will help in interpreting issues that you will meet in many of these subjects. Studying economics can provide important employability skills and is a good preparation for those wishing to progress to higher education. If you intend to study economics at university, you may wish to consider studying mathematics as one of your other AS or A Level subjects.

Find out more about the OCR Economics specifications, or other related qualifications, at www.ocr.org.uk.

Assessment objectives

In common with other economics specifications, OCR Economics entails four assessment objectives. Candidates will thus be expected to:
- demonstrate knowledge of terms/concepts and theories/models to show an understanding of the behaviour of economic agents and how they are affected by and respond to economic issues
- apply knowledge and understanding to various economic contexts to show how economic agents are affected by and respond to economic issues
- analyse issues within economics, showing an understanding of their impact on economic agents
- evaluate economic arguments and use qualitative and quantitative evidence to support informed judgements relating to economic issues.

In the overall assessment of the AS course, a greater weighting is given to the first two objectives. In the A Level course, all four objectives have equal weighting. You will need to develop competence in certain quantitative skills that are relevant to economics, and the assessment of these skills will contribute to a minimum of 15% of the overall AS marks and 20% of the A Level marks.

(See the OCR AS and A Level GCE in Economics specifications at www.ocr.org.uk. Annex 1 of the specifications provides more detail about the quantitative skills expected.)

AS

The AS in Economics is assessed by two examinations, one in microeconomics and one in macroeconomics. Each is a written paper lasting an hour and a half. Each of the question papers contains a combination of multiple-choice questions, a data-response section and an essay (an extended writing question).

A Level

The A Level assessment is based on three examinations at the end of the 2-year course, one in microeconomics, one in macroeconomics and one on themes in economics. Each is a written paper lasting 2 hours. The question papers contain a combination of multiple-choice questions, a data-response section and an essay (an extended writing question). Further details are again provided on the OCR website.

Economics in this book

Economics is different from some other subjects in that relatively few students will have studied it before embarking on the AS or A Level course. The text thus begins from the beginning, and provides a thorough foundation in the subject and its applications. By studying this book, you should develop an awareness of the economist's approach to issues and problems, and the economist's way of thinking about the world.

The study of economics also requires a familiarity with recent economic events in the UK and elsewhere, and candidates will be expected to show familiarity with 'recent historical data' — broadly defined as the last 7 to 10 years. The following websites will help you to keep up to date with recent trends and events:

- Recent and historical data about the UK economy can be found at the website of the Office for National Statistics (ONS) at: www.ons.gov.uk
- Also helpful is the site of HM Treasury at: www.gov.uk/government/ organisations/hm-treasury Especially useful is the Treasury's *Pocket databank*, which is updated weekly, providing major economic indicators and series for both domestic and international economies: www.gov.uk/government/statistics/weekly-economic-indicators
- The Bank of England site is well worth a visit, especially the *Inflation Report* and the Minutes of the Monetary Policy Committee: www.bankofengland.co.uk
- The Institute for Fiscal Studies offers an independent view of a range of economic topics: www.ifs.org.uk

For information about other countries, visit the following:

- www.oecd.org/home
- http://europa.eu.int
- www.worldbank.org
- www.undp.org

How to study economics

There are two crucial aspects of studying economics. The first stage is to study the theory, which helps us to explain economic behaviour. However, in studying AS or A Level Economics it is equally important to be able to apply the theories and concepts that you meet, and to see just how these relate to the real world.

If you are to become competent at this, it is vital that you get plenty of practice. In part, this means carrying out the exercises that you will find in this text. However, it also means thinking about how economics helps us to explain news items and data that appear in the newspapers and on the television. Make sure that you practise as much as you can.

In economics, it is also important to be able to produce examples of economic phenomena. In reading this text, you will find some examples that help to illustrate ideas and concepts. Do not rely solely on the examples provided here, but look around the world to find your own examples, and keep a note of these ready for use in essays and exams. This will help to convince the examiners that you have understood economics. It will also help you to understand the theories.

Enjoy economics

Most important of all, I hope you will enjoy your study of economics. I have always been fascinated by the subject, and hope that you will capture something of the excitement and challenge of learning about how markets and the economy operate. I also wish you every success with your studies.

Acknowledgements

I would like to express my deep gratitude to Mark Russell, whose thorough reading of the book's precursor and insightful and helpful comments were invaluable in improving the scope and focus of this book. I am also grateful to those who have commented on the previous editions; their remarks and suggestions have enabled improvements in the content and style of this new edition. I would also like to thank the team at Hodder Education, especially Naomi Holdstock and Rachel Furse, for their efficiency in production of this book, and for their support and encouragement.

Many of the data series shown in figures in this book were drawn from the data obtained from the National Statistics website: www.ons.gov.uk and contain public sector information licensed under the Open Government Licence v3.0.

Other data were from various sources, including OECD, World Bank, United Nations Development Programme and other sources as specified.

While every effort has been made to trace the owners of copyright material, I would like to apologise to any copyright holders whose rights may have unwittingly been infringed.

Peter Smith

MICROECONOMICS

Part 1
Scarcity and choice

Introducing economics

Welcome to economics. Many of you opening this book will be meeting economics for the first time, and you will want to know what is in store for you as you set out to study the subject. This opening chapter sets the scene by introducing you to some key ideas and identifying the scope of economic analysis. As you learn more of the subject, you will find that economics is a way of thinking that will broaden your perspective on the world around you.

Learning objectives

This chapter will introduce you to:
- the nature and scope of economic analysis
- the concept of opportunity cost
- the distinction between microeconomics and macroeconomics
- the notion of factors of production
- the role of models and assumptions in economics
- the production possibility curve
- the concept of the division of labour
- how specialisation can improve productivity
- the role of markets
- the importance of money and exchange in an economy
- positive and normative statements

The economic problem

Key term

scarcity a situation that arises because people have unlimited wants in the face of limited resources

For any society in the world, the fundamental economic problem faced is that of **scarcity**. You might think that this is obvious for some societies in the less developed world, where poverty and hunger are rife. But it is also true for relatively prosperous economies such as those of Switzerland, the USA and the UK.

It is true in the sense that all societies have *finite resources*, but people have *unlimited wants*. A big claim? Not really. There is no country in the world in which all wants can be met, and this is clearly true at the global level.

A distinction can be drawn between *wants* and *needs*. Everyone needs to breathe and to eat, so air and food are necessary for human life. However, there are also things that people would like to consume, and these are known as wants.

There are some goods that may be regarded as *free goods*. An example might be the earth's atmosphere, which would not normally be regarded as being scarce. Goods which are scarce are known as *economic goods*. Most goods fall into this category.

Talking about *scarcity* in this sense is not the same as talking about *poverty*. Poverty might be seen as an extreme form of scarcity, in which individuals lack the basic necessities of life — whereas even relatively prosperous people face scarcity because resources are limited.

Scarcity and choice

The key issue that arises from the existence of scarcity is that it forces people to make choices. Each individual must choose which goods and services to consume. In other words, everyone needs to prioritise the consumption of whatever commodities they need or would like to have, as they cannot satisfy all their wants. Similarly, at the national level, governments have to make choices between alternative uses of resources.

It is becoming increasingly apparent that the choices forced by scarcity need to take into account the long-term implications of those choices in order to achieve sustainability into the future. A choice made today to clear large areas of rainforest for timber has implications for the sustainability of the forest in the future, which in turn may affect the sustainability of the planet.

It is this need to choose that underlies the subject matter of economics. Economic analysis is about analysing those choices made by individual people, firms and governments.

Opportunity cost

Key term

opportunity cost in decision making, the value of the next-best alternative forgone

Exercise 1.1

Andrew has just started his AS courses, and has chosen to take economics, mathematics, geography and French. Although he was certain about the first three, it was a close call between French and English. What is Andrew's opportunity cost of choosing French?

Study tip

Opportunity cost is a key concept in economics, and will be important in a variety of contexts. Make sure you understand it and watch for situations in which it is relevant.

This raises one of the most important concepts in all of economic analysis — the notion of **opportunity cost**. When an individual chooses to consume one good, she does so at the cost of the item that would have been next in her list of priorities. For example, suppose you are on a strict diet and at the end of the day you can 'afford' either one chocolate or a piece of cheese. If you choose the cheese, the opportunity cost of the cheese is the chocolate that you could have had instead. In other words, the opportunity cost is the value of the next-best alternative forgone.

This important notion can be applied in many different contexts because, whenever you make a decision, you reject an alternative in favour of your chosen option. You have chosen to read this book — when instead you could be watching television or meeting friends.

As you move further into studying economics, you will encounter this notion of opportunity cost again and again. For example, firms take decisions about the sort of economic activity in which to engage. A market gardener with limited land available has to decide whether to plant onions or potatoes; if he decides to grow onions, he has to forgo the opportunity to grow potatoes. From the government's point of view, if it decides to devote more resources to the National Health Service, it will have fewer resources available for, say, defence. The need to balance the relative merits of alternative choices is challenging, but crucial. Economic analysis helps to explain how such choices are made, and how they could be improved.

Economic agents

In analysing the process by which choices are made, it is important to be aware of the various economic agents that are responsible for making decisions. In economic analysis, there are three key groups of decision makers: households, firms and government.

Households make choices about their expenditure. In this role, they are consumers who demand goods and services. In order to be able to buy goods, households need income, so they also take decisions about the supply of their labour, which will be discussed in the next section.

Firms exist in order to produce output of goods or services. Firms also make choices, in particular about which goods or services to produce, and the techniques of production to be used. The prices at which they can sell are also important in economic analysis.

Government fulfils several roles in society. It undertakes expenditure, and influences the economy through its taxation and regulation of markets.

Factors of production

As mentioned above, people in a society play two quite different roles. On the one hand, they are the consumers, the ultimate beneficiaries of the process of production. On the other, they are a key part of the production process in that they are instrumental in producing goods and services.

More generally, it is clear that both *human resources* and *physical resources* are required as part of the production process. These productive resources are known as the factors of production.

The most obvious human resource is *labour*. Labour is a key input into production. Of course, there are many different types of labour, encompassing different skill levels and working in different ways. *Entrepreneurship* is another human resource. An entrepreneur is someone who organises production and identifies projects to be undertaken, bearing the risk of the activity. *Management* is also sometimes classified as a human resource, although it might be seen as a particular form of labour. *Natural resources* are also inputs into the production process. In particular, all economic activities require some use of *land*, and most use some raw materials. An important distinction here is between *renewable resources* such as forests, and *non-renewable resources* such as oil or coal.

There are also *produced resources* — inputs that are the product of a previous manufacturing process. If you like, these can be regarded as a stock of past production used to aid current production. For example, machines are used in the production process; they are resources manufactured for the purpose of producing other goods. These inputs are referred to as *capital*, which includes things like factory buildings and transport equipment as well as plant and machinery.

The way in which these inputs are combined in order to produce output is another important part of the allocation of resources. Firms need to take decisions about the mix of inputs used in order to produce their output. Such decisions are required in whatever form of economic activity a firm is engaged.

> **Key term**
>
> **factors of production** resources used in the production process; *inputs* into production, including labour, capital, land and entrepreneurship

> **Exercise 1.2**
>
> Classify each of the following as human, natural (renewable or non-renewable) or produced resources:
> a timber
> b services of a window cleaner
> c natural gas
> d solar energy
> e a combine harvester
> f a computer programmer who sets up a company to market his software
> g a computer

Factors of production — labour (workers), capital (buildings) and land

The factors of production need to be rewarded for the services provided. The reward to labour is in the form of wages and salaries, whereas profits are seen as the reward for capital services, and rent is the return on land.

By now you should be getting some idea of the subject matter of economics. The US economist Paul Samuelson (who won the Nobel Prize for Economic Sciences in 1970) identified three key questions that economics sets out to investigate:

1   *What?* What goods and services should be produced in a society from its scarce resources? In other words, how should resources be allocated among producing DVD players, potatoes, banking services and so on?
2   *How?* How should the productive resources of the economy be used to produce these various goods and services?
3   *For whom?* Having produced a range of goods and services, how should these be allocated among the population for consumption?

Exercise 1.3

With which of Samuelson's three questions (what, how, for whom) would you associate the following?

a A firm chooses to switch from producing CD players in order to increase its output of DVD recorders.
b The government reduces the highest rate of income tax.
c Faced with increased labour costs, a firm introduces labour-saving machinery.
d There is an increase in social security benefits.
e The owner of a fish-and-chip shop decides to close down and take a job in a local factory.

Summary

- The fundamental problem faced by any society is scarcity, because resources are finite but wants are unlimited. As a result, choices need to be made.
- Each choice has an opportunity cost — the value of the next-best alternative.
- The amount of output produced in a period depends upon the inputs of factors of production.
- Economics deals with the questions of what should be produced, how it should be produced, and for whom.

Models and assumptions

Key term

model a simplified representation of reality used to provide insight into economic decisions and events

Economics sets out to tackle some complex issues concerning what is a very complex real world. This complexity is such that it is essential to simplify reality in some way; otherwise the task would be overwhelming. Economists thus work with **models**. These are simplified versions of reality that are more tractable for analysis, allowing economists to focus on some key aspects of the world.

Often this works by allowing them to focus on one thing at a time. A model almost always begins with assumptions that help economists to simplify their questions. These assumptions can then be gradually relaxed so that the effect of each one of them can be observed. In this way, economists can gradually move towards a more complicated version of reality.

In evaluating a model, it is not a requirement that it be totally realistic. The model's desired objective may be to predict future behaviour, or test empirical evidence collected from the real world. If a model provides insights into how individuals take decisions or helps to explain economic events, then it has some value, even if it seems remote from reality.

However, it is always important to examine the assumptions that are made, and to ask what happens if these assumptions do not hold.

Opportunity cost and the production possibility curve

Key term

production possibility curve (PPC) a curve showing the maximum combinations of goods or services that can be produced in a set period of time given available resources

Economists rely heavily on diagrams to help in their analysis. In exploring the notion of opportunity cost, a helpful diagram is the **production possibility curve (PPC)**, also known as the production possibility frontier. This shows the maximum combinations of goods that can be produced with a given set of resources.

First consider a simple example. In Exercise 1.1, Andrew was studying for his AS. Suppose now that he has got behind with his homework. He has limited time available, and has five economics questions to answer and five maths exercises to do. An economics question takes the same time to answer as a maths exercise.

What are the options? Suppose he knows that in the time available he can tackle either all of the maths and none of the economics, or all of the economics and none of the maths. Alternatively, he can try to keep both teachers happy by doing some of each.

Quantitative skills 1.1

Drawing and interpreting graphs

An important quantitative skill is to be able to draw and interpret graphs. The diagram showing the production possibility curve is a good example to introduce this skill.

Figure 1.1 shows the options that Andrew faces. He can devote all of his efforts to maths, and leave the economics for another day. He will then be at point *A* in the figure, choosing to do 5 maths exercises (which you read off as the value on the vertical axis, but no economics exercises (reading zero on the horizontal axis).

Alternatively, he can do all the economics exercises and no maths, and be at point *B*. The line joining these two extreme points shows the intermediate possibilities. For example, at *C* he does 2 economics exercises and 3 maths problems, again you read off the values from the two axes.

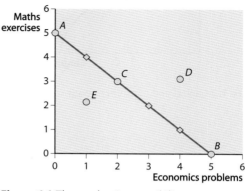

Figure 1.1 The production possibility curve

The line shows the maximum combinations that Andrew can tackle — which is why it is sometimes called a 'frontier'. There is no way he can manage to be beyond the frontier (for example, at point *D*), as to do 3 maths exercises and 4 economics ones would need more time than he has available. However, he could end up *inside* the frontier, at a point such as *E*. This could happen if he gives up, and squanders his time by watching television; that would be an inefficient use of his resources — at least in terms of tackling his homework.

As Andrew moves down the line from left to right, he is spending more time on economics and less on maths. The opportunity cost of tackling an additional economics question is an additional maths exercise forgone. One way of expressing this is that Andrew faces a *trade-off* between the time spent on economics and on maths.

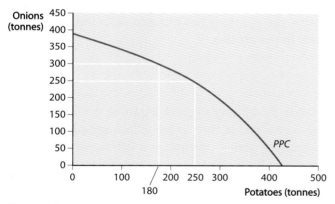

Figure 1.2 Opportunity cost and the *PPC*

Figure 1.2 shows how the *PPC* provides information about opportunity cost. Suppose we have a farmer with 10 hectares of land who is choosing between growing potatoes and onions. The *PPC* shows the combinations of the two crops that could be produced. For example, if the farmer produces 300 tonnes of onions on part of the land, then 180 tonnes of potatoes could be produced from the remaining land. In order to increase production of potatoes by 70 tonnes from 180 to 250, 50 tonnes of onions must be given up. Thus, the opportunity cost of 70 extra tonnes of potatoes is seen to be 50 tonnes of onions. There is a trade-off between the production of potatoes and onions.

Consumption and investment

To move from thinking about an individual to thinking about an economy as a whole, it is first necessary to simplify reality. Assume an economy that produces just two types of good: capital goods and consumer goods. Capital goods are used to increase the future capacity of the economy. For example, you might think of machinery, trucks or factory buildings that will be used to produce other goods in the future. Expenditure on such goods is known as *investment*. In contrast, consumer goods are for present use. They are goods that people consume, such as apples, televisions and private cars. This sort of expenditure is known as *consumption*.

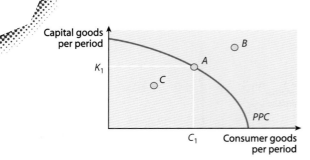

Figure 1.3 Capital and consumer goods

Figure 1.3 illustrates society's options in a particular period. Given the resources available, society can produce any combination of capital and consumer goods along the *PPC*. Thus, point *A* represents one possible combination of outputs, in which the economy produces C_1 consumer goods and K_1 capital goods.

As with the simpler examples, if society were to move to the right along the *PPC*, it would produce more consumer goods — but at the expense of capital goods. Thus, it can be seen that the opportunity cost of producing consumer goods is in terms of forgone opportunities to produce capital goods. Notice that the *PPC* has been drawn as a curve instead of a straight line. This is because not all factors of production are equally suited to the production of both sorts of good. When the economy is well balanced, as at *A*, the factors can be allocated to the uses for which they are best equipped. However, as the economy moves towards complete specialisation in one of the types of good, factors are no longer being best used, and the opportunity cost changes. For example, if nearly all of the workers are engaged in producing consumer goods, it becomes more difficult to produce still more of these, whereas those workers producing machinery find they have too few resources with which to work. In other words, the more consumer goods are being produced, the higher is their opportunity cost.

It is now possible to interpret points *B* and *C*. Point *B* is unreachable given present resources, so the economy cannot produce that combination of goods. This applies to any point outside the *PPC*. On the other hand, at point *C* society is not using its resources efficiently. In this position there is *unemployment* of some resources in the economy. By making better use of the resources available, the economy can move towards the frontier, reducing unemployment in the process.

Economic growth

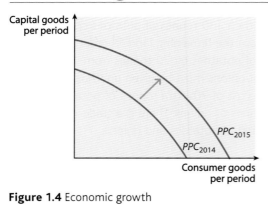

Figure 1.4 Economic growth

Figure 1.3 focused on a single period. However, if the economy is producing capital goods, then in the following period its capacity to produce should increase, as it will have more resources available for production. How can this be shown on the diagram? An expansion in the available inputs suggests that in the next period the economy should be able to produce more of both goods. This is shown in Figure 1.4.

Suppose that in the year 2014 the production possibility curve was at PPC_{2014}. However, in the following year the increased availability of resources enables greater production, and the frontier moves to PPC_{2015}. This is a process of **economic growth**, an expansion of the economy's productive capacity through the increased availability of inputs. Notice that the decision to produce more capital goods today means that fewer consumer goods will be produced today. People must choose between 'more jam today' or 'more jam tomorrow'.

Total output in an economy

Key term

gross domestic product (GDP)
a measure of the economic
activity carried out in an
economy during a period

Remember that the *PPC is* a model: a much simplified version of reality. In a real economy there are many different goods and services produced by a wide range of different factors of production — but it is not possible to draw diagrams to show all of them. The total output of an economy like the UK is measured by its **gross domestic product (GDP)**.

Exercise 1.4

Beverly has been cast away on a desert island, and has to survive by spending her time either fishing or climbing trees to get coconuts. The *PPC* in Figure 1.5 shows the maximum combinations of fish and coconuts that she can gather during a day. Which of the points *A* to *E* represent each of the following?

a a situation where Beverly spends all her time fishing
b an unreachable position
c a day when Beverly goes for a balanced diet — a mixture of coconuts and fish
d a day when Beverly does not fancy fish, and spends all day collecting coconuts
e a day when Beverly spends some of the time trying to attract the attention of a passing ship

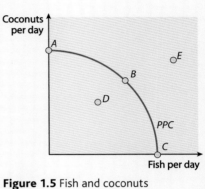

Figure 1.5 Fish and coconuts

Summary

- The production possibility curve shows the maximum combinations of goods or services that can be produced in a period by a given set of resources.
- At any point on the *PPC*, society is making full use of all resources.
- At any point inside the *PPC*, there is unemployment of some resources.
- Points beyond the *PPC* are unattainable.
- In a simple society producing two goods (consumer goods and capital goods), the choice is between consumption and investment for the future.
- As society increases its stock of capital goods, the productive capacity of the economy increases, and the production possibility curve moves outwards: this may be termed 'economic growth'.

Specialisation

How many workers does it take to make a pin? The eighteenth-century economist Adam Smith figured that 10 was about the right number. He argued that when a worker was producing pins on his own, carrying out all the various stages involved in the production process, the maximum number of pins that could be produced in one day was 20 — given the technology of his day, of course. This would imply that 10 workers

Key term

division of labour a process whereby the production procedure is broken down into a sequence of stages, and workers are assigned to particular stages

could produce about 200 pins if they worked in the same way as the lone worker. However, if the pin production process were broken into 10 separate stages, with one worker specialising in each stage, the maximum production for a day's work would be a staggering 48,000. This is known as **division of labour**.

The division of labour is effective because individual workers become skilled at performing specialised tasks. By focusing on a particular stage, they can become highly adept, and thus more efficient, at carrying out that task. In any case, people are not all the same, so some are better at certain activities. Furthermore, this specialisation is more efficient because workers do not spend time moving from one activity to another. Specialisation may also enable firms to operate on a larger scale of production. You will see later that this may be advantageous.

This can be seen in practice in many businesses today, where there is considerable specialisation of functions. Workers are hired for particular tasks and activities. You do not see Wayne Rooney pulling on the goalkeeper's jersey at half time because he fancies a change. Earlier in the chapter, it was argued that 'labour' is considered a factor of production. This idea will now be developed further by arguing that there are different types of labour, having different skills and functions.

Although we refer to the division of labour, we can extend these arguments to consider specialisation among firms, or even among nations. For example, consider car manufacturing. The process of mass producing cars does not all take place within a single firm. One firm may specialise in producing tyres; another may produce windscreens; another may focus on assembling the final product. Here again, specialisation enables efficiency gains to be made.

Employees at a BMW factory. Each worker specialises in a particular task, creating an efficient assembly line

At national level, specialisation again takes place, simply because some countries are better equipped to produce some products than others. For example, it would not make sense for the UK to go into commercial production of pineapples or mangoes. There are other countries with climatic conditions that are much more suitable for producing these products. On the other hand, most Formula 1 racing teams have their headquarters in the UK, and there are benefits from this specialisation.

The benefits from specialisation

Everyone is different. Individuals have different natural talents and abilities that make them good at different things. Indeed, there are some lucky people who seem to be good at everything.

Consider this example. Matthew and Sophie try to supplement their incomes by working at weekends. They have both been to evening classes and have attended pottery and jewellery-making classes. At weekends they make pots and bracelets. Depending on how they divide their time, they can make differing combinations of these goods; some of the possibilities are shown in Table 1.1.

Table 1.1 Matthew and Sophie's production

Matthew		Sophie	
Pots	Bracelets	Pots	Bracelets
12	0	18	0
9	3	12	12
6	6	6	24
3	9	3	30
0	12	0	36

The first point to notice is that Sophie is much better at both activities than Matthew. If they each devote all their time to producing pots, Matthew produces only 12 to Sophie's 18. If they each produce only bracelets, Matthew produces 12 and Sophie, 36. There is another significant feature of this table. Although Sophie is better at producing both goods, the difference is much more marked in the case of bracelet production than pot production. So Sophie is relatively more proficient in bracelet production: in other words, she faces a lower opportunity cost in making bracelets. If Sophie switches from producing pots to producing bracelets, she gives up 6 pots for every 12 additional bracelets that she makes.

The opportunity cost of an additional bracelet is thus $\frac{6}{12} = 0.5$ pots.

For Matthew, there is a one-to-one trade-off between the two, so his opportunity cost of a bracelet is 1 pot.

More interesting is what happens if the same calculation is made for Matthew and pot making. Although Sophie is absolutely better at making pots, if Matthew increases his production of pots, his opportunity cost in terms of bracelets is still 1. But for Sophie the opportunity cost of making pots in terms of bracelets is $\frac{12}{6} = 2$, so Matthew has the lower opportunity cost.

Why does this matter? It illustrates the potential benefits to be gained from specialisation. Suppose that both Matthew and Sophie divide their time between the two activities in such a way that Matthew produces 6 pots and 6 bracelets, and Sophie produces 6 pots and 24 bracelets. Between them, they will have produced 12 pots and 30 bracelets. However, if they each specialise in the product in which they face the lower opportunity cost, their joint production will increase. If Matthew devotes all his time to pottery, he produces 12 pots, while Sophie, focusing only on bracelets, produces 36. So between them they will have produced the same number of pots as before — but 6 extra bracelets.

One final point before leaving Matthew and Sophie. Figure 1.6 shows their respective production possibility curves. You can check this by graphing the points in Table 1.1 and joining them up. In this case the *PPC*s are straight lines. You can see that because Sophie is better at both activities, her *PPC* lies entirely above Matthew's. The differences in opportunity cost are shown by the fact that the two *PPC*s have different slopes, as the opportunity cost element is related to the slope of the *PPC* — the rate at which one good is sacrificed for more of the other.

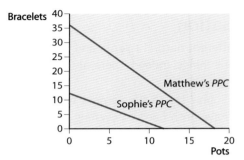

Figure 1.6 Matthew's and Sophie's production possibilities

The dangers of over-specialisation

Although there may be many disadvantages that flow from specialisation, it is also important to realise that there may be a downside if individuals, firms or countries overspecialise. If Matthew spends all his time producing pots, while Sophie produces only bracelets, they may each get bored and begin to lose concentration and job satisfaction. This may be even more of a danger in the case of Adam Smith's pin production. If workers find themselves carrying out the same task day after day, the tedium may lead them to become careless and inefficient.

If a firm focuses on production of a narrow range of products and then finds that demand is falling for those products, it will face difficulties. It may thus be advisable to maintain some diversity in the output range, in the hope that demand will not fall for all products simultaneously. Complete specialisation may not always be the best way for a firm to become successful in the long run.

Nations may also find problems if they overspecialise. For example, it could be argued that all nations should retain some agricultural activity for strategic reasons. If a nation were to be completely dependent on imported foodstuffs and then became engaged in a war, this could leave the country in a vulnerable position. Indeed, this was one of the motivations for the establishment of what would become the European Union.

Summary
- Adam Smith introduced the notion of division of labour, which suggests that workers can become more productive by specialising in stages of the production process.
- Specialisation opens up the possibility of trade.
- The gains from specialisation and trade result from differences in opportunity cost.

Markets

You will find that in economics the term **market** is used frequently, so it is important to be absolutely clear about what is meant by it.

A market need not be a physical location (although it could be — you might regard the local farmers' market as an example of 'a set of arrangements that allows transactions to take place'). With the growth of the internet, everyone is becoming accustomed to ways of buying and selling that do not involve direct physical contact between buyer and seller, so the notion of an abstract market should not be too alien a concept.

In relation to a particular product, a market brings together potential buyers and sellers. This will be explored in the following chapters.

Markets are very important in the process of resource allocation, with prices acting as a key signal to potential buyers and sellers. If a firm finds that it cannot sell its output at the price it has chosen, this is a signal about the way that buyers perceive the product. Price is one way that firms find out about consumers and their willingness to pay for a particular product. This will be explored more fully in Chapter 5.

Money and exchange

Imagine a world without money. It is lunchtime, and you fancy a banana. In your bag you have an apple. Perhaps you can find someone with a banana who fancies an apple? But the only person with a banana available fancies an ice cream. The problem with such a *barter economy* is that you need to find someone who wants what you have and who has what you want — a *double coincidence of wants*. If this problem were to be faced by a whole economic system, undertaking transactions would be so inefficient as to be impossible. Hence the importance of *money* as a *medium of exchange*.

In order to fulfil this role, money must be something that is acceptable to both buyers and sellers. Nobody would accept money in payment for goods or services if they did not trust that they could proceed to use money for further transactions. Money must thus also act as a *store of value*: it must be possible to use it for future transactions. This quality of money means that it can be used as one way of storing wealth for future purchases. Money also allows the value of goods, services and other assets to be compared — it provides a *unit of account*. In this sense, prices of goods reflect the value that society places on them, and must be expressed in money terms.

A further role for money is that it acts as a *standard of deferred payment*. For example, a firm may wish to agree a contract for the future delivery of a good, or may wish to hire a worker to be paid at the end of the month. Such contracts are typically agreed in terms of a money value.

All of these *functions of money* are important to the smooth operation of markets, and are crucial if prices are to fulfil their role in allocating resources within society. This will become apparent as you learn more about economics.

Microeconomics and macroeconomics

The discussion so far has focused sometimes on individual decisions, and sometimes on the decisions of governments, or of 'society' as a whole. Economic thinking is applied in different ways, depending on whether the focus is on the decisions taken by individual agents in the economy or on the interaction between economic variables at the level of the whole economy.

Microeconomics deals with individual decisions taken by households or firms, or in particular markets.

Macroeconomics examines the interactions between economic variables at the level of the aggregate economy. For example, it might examine the effect of a change in income taxes on the level of unemployment, or of the interest rate on total demand and the rate of inflation.

In some ways the division between the two types of analysis is artificial. The same sort of economic reasoning is applied in both types, but the focus is different.

Key terms

microeconomics the study of economic decisions taken by individual economic agents, including households and firms
macroeconomics the study of the interrelationships between economic variables at an aggregate (economy-wide) level

Exercise 1.5

Think about the following, and see whether you think each represents a macroeconomic or microeconomic phenomenon:
a the overall level of prices in an economy
b the price of ice cream
c the overall rate of unemployment in the UK
d the unemployment rate among catering workers in Aberdeen
e the average wage paid to construction workers in Southampton

Positive and normative statements

Key terms

positive statement a statement about what *is*, i.e. about *facts*
normative statement a statement involving a value judgement that is about what *ought to be*

Economics tries to be objective in analysis. However, some of its subject matter requires careful attention in order to retain an objective distance. In this connection, it is important to be clear about the difference between **positive** and **normative statements**.

In short, a positive statement is about *facts*. In contrast, a normative statement is about *what ought to be*. Another way of looking at this is that a statement becomes normative when it involves a *value judgement*.

Suppose the government is considering raising the tax on cigarettes. It may legitimately consult economists to discover what effect a higher tobacco tax will have on the consumption of cigarettes and on government revenues. This would be a *positive* investigation, in that the economists are being asked to use economic analysis to forecast what will happen when the tax is increased.

A very different situation will arise if the government asks whether it *should* raise the tax on cigarettes. This moves the economists beyond positive analysis because it entails a value judgement — so it is now a *normative* analysis. There are some words that betray normative statements, such as 'should' or 'ought to' — watch for these.

Most of this book is about positive economics. However, you should be aware that positive analysis is often called upon to inform normative judgements. If the aim of a policy is to stop people from smoking (which reflects a normative judgement about what ought to happen), then economic analysis may be used to highlight the strengths and weaknesses of alternative policy measures in a purely positive fashion.

Critics of economics often joke that economists always disagree with one another: for example, it has been said that if you put five economists in a room together, they will come up with at least six conflicting opinions. However, although economists may arrive at different value judgements, and thus have differences when it comes to normative issues, there is much greater agreement when it comes to positive analysis.

Summary

- A market is a set of arrangements that allows transactions to take place.
- A barter economy is a highly inefficient way of conducting transactions, hence the importance of money in enabling exchange to take place.
- Money plays key roles as a medium of exchange, a store of value, a unit of account, and a standard of deferred payment.
- By fulfilling these various roles, money enables the smooth operation of markets, and allows prices to act as a guide in allocating resources.
- Microeconomics deals with individual decisions made by consumers and producers, whereas macroeconomics analyses the interactions between economic variables in the aggregate — but both use similar ways of thinking.
- Positive statements are about what is, whereas normative statements involve value judgements and are about what ought to be.

Case study 1.1

Jacob is a subsistence farmer who lives in Nangare, a village in the west of Uganda. He lives in a mud hut and owns two sheep, two chickens and one mattress for his household of ten people. He farms a small piece of land, on which he grows plantains (a staple food crop in Uganda, related to the banana) and some tobacco. One of the key decisions that Jacob faces is how to allocate his land between plantains and tobacco. If he chooses to plant more tobacco in his field, he faces a cost, as growing more tobacco means growing fewer plantains.

A number of factors are likely to influence this decision. For example, the prices of plantains and tobacco may be important, and it may be that the costs involved in growing the two crops are different. Or it may be that some parts of the land are more suitable for growing

one of the crops. There may also be other crops that could be grown on the land. All of these factors could affect Jacob's decisions.

Plantains or tobacco? How will Jacob allocate his land?

Follow-up questions

a With reference to Jacob's choice between growing plantains and tobacco, explain the concept of **opportunity cost**.

b Draw a possible **production possibility curve** to illustrate Jacob's choice of producing plantains and tobacco.

c Identify a point on the diagram that you drew for part (b) to illustrate a situation in which:

   i   Jacob uses his land to produce only plantains.

   ii Jacob uses his land to produce a combination of plantains and tobacco.

   iii Jacob does not use all of the land available, but produces a combination of the two crops.

MICROECONOMICS

Part 2
How competitive markets work

The coordination problem

The complexity of organising production, consumption, investment and government activity in an economy is extreme. Decisions need to be taken about Samuelson's three questions of what to produce, how to produce it and for whom. But how can this be achieved in a way that ensures that the right things are produced in the right way and that the right people get to consume them? This chapter explores some of the issues that arise in this context and looks at some different approaches that have been adopted to cope with the problem of coordinating the activity of the various economic agents introduced in the previous chapter.

Learning objectives

After studying this chapter, you should:
- understand what is meant by resource allocation
- be familiar with the possible objectives of economic agents
- understand what is meant by maximisation in the context of economic thinking
- be familiar with the impact of incentives in influencing the behaviour of economic agents
- be aware of the importance and effectiveness of incentives in determining the behaviour of economic agents and how this affects resource allocation
- be able to explain how market, planned and mixed economies allocate resources
- be able to evaluate the advantages and disadvantages of different types of economy in allocating resources

Resource allocation

Key term

resource allocation the way in which a society's productive assets are used amongst their alternative uses

Chapter 1 highlighted the importance of scarcity as being the fundamental economic problem. This is because people have unlimited wants, but all societies have finite resources. This then forces choices to be made about how to make use of the resources at society's disposal. These choices are complicated by the fact that many of society's resources can be deployed in different ways or may have alternative functions. The choices about **resource allocation** are thus choices about how to deploy society's available resources between their alternative uses, particularly in relation to society's productive assets.

As an example, think about a society that can use its productive assets (labour, land, capital, etc.) to produce either food for people to consume today or machinery to improve its potential for producing goods in the future. If resources are allocated entirely to improving the potential for future production, people may starve today and not get to benefit from those future improvements. On the other hand, if all resources are used to produce food for today's consumers, society will not benefit in the future from gains in production. Jam today? Or jam tomorrow?

In practice, the choices are much more complex than that in a real economy, where there are so many alternative options for allocating resources — and so many people involved in the decision-making process. Making sense of this is one of the key challenges of economic analysis.

The behaviour of economic agents

Resource allocation is determined by the actions of the three key economic agents that operate in the economy: households, firms and the government. All take decisions that will influence the allocation of resources.

Think first about households, and the choices that they will make about economic issues. In their role as consumers, households take decisions about what goods and services they wish to consume. Of course, the range of goods and services that a household will consume is wide. Households consume food and drink, but also household goods, housing, leisure goods and services, education, healthcare...any number of different items. Even within these broadly defined items, there are decisions to be made about what sort of foodstuffs, what variety of drinks, and so on. This underlines the notion of the complexity of economic decisions.

Households also need to take decisions about their work patterns. What occupations should they pursue, which firms should they consider joining, how many hours of work should they offer?

Firms face decisions about what goods and services to produce, and about the technology and techniques of production to be employed. How many workers should they hire? How much land do they need to rent in order to be able to conduct their business?

Governments also take decisions about expenditure, impose taxation and establish the framework in which decisions can be taken by the other economic agents — for example, by regulating economic activity in various ways.

In their role as consumers, households take decisions about what goods and services they wish to consume

Objectives of economic agents

In order to begin to analyse these decisions that will determine resource allocation, it is important to understand what it is that economic agents are trying to achieve (their motivations). In turn, this will set the incentives that will affect their behaviour.

For example, when a household takes decisions about how to allocate its expenditure, what is it that they are trying to achieve by their spending on goods and services? Economists typically think of this in terms of the satisfaction (or utility) that households receive from consuming goods and services. In other words, if you buy an apple, you do not simply want to own it and know that you have it, you want to be able to eat it, because that is what gives you satisfaction.

Similarly, if you choose to work stacking shelves in the supermarket at the weekends, you do this not because you enjoy stacking shelves, but because this provides you with income that can be used to buy goods that will give you satisfaction. So the decisions made by households will be influenced by the satisfaction that they will ultimately gain from consuming goods and services.

Firms also have objectives — and we will see later that different firms may have different objectives. For the moment, the assumption will be made that firms set out with the objective of making profits on their activities. They decide to produce particular goods or services, and to use labour, land and capital in order to receive a return on their efforts.

The government may have different objectives. It needs to raise revenue through taxation, pursue its expenditure programme and provide the framework within which the economy can operate. This incorporates the need to ensure the stability of the economy, meet environmental targets, avoid excessive unemployment and enable the economy to grow over time. It may also wish to influence resource allocation directly: for example, pursuing long-term plans or redistributing income to protect vulnerable members of society.

Maximisation

Given these objectives of economic agents, a next step is to take a view about how they will choose to pursue those objectives. At this point, economists have tended to make the assumption that economic agents behave rationally. In the case of households, this would be interpreted as saying that households not only set out to gain satisfaction from their activities, but set out to get *as much* satisfaction as they possibly can, relative to the costs of achieving this. In other words, they set out to *maximise* satisfaction. Similarly, firms may be assumed to set out to maximise their profits.

This maximisation process underpins much of economic analysis. In practice, some recent economics research has suggested that economic agents do not always act rationally by using maximising behaviour. Some of the findings of *behavioural economics* will be discussed in a later chapter.

Study tip

Make sure that you understand the objectives for the three main types of economic agent — households, firms and government. This is important as it is one of the building blocks of economic analysis.

Incentives

Given the objectives of economic agents and the maximisation process, it is possible to begin to analyse how decisions are taken. Take the case of a household seeking to maximise satisfaction from consuming a particular product. The decision will turn on the benefits gained from consuming a good relative to the costs involved. The costs here will depend partly upon the *price* of the good, but also on the opportunity cost — the fact that in order to consume more of one product, some consumption of other products will need to be sacrificed.

In terms of resource allocation, the price of a product is especially important, as this will be seen as a signal from firms to households about the conditions under which they are prepared to provide the good, and a signal from households to firms about how much they are prepared to spend. This is crucial in helping to coordinate the actions of firms and households, as will be explained.

Also important is that economic agents are seen to respond to *incentives*. For example, suppose a household realises that the price of a particular good has fallen. There is then an incentive to consume more of it, as the cost has fallen relative to the benefit. Conversely, if a firm realises that the price of a good has risen, it has an incentive to supply more of it if this allows a higher return on producing it.

If economic agents understand the incentives faced by other agents, they may be able to influence behaviour. For example, if firms know that consumers have an incentive to consume more of a good at a lower price, then they may be able to use this to encourage higher sales, and thus affect their own position in a market. Knowledge about the effect of incentives can also be crucial for government. For example, a government may wish to influence the consumption of certain products such as tobacco. Knowing the incentives that people face, a government may be able to influence their behaviour.

Exercise 2.1

For each of the following situations, identify an incentive that would induce the change in behaviour described:

a a reduction in the consumption of alcohol by consumers

b an increase in the production of medical drugs by pharmaceutical firms

c an increase in the number of plumbers

d an improvement in air quality in cities

e a fall in the number of cars on the roads during peak hours

---

The coordination problem

Key terms

market economy market forces are allowed to guide the allocation of resources within a society

centrally planned economy decisions on resource allocation are guided by the state

mixed economy resources are allocated partly through price signals and partly on the basis of direction by government

With so many different individuals and organisations (consumers, firms, governments) all taking decisions, a major question is how it all comes together. How are all these separate decisions coordinated so that the overall allocation of resources in a society is coherent? In other words, how can it be ensured that firms produce the commodities that consumers wish to consume? And how can the distribution of these products be organised? These are some of the basic questions that economics sets out to answer. In reality, different societies have adopted different approaches to the coordination problem.

A **market economy** is one in which market forces are allowed to guide the allocation of resources within a society, whereas a **centrally planned economy** is one in which the government undertakes the coordination role by planning and directing the allocation of resources. However, most economies operate a **mixed economy** system, in which market forces are complemented by some state intervention.

The working of a market economy

The role of prices is at the heart of a free market economy. Consumers express changes in their preferences by their decisions to buy (or not to buy) at the going price. This is then a signal to firms, which are able to respond to changes in consumer demand, given the incentive of profitability, which is related to price.

This sort of system of resource allocation is often referred to as **capitalism**. The key characteristic of capitalism is that individuals own the means of production, and can pursue whatever activities they choose — subject, of course, to the legal framework within which they operate.

The government's role in a free capitalist economy is limited, but nonetheless important. A basic framework of *property rights* is essential, together with a basic legal framework. However, the state does not intervene in the production process directly. Secure property rights are significant, as this assures the incentives for the owners of capital.

Within such a system, consumers try to maximise the satisfaction they gain from consuming a range of products, and firms seek to maximise their profits by responding to consumer demand through the medium of price signals.

As has been shown, this is a potentially effective way of allocating resources. In the eighteenth century Adam Smith discussed this mechanism, arguing that when consumers and firms respond to incentives in this way, resources are allocated effectively through the operation of an **invisible hand**, which guides firms to produce the goods and services that consumers wish to consume. Although individuals pursue their self-interest, the market mechanism ensures that their actions will bring about a good result for society overall. A solution to the coordination problem is thus found through the free operation of markets. Such market adjustments provide a solution to Samuelson's three fundamental economic questions of what? how? and for whom?

In terms of resource allocation, the price of a product is especially important

Centrally planned economies

Given the complexity of modern economies, reliance on central planning poses enormous logistical problems. In order to achieve a satisfactory allocation of resources across the economy, the government needs to make decisions on thousands of individual matters.

One example of this emerges from the experience of central planning in Russia after the revolution in 1917. Factories were given production targets to fit in with the overall plan for the development of the economy. These targets then had to be met by the factory managers, who faced strong incentives to meet those targets. Factories producing nails were given two sorts of target. Some factories were given a target to produce a certain number of nails, whereas others were given targets in weight terms. The former responded by producing large numbers of very small nails; the latter produced a very small number of very big nails. Neither was what the planners had in mind!

Micromanagement on this sort of scale proved costly to implement administratively. The collapse of the Soviet bloc in the 1990s largely discredited this approach, although a small number of countries (such as North Korea and Cuba) continue to stick with central planning. China has moved away from pure central planning by beginning to allow prices to be used as signals.

A mixed economy

Most countries now operate a mixed system, in which prices provide signals to firms and consumers, but the government intervenes by providing market infrastructure and influencing the allocation of resources by a pattern of taxes and expenditure and by regulation. As this course progresses, you will see a variety of ways in which such intervention takes place, and will come to understand the reasoning that underpins such intervention — especially in situations where the free market fails to produce the best possible allocation of resources.

Exercise 2.2

Discuss the relative merits of market and centrally planned economies.

Summary

- Resource allocation concerns the way in which a society deploys its productive assets among alternative uses.
- Alternative choices about resource allocation have implications for the wellbeing of society.
- Economic agents take important decisions that affect resource allocation.
- Households, firms and government have differing objectives.
- If economic agents act rationally, they will set out to maximise achievement of these objectives.
- In setting out to take good decisions, economic agents respond to incentives.
- Economic behaviour may be influenced by changing incentives.
- Society faces a coordination problem in seeking to find a good pattern of resource allocation.
- The coordination problem is tackled in different ways in market, centrally planned and mixed economies.

The nature of demand

The demand and supply model is perhaps the most famous of all pieces of economic analysis; it is also one of the most useful. It has many applications that help explain the way markets work in the real world. It is thus central to understanding economics. This chapter introduces the demand side of the model. Chapter 4 will introduce supply.

> ## Learning objectives
> After studying this chapter, you should:
> - be familiar with the notion of the demand for a good or service
> - be aware of the relationship between the demand for a good and its price
> - be familiar with the demand curve and the law of demand
> - understand the distinction between a movement along the demand curve and a shift in its position
> - be aware of the distinction between normal and inferior goods
> - understand the other influences that affect the position of the demand curve
> - understand the meaning and significance of consumer surplus

Demand

Key term

demand the quantity of a good or service that consumers are willing and able to buy at any possible price in a given period

Consider an individual consumer. Think of yourself, and a product that you consume regularly. What factors influence your **demand** for that product? Put another way, what factors influence how much of the product you choose to buy?

When thinking about the factors that influence your demand for your chosen product, common sense will probably mean that you focus on a range of different points. You may think about why you enjoy consuming the product. You may focus on how much it will cost to buy the product, and whether you can afford it. You may decide that you have consumed a product so much that you are ready for a change; or perhaps you will decide to try something that has been advertised on television, or is being bought by a friend.

Whatever the influences you come up with, they can probably be categorised under four headings that ultimately determine your demand for a good. First, the *price* of the good is an important influence on your demand for it, and will affect the quantity of it that you choose to buy. Second, the *price of other goods* may be significant. Third, your *income* will determine how much of the good you can afford to purchase. Finally, almost any other factors that you may have thought of can be listed as part of your *preferences*.

This common-sense reasoning provides the basis for the economic analysis of demand. You will find that a lot of economic analysis begins in this way, by finding a way to construct a model that is rooted in how we expect people or firms to behave.

Individual and market demand

A similar line of argument may apply if we think in terms of the demand for a particular product — say, DVDs. The market for DVDs can thus be seen as bringing together all the potential buyers (and sellers) of the product, and market demand can be analysed in terms of the factors that influence all potential buyers of that good or service. In other words, market demand can be seen as the total quantity of a good or service that all potential buyers would choose to buy at any given price. The same four factors that influence your own individual decision to buy will also influence the total market demand for a product. In addition, the number of potential buyers in the market will clearly influence the size of total demand at any price. Notice that the market for DVDs could be viewed as a *sub-market* of the market for entertainment products.

Derived, joint and composite demand

The nature of demand for a product may depend upon its characteristics. For example, think about the demand for a machine. A firm's demand for a machine arises not because of the innate attractiveness of the machine, but for the output that will be produced by it. The demand for a machine is thus a derived demand. Similarly, the demand for labour is derived from the output that will be produced; it is not a demand for labour itself.

Some products may be joint products, such as printers and print cartridges. There is no point buying a printer unless you also buy a printer cartridge; nor would you buy cartridges if you did not have a printer. These goods are demanded together as a joint demand. Such goods are complements. Some goods have multiple uses, so in these cases demand is seen as a composite demand. For example, water has multiple uses — for drinking, washing, watering the plants and so on. However, for many goods, demand is competitive. A good is in competition with other goods, as they are substitutes for each other.

Key terms

derived demand demand for a factor of production or a good which derives not from the factor or the good itself, but from the goods it produces

joint demand demand for goods which are interdependent, such that they are demanded together

composite demand demand for a good that has multiple uses

competitive demand demand for goods that are in competition with each other

Demand and the price of a good

Key term

ceteris paribus a Latin phrase meaning 'other things being equal'; it is used in economics when we focus on changes in one variable while holding other influences constant

Assume for the moment that the influences mentioned above, other than the price of the good, are held constant, so that the focus is only on the extent to which the price of a good influences the demand for it. This is a common assumption in economics, which is sometimes expressed by the Latin phrase ceteris paribus, meaning 'other things being equal'. Given the complexity of the real world, it is often helpful to focus on one thing at a time.

This ceteris paribus assumption is used a lot in economics, and is a powerful tool. Focusing on one influence at a time is a way of coping with the complexities of the real world and makes the analysis of economic issues much clearer than if we try to analyse everything at once. You will see many instances of it as the course proceeds.

So how is the demand for DVDs influenced by their price? Other things being equal (ceteris paribus), you would expect the demand for DVDs to be higher when the price is low, and lower when the price is high. In other words, you would expect an inverse relationship between the price and the quantity demanded. This is such a strong phenomenon that it is referred to as the **law of demand**.

If you were to compile a list that showed how many DVDs would be bought at any possible price and plotted these on a diagram, this would be called the **demand curve**. Figure 3.1 shows what this might look like. As it is an inverse relationship, the demand curve slopes downwards. Notice that the demand curve need not be a straight line: its shape depends upon how consumers react at different prices.

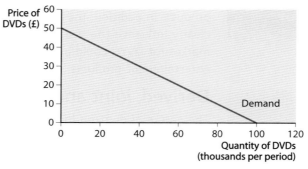

Figure 3.1 A demand curve for DVDs

Table 3.1 shows how the demand for oojits varies with their price. Draw the demand curve.

Table 3.1 The demand for oojits

Price	Quantity
100	0
90	3
80	7
70	15
60	25
50	40
40	60
30	85
20	120

Study tip

In order to emphasise the difference between a shift of the demand curve and a movement along it, the convention is adopted to use an *extension* (or *contraction*) of demand for a movement along the demand curve, and to use an *increase* (or *decrease*) to denote a shift of the curve.

As the price of a good changes, a movement along the demand curve can be observed as consumers adjust their buying pattern in response to the price change.

Notice that the demand curve has been drawn under the ceteris paribus assumption. In other words, it was assumed that all other influences on demand were held constant in order to focus on the relationship between demand and price. There are two important implications of this procedure.

First, the price drawn on the vertical axis of a diagram such as Figure 3.1 is the *relative* price — it is the price of DVDs under the assumption that all other prices are constant.

Second, if any of the other influences on demand changes, you would expect to see a shift of the whole demand curve. It is very important to distinguish between factors that induce a movement *along* a curve, and factors that induce a shift *of* a curve. This applies not only in the case of the demand curve — there are many other instances where this is important.

The two panels of Figure 3.2 show this difference. In panel (a) of the figure, the demand curve has shifted to the right because of a change in one of the factors that influences demand. In panel (b), the price of DVDs falls from P_0 to P_1, inducing a movement along the demand curve as demand expands from Q_0 to Q_1.

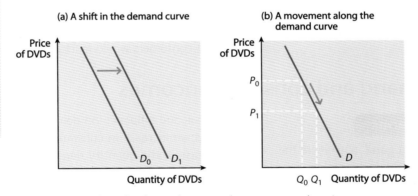

Figure 3.2 A shift in the demand curve and a movement along it

Snob effects

It is sometimes argued that for some goods a 'snob effect' may lead to the demand curve sloping upwards. The argument is that some people may value certain goods more highly simply because their price is high, especially if they know that other people will observe them consuming these goods; an example might be Rolex watches. In other words, people gain value from having other people notice that they are rich enough to afford to consume a particular good. There is thus a *conspicuous consumption* effect, which was first pointed out by Thorstein Veblen at the end of the nineteenth century.

Rolex watches may benefit from the conspicuous consumption effect

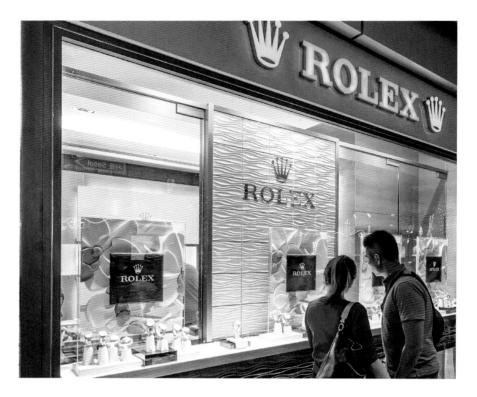

However, although there may be some individual consumers who react to price in this way, there is no evidence to suggest that there are whole markets that display an upward-sloping demand curve for this reason. In other words, most consumers would react normally to the price of such goods.

Demand and consumer incomes

Key terms

normal good one where the quantity demanded increases in response to an increase in consumer incomes

inferior good one where the quantity demanded decreases in response to an increase in consumer incomes

The second influence on demand is consumer incomes. For a **normal good**, an increase in consumer incomes will, ceteris paribus, lead to an increase in the quantity demanded at any given price. Foreign holidays are an example of a normal good because, as people's incomes rise, they will tend to demand more foreign holidays at any given price.

Figure 3.3 illustrates this. D_0 here represents the initial demand curve for foreign holidays. An increase in consumers' incomes causes demand to be higher at any given price, and the demand curve shifts to the right — to D_1.

However, demand does not always respond in this way. For example, think about bus journeys. As incomes rise in a society, more people can afford to have a car, or to use taxis. This means that, as incomes rise, the demand for bus journeys may tend to fall. Such goods are known as **inferior goods**.

This time an increase in consumers' incomes in Figure 3.4 causes the demand curve to shift to the left, from its initial position at D_0, to D_1 where less is demanded at any given price.

The relationship between quantity demanded (*QDI*) and income can be shown more directly on a diagram. Panel (a) of Figure 3.5 shows how this would look for a normal good. It is upward sloping, showing that the quantity demanded is higher when consumer incomes are higher. In contrast, the income–demand curve for an inferior good, shown in panel (b) of the diagram, slopes downwards, indicating that the quantity demanded will be lower when consumer incomes are relatively high.

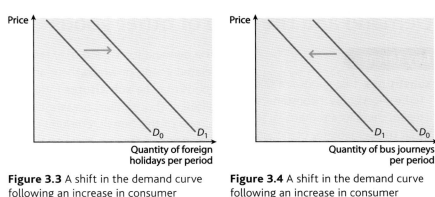

Figure 3.3 A shift in the demand curve following an increase in consumer incomes (a normal good)

Figure 3.4 A shift in the demand curve following an increase in consumer incomes (an inferior good)

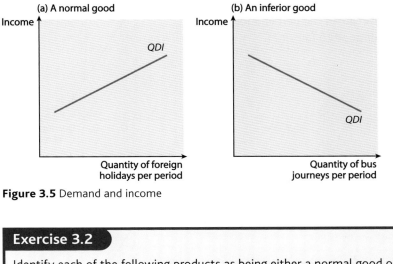

Figure 3.5 Demand and income

Exercise 3.2

Identify each of the following products as being either a normal good or an inferior good:

a digital camera   c potatoes   e fine wine

b magazine   d bicycle   f cheap wine

Extension material

A Giffen good

Remember that a consumer's response to a change in the price of a good is made up of a substitution effect and a real income effect (see the extension material on page 26). The substitution effect always acts in the opposite direction to the price change: in other words, an increase in the price of a good always induces a switch *away* from the good towards other goods. However, it can now be seen that the real income effect may operate in either direction, depending on whether it is a normal good or an inferior good that is being considered.

Suppose there is a good that is *very* inferior. A fall in the price of a good induces a substitution effect towards the good, but the real income effect works in the opposite

direction. The fall in price is equivalent to a rise in real income, so consumers will consume less of the good. If this effect is really strong, it could overwhelm the substitution effect, and the fall in price could induce a fall in the quantity demanded: in other words, for such a good the demand curve could be upward sloping.

Such goods are known as *Giffen goods*, after Sir Robert Giffen, who pointed out that this could happen. However, in spite of stories about the reaction of demand to a rise in the price of potatoes during the great Irish potato famine, there have been no authenticated sightings of Giffen goods. The notion remains a theoretical curiosity.

Demand and the price of other goods

Key terms

substitutes two goods are said to be substitutes if consumers regard them as alternatives, so that the demand for one good is likely to rise if the price of the other good rises

complements two goods are said to be complements if people tend to consume them jointly, so that an increase in the price of one good causes the demand for the other good to fall

The demand for a good may respond to changes in the price of other related goods, of which there are two main types. On the one hand, two goods may be **substitutes** for each other. For example, consider two different (but similar) breakfast cereals. If there is an increase in the price of one of the cereals, consumers may switch their consumption to the other, as the two are likely to be close substitutes for each other. Not all consumers will switch, of course — some may be deeply committed to one particular brand — but some of them are certainly likely to change over.

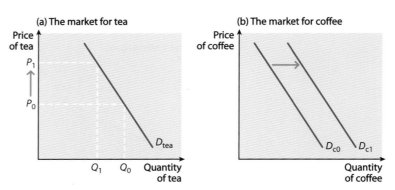

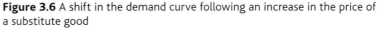

Figure 3.6 A shift in the demand curve following an increase in the price of a substitute good

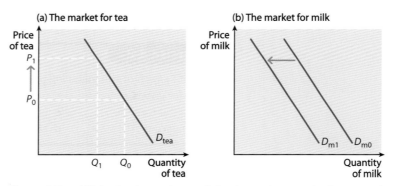

Figure 3.7 A shift in the demand curve following an increase in the price of a complementary good

On the other hand, there may also be goods that are **complements** — for example, products that are consumed jointly, such as breakfast cereals and milk, or cars and petrol. Here a fall in the price of one good may lead to an increase in demand for *both* products.

Whether goods are substitutes or complements determines how the demand for one good responds to a change in the price of another. Figure 3.6 shows the demand curves (per period) for two goods that are substitutes — tea and coffee.

If there is an increase in the price of tea from P_0 to P_1 in panel (a), more consumers will switch to coffee and the demand curve in panel (b) will shift to the right — say, from D_{c0} to D_{c1}.

For complements the situation is the reverse: in Figure 3.7 an increase in the price of tea from P_0 to P_1 in panel (a) causes the demand curve for milk to shift leftwards, from D_{m0} to D_{m1}.

Demand, consumer preferences and other influences

The discussion has shown how the demand for a good is influenced by the price of the good, the price of other goods, and consumer incomes. It was stated earlier that almost everything else that determines demand for a good can be represented as 'consumer preferences'. In particular, this refers to whether you like or dislike a good. There may be many things that influence whether you like or dislike a product. In part it simply depends upon your own personal inclinations — some people like dark chocolate, others prefer milk chocolate. However, firms may try to influence your preferences through advertising, and sometimes they succeed. Or you might be one of those people who get so irritated by television advertising that you compile a blacklist of products that you will never buy! Even this is an influence on your demand.

In some cases, your preferences may be swayed by other people's demand — again, this may be positive or negative. Fashions may influence demand, but some people like to buck (or lead) the trend.

You may also see a movement of the demand curve if there is a sudden surge in the popularity of a good — or, indeed, a sudden collapse in demand.

Exercise 3.3

Sketch some demand curves for the following situations, and think about how you would expect the demand curve to change (if at all):

a the demand for chocolate following a campaign highlighting the dangers of obesity

b the demand for oranges following an increase in the price of apples

c the demand for oranges following a decrease in the price of oranges

d the demand for DVDs following a decrease in the price of DVD players

e the demand for VCRs following a decrease in the price of DVD recorders

f the demand for private transport following an increase in consumer incomes

g the demand for public transport following an increase in consumer incomes

Study tip

As you proceed through your study of economics, it is useful to keep track of some key issues. An example is the key influences on the demand for a good, which are:

- the price of the good
- the prices of other goods — in particular, the substitutes and complements
- consumer incomes
- consumer preferences
- the time period over which demand is being considered

Keep a note of these and be ready to make use of them.

The above discussion has covered most of the factors that influence the demand for a good. However, in some cases it is necessary to take a time element into account. Not all of the goods bought are consumed instantly. In some cases, consumption is spread over long periods of time. Indeed, there may be instances where goods are not bought for consumption at all, but are seen by the buyer as an investment, perhaps for resale at a later date. In these circumstances, expectations about future price changes may be relevant. For example, people may buy fine wine or works of art in the expectation that prices will rise in the future. There may also be goods whose prices are expected to fall in the future. This has been common with many high-tech products; initially a newly launched product may sell at a high price, but as production levels rise, costs may fall, and prices too. People may therefore delay purchase in the expectation of future price reductions.

Consumer surplus

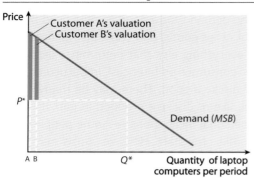
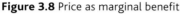

Figure 3.8 Price as marginal benefit

Think a little more carefully about what the demand curve represents. Figure 3.8 shows the demand curve for laptop computers. Suppose that the price is set at P^* and quantity demanded is thus Q^*. P^* can be seen as the value that the last customer places on a laptop. In other words, if the price were even slightly above P^*, there would be one consumer who would choose not to buy: this individual will be referred to as the *marginal consumer*.

To that marginal consumer, P^* represents the marginal (that is, the additional) benefit derived from consuming this good — it is the price that just reflects the consumer's benefit from a laptop, as it is the price that just induces her to buy. Thinking of the society as a whole (which is made up of all the consumers within it), P^* can be regarded as the **marginal social benefit (MSB)** derived from consuming this good. The same argument could be made about any point along the demand curve, so the demand curve can be interpreted as the marginal benefit to be derived from consuming laptop computers.

In most markets, all consumers face the same prices for goods and services. This leads to an important concept in economic analysis. P^* may represent the value of laptops to the *marginal* consumer, but what about all the other consumers who are also buying laptops at P^*? They would all be willing to pay a higher price for a laptop. Indeed, consumer A in Figure 3.8 would pay a very high price indeed, and thus values a laptop much more highly than P^*. When consumer A pays P^* for a laptop, he gets a great deal, as he values the good so much more highly — as represented by the vertical green line on Figure 3.8. Consumer B also gains a surplus above her willingness to pay (the blue line).

If all these surplus values are added up, they sum to the total surplus that society gains from consuming laptops. This is known as the **consumer surplus**, represented by the shaded triangle in Figure 3.9. It can be interpreted as the welfare that society gains from consuming the good, over and above the price that has to be paid for it. Notice that if the price of a good increases, this will reduce the overall size of consumer surplus, and thus affects the welfare that society receives from consuming the good.

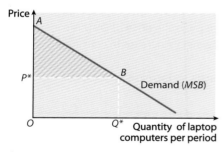

Figure 3.9 Consumer surplus

Exercise 3.4

Table 3.2 shows the price at which each of six consumers would be prepared to buy a good.

Table 3.2

Consumer A	£20
Consumer B	£18
Consumer C	£16
Consumer D	£14
Consumer E	£12
Consumer F	£10

Suppose the market price is at £14.

a Which of the consumers would choose to buy the good?

b What would be Consumer A's consumer surplus at this price?

c What would be the total consumer surplus enjoyed by the consumers purchasing the good?

d What would be the total consumer surplus if the price were to increase to £16?

Summary

- A market is a set of arrangements that enables transactions to take place.
- The market demand for a good depends upon the price of the good, the price of other goods, consumers' incomes and preferences, and the number of potential consumers.
- The demand curve shows the relationship between demand for a product and its price, ceteris paribus.
- The demand curve is downward sloping, as the relationship between demand and price is an inverse one.
- A change in price induces a movement along the demand curve, whereas a change in the other determinants of demand induces a shift of the demand curve.
- When the demand for a good rises as consumer incomes rise, that good is referred to as a normal good; when demand falls as income rises, the good is referred to as an inferior good.
- A good or service may be related to other goods by being either a substitute or a complement.
- For some products, demand may be related to expected future prices.
- Consumer surplus represents the benefit that consumers gain from consuming a product, over and above the price they pay for that product.

Case study 3.1

Smoothies and Cola

A few years ago, growing concerns about obesity in the British population led the government to launch a campaign to encourage healthier eating. Part of this campaign aimed to encourage people to consume more fruit and vegetables, which was reinforced by the 'five-a-day' slogan, the idea being that five portions per day of fruit and vegetables were an essential part of a balanced diet.

Firms selling food products naturally tried to take advantage of the campaign by emphasising in their advertising that their products contributed in some way to the five-a-day. Smoothies were one such product advertised in this way as helping people to meet their five-a-day quota. One result was that sales of cola and other soft drinks were affected, with people keen to switch to smoothies as a healthier alternative.

Smoothies – part of your five-a-day?

Whether this was actually true was another matter, and some people argued that the sugar content of smoothies was in fact much higher than that of some other fizzy drinks…but that's another story.

Follow-up questions

a Consider the factors that influence demand. Which of these explains the increase in demand for smoothies following the campaign?

b What effect would the campaign have on the demand curve for smoothies and fizzy drinks such as cola?

c Would you see smoothies and fizzy soft drinks as being substitutes or complements? Explain your answer.

The nature of supply

The previous chapter introduced you to the demand curve. The other key component of the demand and supply model is, of course, supply. For any market transaction, there are two parties, buyers and sellers. The question to be considered in this chapter is what determines the quantity that sellers will wish to supply to the market.

Learning objectives

After studying this chapter, you should:
- be familiar with the notion of the supply of a good or service
- be aware of the relationship between the supply of a good and its price in a competitive market
- understand what is meant by the supply curve and the factors that influence its shape and position
- be able to distinguish between shifts of the supply curve and movements along it
- be aware of the effect of taxes and subsidies on the supply curve
- understand the meaning and significance of producer surplus

Supply

Key term

firm an organisation that brings together factors of production in order to produce output

In discussing demand, the focus of attention was on consumers, and on their willingness to pay for goods and services. In thinking about supply, attention switches to firms, as it is firms that take decisions about how much output to supply to the market. It is important at the outset to be clear about what is meant by a 'firm'. A **firm** exists to organise production: firms bring together various factors of production, and organise the production process in order to produce output.

There are various forms that the organisation of a firm can take. A firm could be a *sole proprietor*: probably a small business such as a newsagent where the owner of the firm also runs the firm. A firm could be in the form of a *partnership* — for example, a dental practice in which profits (and debts) are shared between the partners in the business. Larger firms may be organised as private or public *joint stock companies*, owned by shareholders. The difference between private and public joint stock companies is that the shares of a public joint stock company are traded on the stock exchange, whereas this is not the case with the private company.

In order to analyse how firms decide how much of a product to supply, it is necessary to make an assumption about what it is that firms are trying to achieve. Assume that they aim to maximise their profits, where 'profits' are defined as the difference between a firm's total revenue and its total costs.

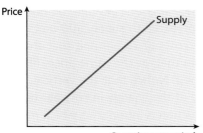

Figure 4.1 A supply curve

Exercise 4.1

Table 4.1 shows how the supply of oojits varies with their price. Draw the supply curve.

Table 4.1 The supply of oojits

Price	Quantity
100	98
90	95
80	91
70	86
60	80
50	70
40	60
30	50
20	35
10	18

As discussed in Chapter 3, the demand curve shows a relationship between quantity demanded and the price of a good or service. A similar relationship between the quantity supplied by firms and the price of a good can be identified in relation to the behaviour of firms in a **competitive market** — that is, a market in which individual firms cannot influence the price of the good or service that they are selling, because of competition from other firms.

As with the demand curve, there is a distinction between the supply curve of an individual firm, and the supply curve for a *market*. The individual supply curve shows the amount that an individual firm is prepared to supply at any given price. The market supply curve shows the total amount of a product that firms wish to supply at any given price.

In such a market it may well be supposed that firms will be prepared to supply more goods at a high price than at a lower one (ceteris paribus), as this will increase their profits. The **supply curve** illustrates how much the firms in a market will supply at any given price, as shown in Figure 4.1. As firms are expected to supply more goods at a high price than at a lower price, the supply curve will be upward sloping, reflecting this positive relationship between quantity and price.

Quantitative skills 4.1

Interpreting lines on a graph

Be clear about why the upward-sloping nature of the supply curve reflects the fact that firms are willing to supply more output at a higher price, whereas the downward-sloping nature of the demand curve reflects the way that consumers are willing to purchase more of a good when the price is relatively low. This is bound up with the way in which we interpret the supply (or demand) curve. In Figure 4.1, think about how firms behave when the price is relatively low — that is when you pick a price low down on the vertical axis. The quantity that firms are willing to supply is read off from the supply curve — and is relatively low. However, if you read off the quantity from a higher price level, the quantity is also higher. You need to become accustomed to interpreting lines and curves on a diagram in this way. The shape of the line (or curve) shows the extent to which firms respond at different prices.

Notice that the focus of the supply curve is on the relationship between quantity supplied and the price of a good in a given period, ceteris paribus — that is, holding other things constant. As with the demand curve, there are other factors affecting the quantity supplied. These other influences on supply will determine the position of the supply curve: if any of them changes, the supply curve can be expected to shift.

What influences supply?

We can identify five important influences on the quantity that firms will be prepared to supply to the market at any given price:
- production costs
- the technology of production
- taxes and subsidies
- the price of related goods
- firms' expectations about future prices

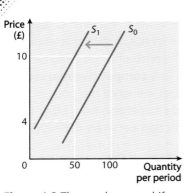

Figure 4.2 The supply curve shifts to the left if production costs increase

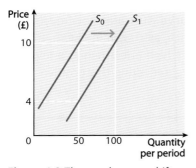

Figure 4.3 The supply curve shifts to the right if production costs fall

Costs and technology

If firms are aiming to maximise profits, an important influence on their supply decision will be the costs of production that they face. Chapter 1 explained that in order to produce output, firms need to use inputs of the factors of production — labour, capital, land, etc. If the cost of those inputs increases, firms will in general be expected to supply less output at any given price. The effect of this is shown in Figure 4.2, where an increase in production costs induces firms to supply less output at each price. The curve shifts from its initial position at S_0 to a new position at S_1. For example, suppose the original price was £10 per unit; before the increase in costs, firms would have been prepared to supply 100 units of the product to the market. An increase in costs of £6 per unit that shifted the supply curve from S_0 to S_1 would mean that, at the same price, firms would now supply only 50 units of the good. Notice that the vertical distance between S_0 and S_1 is the amount of the change in cost per unit.

In contrast, if a new technology of production is introduced, which means that firms can produce more cost effectively, this could have the opposite effect, shifting the supply curve to the right. This is shown in Figure 4.3, where improved technology induces firms to supply more output at any given price, and the supply curve shifts from its initial position at S_0 to a new position at S_1. Thus, if firms in the initial situation were supplying 50 units with the price at £10 per unit, then a fall in costs of £6 per unit would induce firms to increase supply to 100 units (if the price remained at £10).

Taxes and subsidies

Suppose the government imposes a sales tax such as VAT on a good or service. The price paid by consumers will be higher than the revenue received by firms, as the tax has to be paid to the government. This means that firms will (ceteris paribus) be prepared to supply less output at any given market price. Again, the supply curve shifts to the left. This is shown in panel (a) of Figure 4.4, which assumes a fixed per unit tax. The supply curve shifts, as firms supply less at any given market price. On the other hand, if the government pays firms a subsidy to produce a particular good, this will reduce their costs, and induce them to supply more output at any given price. The supply curve will then shift to the right, as shown in panel (b).

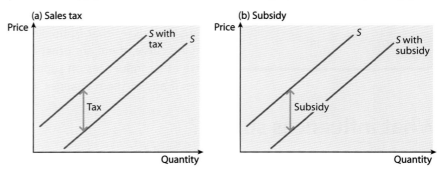

Figure 4.4 The effects of taxes and subsidies on supply

Prices of other goods

It was shown in Chapter 3 that from the consumers' perspective, two goods may be substitutes for each other, such that if the price of one good increases, consumers may be induced to switch their consumption

Wine producers have to take supply decisions based on expected future prices

to substitute goods. Similarly, there may be substitution on the supply side. A firm may face a situation in which there are alternative uses to which its factors of production may be put: in other words, it may be able to choose between producing a range of different products: a situation of **competitive supply**. A rise in the price of a good raises its profitability, and therefore may encourage a firm to switch production from other goods. This may happen even if there are high switching costs, provided the increase in price is sufficiently large. For example, a change in relative prices of potatoes and organic swedes might encourage a farmer to stop planting potatoes and grow organic swedes instead.

In other circumstances, a firm may produce a range of goods jointly. Perhaps one good is a by-product of the production process of another. An increase in the price of one of the goods may mean that the firm will produce more of both goods. This notion of **joint supply** is similar to the situation on the demand side where consumers regard two goods as complements. As with demand, there may also be **composite supply**, in which a product is supplied to various different sources of demand.

Expected prices

Because production takes time, firms often take decisions about how much to supply on the basis of expected future prices. Indeed, if their product is one that can be stored, there may be times when a firm will decide to allow stocks of a product to build up in anticipation of a higher price in the future, perhaps by holding back some of its production from current sales. In some economic activities, expectations about future prices are crucial in taking supply decisions because of the length of time needed in order to increase output. For example, a firm producing palm oil, rubber or wine needs to be aware that newly planted trees or vines need several years to mature before they are able to yield their product.

Movements along and shifts of the supply curve

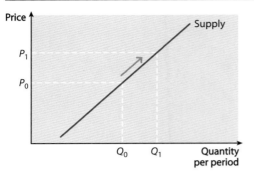

Figure 4.5 A movement along a supply curve in response to a price change

As with the demand curve, it is very important to remember that there is a distinction between movements *along* the supply curve, and shifts *of* the supply curve. If there is a change in the market price, this induces a movement along the supply curve. After all, the supply curve is designed to reveal how firms will react to a change in the price of the good. For example, in Figure 4.5, if the price is initially at P_0 firms will be prepared to supply the quantity Q_0, but if the price then increases to P_1 this will induce a movement along the supply curve as firms increase supply to Q_1.

In contrast, as seen in the previous section, a change in any of the other influences on supply will induce a shift of the whole supply curve, as this affects the firms' willingness to supply at any given price.

Study tip

As with the discussion of demand, it is important to be clear about the difference between a shift of the supply curve and a movement along it. Again, the convention is adopted to use an *extension* (or *contraction*) of supply for a movement along the supply curve, and to use an *increase* (or *decrease*) to denote a shift of the curve. It is also helpful to distinguish between those factors that affect the position of the supply curve and those that affect the position of the demand curve. The factors that affect the position of the supply curve are:
- production costs
- the technology of production
- taxes and subsidies
- the price of related goods
- firms' expectations about future prices

Exercise 4.2

For each of the following, decide whether the demand curve or the supply curve will move, and in which direction:
a Consumers are convinced by arguments about the benefits of organic vegetables.
b A new process is developed that reduces the amount of inputs that firms need in order to produce bicycles.
c There is a severe frost in Brazil that affects the coffee crop.
d The government increases the rate of value added tax.
e Real incomes rise.
f The price of tea falls: what happens in the market for coffee?
g The price of sugar falls: what happens in the market for coffee?

Producer surplus

Parallel to the notion of consumer surplus is the concept of **producer surplus**. Think about the nature of the supply curve: it reveals how much output firms are prepared to supply at any given price in a competitive market. Figure 4.6 depicts a supply curve. Assume the price is at P^*, and that all units are sold at that price. P^* represents the value to firms of

Key terms

producer surplus the difference between the price received by firms for a good or service and the price at which they would have been prepared to supply that good or service
marginal cost the cost of producing an additional unit of output

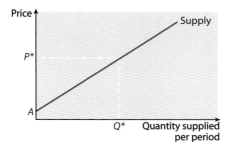

Figure 4.6 A supply curve

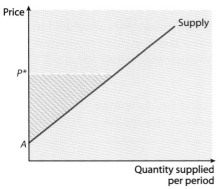

Figure 4.7 Producer surplus

the marginal unit sold. In other words, if the price had been set slightly below P^*, the last unit would not have been supplied, as firms would not have found this profitable.

Notice that the threshold at which a firm will decide it is not profitable to supply is the point at which the price received by the firm reaches the cost to the firm of producing the last unit of the good. Thus, in a competitive market the supply curve reflects **marginal cost**.

The supply curve shows that, in the range of prices between point A and P^*, firms would have been willing to supply positive amounts of this good or service. So at P^*, they would gain a surplus value on all units of the good supplied below Q^*. The total area is shown in Figure 4.7 — it is the area above the supply curve and below P^*, shown as the shaded triangle. One way of defining this producer surplus is as the surplus earned by firms over and above the minimum that would have kept them in the market. It is the *raison d'être* of firms.

Table 4.2 shows the quantity of a good that a firm would be prepared to supply at various prices. At a price of £10, the firm would only supply 1 unit of the good. However, at a price of £12, the firm would supply 2 units, but receives that price for both units of the good supplied. The firm would have been prepared to supply one of these units at £10, but receives £12, thus making a surplus of £2. As the price of the good rises, the firm receives more producer surplus.

Table 4.2 A firm's supply decision

Price (£)	Quantity (units)
10	1
12	2
14	3
16	4
18	5
20	6

The producer surplus that a firm receives is important, as it provides an incentive for firms to respond to changes in the prevailing price. Indeed, this helps to explain why the supply curve is upward sloping.

Extension material

The notions of producer and consumer surplus are important when we come to think about the total welfare that economic agents receive from their economic activities. For consumers, the consumer surplus represents the surplus that they receive over and above what they are willing to pay for a good or service. For firms, the producer surplus represents the surplus that they receive over and above their costs of production. There is thus a sense in which we interpret the sum of these two surpluses as being the net welfare that society as a whole gains from the production and consumption of this good or service. It could be argued that efficient resource allocation is achieved when this is maximised.

Summary

- Other things being equal, firms in a competitive market can be expected to supply more output at a higher price.
- The supply curve traces out this positive relationship between price and quantity supplied.
- Changes in the costs of production, technology, taxes and subsidies, or the prices of related goods may induce shifts of the supply curve, with firms being prepared to sell more (or less) output at any given price.
- Expectations about future prices may affect current supply decisions.

Case study 4.1

Champagne

The market for champagne has been changing in recent years. Champagne has always commanded a premium price compared with other sparkling wines because of its reputation and status as the wine for celebrations of all kinds. Christmas is one such focus for drinking champagne, and major events such as the millennium celebrations cause blips in demand, with no party being complete without a few bottles of champagne. However, the increased availability of good-quality alternatives to champagne at competitive prices has affected champagne producers. It has even been known for some English sparkling wines to fare well at blind tastings compared with some champagnes. Nonetheless champagne production has remained profitable as consumer incomes have risen. Mechanisation of some parts of the production process has benefited producers.

There are strict rules governing the production of champagne. Indeed, champagne can only be called by that name if it comes from a particular designated area in France, and this has effectively limited the amount

More affordable alternatives have affected the market for champagne

that can be produced. In early 2008, it was announced that consideration was being given to expanding the area that could be recognised as producing champagne. The proposal was accepted, and the first vines were expected to be planted around 2015. This will not affect the market for some period, as it takes time for newly planted vines to produce grapes that can be used to make wine. It is unlikely that any of this new-region champagne will come to market before about 2021.

Follow-up questions
a From the passage, identify factors that would be expected to affect the demand curve for champagne.
b From the passage, identify factors that would be expected to affect the supply curve for champagne.

Market equilibrium and the price system

The previous chapters introduced the notions of demand and supply, and it is now time to bring these two curves together in order to meet the key concept of market equilibrium. The model can then be further developed to see how it provides insights into how markets operate. You will encounter demand and supply in a wide variety of contexts, and begin to glimpse some of the ways in which the model can help to explain how the economic world works.

Learning objectives

After studying this chapter, you should:

- understand the notion of equilibrium and its relevance in the demand and supply model
- be aware of what is meant by comparative static analysis
- understand the concept of elasticity measures and appreciate their importance and applications

Market equilibrium

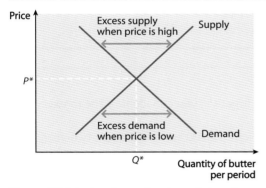

Figure 5.1 Bringing demand and supply together

The previous chapters have described the components of the demand and supply model. It only remains to bring them together, for this is how the power of the model can be appreciated. Figure 5.1 shows the demand for and supply of butter.

Suppose that the price were to be set relatively high (above P^*). At such a price, firms wish to supply lots of butter to the market. However, consumers are not very keen on butter at such a high price, so demand is not strong. Firms now have a problem: they find that their stocks of butter are building up. What has happened is that the price has been set at a level that exceeds the value that most consumers place on butter, so they will not buy it. There is *excess supply*. The only thing that the firms can do is to reduce the price in order to clear their stocks.

Suppose they now set their price relatively low (below P^*). Now it is the consumers who have a problem, because they would like to buy more butter at the low price than firms are prepared to supply. There is *excess demand*. Some consumers may offer to pay more than the going price in order to obtain their butter supplies, and firms realise that they can raise the price.

How will it all end? When the price settles at *P** in Figure 5.1, there is a balance in the market between the quantity that consumers wish to demand and the quantity that firms wish to supply, namely *Q**. This is the **market equilibrium**. In a free market the price can be expected to converge on this equilibrium level, through movements along both demand and supply curves.

Quantitative skills 5.1

Identifying and interpreting an intersection on a graph
You will meet many diagrams in economics where there are upward- and downward-sloping lines that intersect at some point. Such intersection points are almost always significant. In the case of demand and supply, the downward-sloping line represents demand, and the upward-sloping curve shows supply. Only at the point where the two lines meet are the decisions of consumers and firms mutually consistent. In other words, consumers are choosing to demand exactly the quantity that firms are willing to supply. The important question to explore is the mechanism that will lead to this equilibrium point. This in turn depends on the incentives facing economic agents if the starting point is away from the intersection point.

Exercise 5.1

Identify the equilibrium market price if demand and supply are as in Figure 5.2.

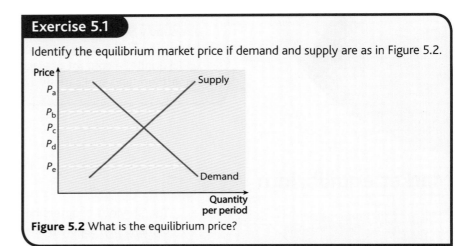

Figure 5.2 What is the equilibrium price?

Summary
- Bringing demand and supply together, you can identify the market equilibrium.
- The equilibrium price is the unique point at which the quantity demanded by consumers is just balanced by the quantity that firms wish to supply.
- In a free market, natural forces can be expected to encourage prices to adjust to the equilibrium level.

Examples of markets

The markets that have been discussed so far have been product markets, such as the market for DVDs, tea or butter. However, the model is much more widely applicable than this, as is shown by the examples that follow.

The labour market

Within the economy, firms demand labour and employees supply
labour — so why not use demand and supply to analyse the market?
This can indeed be done.

From the firms' point of view, the demand for labour is a **derived
demand**. In other words, firms want labour not for its own sake, but for the
output that it produces. When the 'price' of labour is low, firms will tend to
demand more of it than when the 'price' of labour is high. The wage rate
can be regarded as this 'price' of labour. On the employee side, it is argued
that more people tend to offer themselves for work when the wage is
relatively high.

On this basis, the demand for labour is expected to be downward
sloping and the supply of labour upward sloping, as in Figure 5.3. As usual,
the equilibrium in a free market will be at the intersection of demand and
supply, so firms will hire L^* labour at a wage rate of w^*.

The consequences of such a market being away from equilibrium are
important. Consider Figure 5.4. Suppose the wage rate is set above the
equilibrium level at w_1. The high wage rate encourages more people to
offer themselves for work — up to the amount of labour L_s. However,
at this wage rate employers are prepared to hire only up to L_d labour.
Think about what is happening here. There are people offering themselves
for work who cannot find employment: in other words, there is
unemployment. Thus, one possible cause of unemployment is a wage rate
that is set above the equilibrium level.

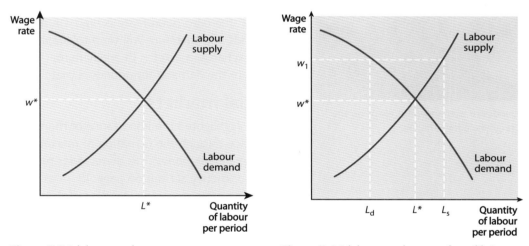

Figure 5.3 A labour market   **Figure 5.4** A labour market out of equilibrium

The foreign exchange market

When you take your holidays in Spain, you need to buy euros. Equally,
when German tourists come to visit London, they need to buy pounds. If
there is buying going on, then there must be a market — remember from
Chapter 1 that a market is a set of arrangements that enable transactions
to be undertaken. So here is another sort of market to be considered. The
exchange rate is the price at which two currencies exchange, and it can be
analysed using demand and supply.

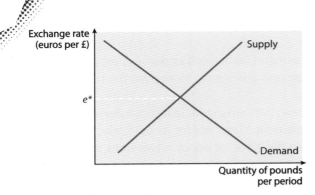

Exchange rate
(euros per £)

Supply

e*

Demand

Quantity of pounds
per period

Figure 5.5 The market for pounds

Pounds are exchanged for euros on the foreign exchange market

Consider the market for pounds, and focus on the exchange rate between pounds and euros, as shown in Figure 5.5. Think first about what gives rise to a demand for pounds. It is not just German tourists who need pounds to spend on holiday: anyone holding euros who wants to buy UK goods needs pounds in order to pay for them. So the demand for pounds comes from people in the euro area who want to buy UK goods or services — or assets. When the exchange rate for the pound in euros is high, potential buyers of UK goods get relatively few pounds per euro, so the demand will be relatively low, whereas if the euro per pound rate is relatively low, they get more for their money. Hence the demand curve is expected to be downward sloping.

Foreign exchange as a derived demand

One point to notice from this is that foreign exchange is another example of a derived demand, in the sense that people want pounds not for their own sake, but for the goods or services that they can buy. One way of viewing the exchange rate is as a means by which to learn about the international competitiveness of UK exports. When the exchange rate is high, UK goods are less competitive in Europe, ceteris paribus. Notice the ceteris paribus assumption here. This is important because the exchange rate is not the only determinant of the competitiveness of UK goods: this also depends on the relative price levels in the UK and Europe.

How about the supply of pounds? Pounds are supplied by UK residents wanting euros to buy goods or services from Europe. From this point of view, when the euro/pound rate is high, UK residents get more euros for their pounds and therefore will tend to supply more pounds.

If the exchange market is in equilibrium, the exchange rate will be at e*, where the demand for pounds is matched by the supply.

Financial markets

Chapter 1 highlighted the importance of money in enabling exchange to take place through the operation of markets. This implies that people have a *demand for money*. This demand for money is associated with the functions of money set out on page 13 — as a medium of exchange, store of value, unit of account and standard of deferred payment. If there is a demand for money, then perhaps there should also be a market for money?

The demand for and supply of money

We can think of the demand for money depending on a number of factors — in particular, upon the number of transactions that people wish to undertake — which probably depends upon income. But is there a price of money? The price of money can be viewed in terms of opportunity cost. When people choose to hold money, they incur an opportunity cost, which can be seen as the next best alternative to holding money. For example, instead of holding money, you could decide to purchase a financial asset that would provide a rate of return, represented by the rate of interest. This rate of interest can thus be interpreted as the price of holding money.

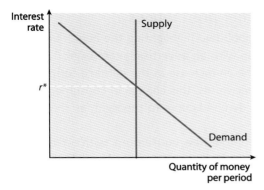

Interest rate

Supply

r^*

Demand

Quantity of money per period

Figure 5.6 The market for money

How about the supply of money? This will be discussed much later in the course, but for now, it can be assumed that the supply of money is determined by the Bank of England, and it can be assumed that this money supply will not depend upon the rate of interest. Figure 5.6 illustrates the market for money. The demand for money is shown to be downward sloping, as the higher the rate of interest, the greater the return that is sacrificed by holding money, so the smaller will be the demand for money. The supply of money does not depend upon the rate of interest (by assumption), so is shown as a vertical line. The market is in equilibrium when the rate of interest is at r^*, the level at which the demand and supply of money are equal.

Summary

- In the labour market, equilibrium is achieved through the wage rate. If the wage rate is set too high, it leads to unemployment.
- Demand and supply enable you to examine how the foreign exchange rate is determined.
- The model can also be applied to analyse the money market.

Changes to the market equilibrium

In order to make good use of the demand and supply model, it is necessary to introduce another of the economist's key tools. You have seen the way in which a market moves towards equilibrium between demand and supply through price adjustments and movements along the demand and supply curves. This is static analysis, in the sense that a ceteris paribus assumption is imposed by holding constant the factors that influence demand and supply, and focusing on the way in which the market reaches equilibrium.

In the next stage, one of these background factors is changed, and the effect of this change on the market equilibrium is then analysed. In other words, beginning with a market in equilibrium, one of the factors affecting either demand or supply is altered, and the new market equilibrium is then studied. In this way, two static equilibrium positions — before and after — will be compared. This approach is sometimes known as **comparative static analysis**, and is a device often used by economists.

> **Key term**
>
> **comparative static analysis** examines the effect on equilibrium of a change in the external conditions affecting a market

A market for dried pasta

Begin with a simple market for dried pasta, a basic staple foodstuff obtainable in any supermarket. Figure 5.7 shows the market in equilibrium. D_0 represents the demand curve in this initial situation, and S_0 is the supply curve. The market is in equilibrium with the price at P_0, and the quantity being traded is Q_0. It is equilibrium in the sense that pasta producers are supplying just the amount of pasta that consumers wish to buy at that price. This is the 'before' position. Some experiments will now be carried out with this market by disturbing the equilibrium.

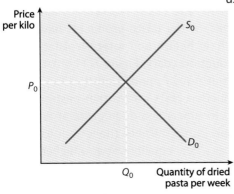

Price per kilo

S_0

P_0

D_0

Q_0 — Quantity of dried pasta per week

Figure 5.7 A market for dried pasta

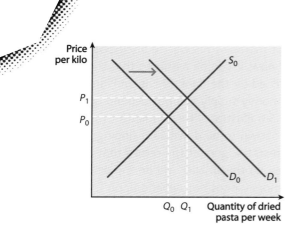

Figure 5.8 A change in consumer preferences for dried pasta

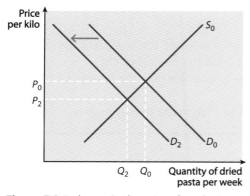
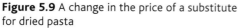

Figure 5.9 A change in the price of a substitute for dried pasta

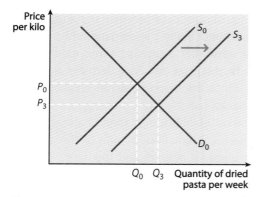

Figure 5.10 New pasta-making technology

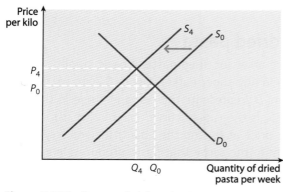

Figure 5.11 An increase in labour costs

A change in consumer preferences

Suppose that a study is published highlighting the health benefits of eating pasta, backed up with an advertising campaign. The effect of this is likely to be an increase in the demand for pasta at any given price. In other words, this change in consumer preferences will shift the demand curve to the right, as shown in Figure 5.8.

The market now adjusts to a new equilibrium, with a new price P_1, and a new quantity traded at Q_1. In this case, both price and quantity have increased as a result of the change in preferences. There has been a movement along the supply curve.

A change in the price of a substitute

A second possibility is that there is a fall in the price of fresh pasta. This is likely to be a close substitute for dried pasta, so the probable result is that some former consumers of dried pasta will switch their allegiance to the fresh variety. This time the demand curve for dried pasta moves in the opposite direction, as can be seen in Figure 5.9. Here the starting point is the original position, with market equilibrium at price P_0 and a quantity traded Q_0. After the shift in the demand curve from D_0 to D_2, the market settles again with a price of P_2 and a quantity traded of Q_2. Both price and quantity traded are now lower than in the original position.

An improvement in pasta technology

Next, suppose that a new pasta-making machine is produced, enabling dried pasta makers to produce at a lower cost than before. This advancement reduces firms' costs, and consequently they are prepared to supply more dried pasta at any given price. The starting point is the same initial position, but now it is the supply curve that shifts — to the right. This is shown in Figure 5.10.

Again, comparative static analysis can be undertaken. The new market equilibrium is at price P_3, which is lower than the original equilibrium, but the quantity traded is higher at Q_3.

An increase in labour costs

Finally, suppose that pasta producers face an increase in their labour costs. Perhaps the Pasta Workers' Union has negotiated higher wages, or the pasta producers have become subject to stricter health and safety legislation, which raises their production costs. Figure 5.11 starts as usual with equilibrium at price P_0 and quantity Q_0.

The increase in production costs means that pasta producers are prepared to supply less dried pasta at any given price, so the supply curve shifts to the left — to S_4. This takes the market to a new equilibrium at a higher price than before (P_4), but with a lower quantity traded (Q_4).

Changes in consumer preferences are just one factor affecting the market for dried pasta

Interrelated markets

There are situations in which a change in one market will have knock-on effects in other markets. For example, suppose that for some reason the price of pizza falls, perhaps because of a fall in the costs faced by pizza producers, so there is a fall in the equilibrium price of pizza. This could well lead to a decrease in demand for dried pasta, resulting in a lower equilibrium price and quantity. There will also be a decrease in demand for labour by producers of dried pasta, and a resulting reduction in wages. There is therefore a series of knock-on effects spreading across markets because they are interrelated.

Using the demand and supply model

The demand and supply model can help in understanding how market equilibrium may be determined, and how it may change as conditions change. For example, think about the market for a commodity such as cocoa, and the way it may change over time. Cocoa is a key ingredient of chocolate, so the demand for cocoa will reflect movements in the demand for chocolate. The supply of cocoa is dependent upon the number of producers, and on the factors that affect the success of the cocoa harvest — weather conditions, the incidence of disease or parasites and so on.

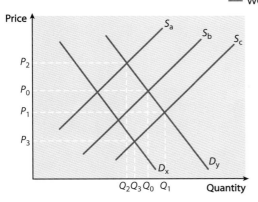

Figure 5.12 The demand and supply of cocoa

Cocoa prices have been quite volatile over recent years, and the demand and supply model can help to provide an explanation. Consider Figure 5.12, which shows possible positions for the demand curve (D_x and D_y) and the supply curve (S_a, S_b and S_c).

Suppose that in one period, the demand curve is D_y and supply is at S_b, which might perhaps be a year in which there is a 'normal' harvest. The equilibrium price here is P_0. Suppose that in the following period, there is an exceptional 'glut' harvest, so the supply curve shifts to S_c, but with the demand curve remaining at D_y. The price falls to a new equilibrium at P_1. If the following period brings a poor harvest, such that supply shifts to S_a, price finds a new equilibrium up at P_2. If in the following period, a big harvest is accompanied by a decrease in demand (perhaps because of a recession), the market could end up with supply at S_c and demand at D_x, with an equilibrium price at P_3. The model thus helps by suggesting possible explanations for volatility in prices in commodity markets.

The same sort of reasoning can be applied to other markets as well, whether in looking for an explanation of rising house prices, or in seeking to analyse the demand for public transport.

Exercise 5.2

Discuss how the demand and supply model could help to explain variations in house prices.

Exercise 5.3

For each of the following market situations, sketch a demand and supply diagram, and undertake a comparative static analysis to see what happens to the equilibrium price and quantity. Explain your answers.

a An increase in consumer incomes affects the demand for bus travel.
b New regulations on environmental pollution force a firm making paint to increase outlay on reducing its emission of toxic fumes.
c A firm of accountants brings in new, faster computers, which have the effect of reducing the firm's costs.
d An outbreak of bird flu causes consumers of chicken to buy burgers instead. (What is the effect on both markets?)

Summary

- Comparative static analysis enables you to analyse the way in which markets respond to external shocks, by comparing market equilibrium before and after a shock.
- All you need to do is to figure out whether the shock affects demand or supply, and in which direction.
- The size and direction of the shifts of the demand and supply curves determine the overall effect on equilibrium price and quantity traded.
- Where markets are related, the effects of a change in conditions in one market may have knock-on effects elsewhere.

Case study 5.1

Profits and superships

In August 2001 the *Financial Times* reported that ship-owners were facing serious problems. Shipping rates (the prices that ship-owners charge for carrying freight) had fallen drastically in the second quarter of 2001.

For example, on the Europe–Asia route, rates fell by 8% eastbound and 6% westbound, causing the ship-owners' profits to be squeezed. Here are some relevant facts and issues:

1 New 'superships', having been ordered a few years earlier, were coming into service with enhanced capacity for transporting freight.
2 A worldwide economic slowdown was taking place; Japan was in lengthy recession and the US economy was also slowing, affecting the growth of world trade.
3 Fuel prices were falling.
4 The structure of the industry is fragmented, with ship-owners watching each other's orders for new ships.
5 New ships take a long time to build.
6 Shipping lines face high fixed costs with slender margins.

Shipping rates fell drastically in 2001

Case study 5.1 (continued)

Follow-up questions

Assume that this is a competitive market. (This will allow you to draw supply and demand curves for the market.) There is some evidence for this, as shipping lines face 'slender margins' (see 6). This suggests that the firms face competition from each other, and are unable to use market power to increase profit margins.

a How would you expect the demand and supply curves to move in response to the first three factors mentioned (i.e. 1, 2 and 3)? Sketch a diagram for yourself.

b Why should the shipping lines undertake a large-scale expansion at a time of falling or stagnant demand?

Elasticity: the sensitivity of demand and supply

Key terms

elasticity a measure of the sensitivity of one variable to changes in another variable

price elasticity of demand (PED) a measure of the sensitivity of quantity demanded to a change in the price of a good or service. It is measured as:

$$\frac{\text{\% change in quantity demanded}}{\text{\% change in price}}$$

Both the demand for and the supply of a good or service can be expected to depend upon its price as well as other factors. It is often interesting to know just how sensitive demand and/or supply will be to a change in either price or one of the other determinants — for example, in predicting how market equilibrium will change in response to a change in the market environment. The sensitivity of demand or supply to a change in one of its determining factors can be measured by its **elasticity**.

The price elasticity of demand

The most common elasticity measure is the **price elasticity of demand (PED)**. This measures the sensitivity of the quantity demanded of a good or service to a change in its price.

The elasticity is defined as the percentage change in quantity demanded divided by the percentage change in the price.

We define the percentage change in price as $100 \times \Delta P/P$ (where Δ means 'change in' and P stands for 'price'). Similarly, the percentage change in quantity demanded is $100 \times \Delta Q/Q$.

When the demand is highly price sensitive, the percentage change in quantity demanded following a price change will be large relative to the percentage change in price. In this case, *PED* will take on a value that is numerically greater than 1. For example, suppose that a 2% change in price leads to a 5% change in quantity demanded; the elasticity is then −5 divided by 2 = −2.5. When the elasticity is numerically greater than 1, demand is referred to as being *price elastic*.

There are two important things to notice about this. First, because the demand curve is downward sloping, the elasticity will always be negative. This is because the changes in price and quantity are always in the opposite direction. Second, you should try to calculate the elasticity only for a relatively small change in price, as it becomes unreliable for very large changes.

When demand is not very sensitive to price, the percentage change in quantity demanded will be smaller than the original percentage change in price, and the elasticity will then be numerically less than 1. For example, if a 2% change in price leads to a 1% change in quantity demanded, then the value of the elasticity will be −1 divided by 2 = −0.5. In this case, demand is referred to as being *price inelastic*.

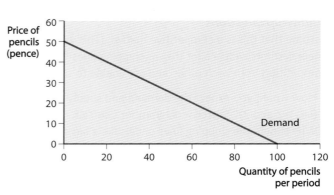
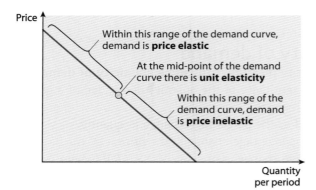

Figure 5.14 The own-price elasticity of demand varies along a straight line

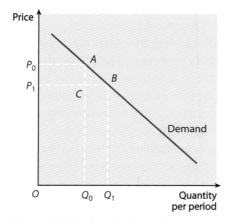

Figure 5.15 Demand and total revenue

This phenomenon is true for any straight-line demand curve: in other words, demand is price elastic at higher prices and inelastic at lower prices. At the halfway point the elasticity is exactly −1, which is referred to as *unit elasticity*.

Why should this happen? The key is to remember that elasticity is defined in terms of the percentage changes in price and quantity. Thus, when price is relatively high, a 1p change in price is a small percentage change, and the percentage change in quantity is relatively large — because when price is relatively high, the initial quantity is relatively low. The reverse is the case when price is relatively low. Figure 5.14 shows how the elasticity of demand varies along a straight-line demand curve.

The price elasticity of demand and total revenue

One reason why firms may have an interest in the price elasticity of demand is that, if they are considering changing their prices, they will be eager to know the extent to which demand will be affected. For example, they may want to know how a change in price will affect their total revenue. As it happens there is a consistent relationship between the price elasticity of demand and total revenue.

Total revenue is given by price multiplied by quantity. In Figure 5.15, if price is at P_0, quantity demanded is at Q_0 and total revenue is given by the area of the rectangle OP_0AQ_0. If price falls to P_1 the quantity demanded rises to Q_1, and you can see that total revenue has increased, as it is now given by the area OP_1BQ_1. This is larger than at price P_0, because in moving from P_0 to P_1 the area P_1P_0AC is lost, but the area Q_0CBQ_1 is gained, and the latter is the larger. As you move down the demand curve, total revenue at first increases like this, but then decreases — try sketching this for yourself to check that it is so.

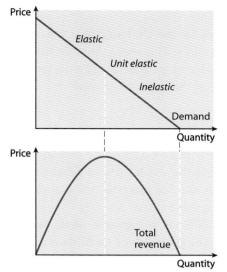

Figure 5.16 Elasticity and total revenue

Elasticity and a straight-line demand curve

For the case of a straight-line demand curve the relationship is illustrated in Figure 5.16. Remember that demand is price elastic when price is relatively high. This is the range of the demand curve in which total revenue rises as price falls. This makes sense, as in this range the quantity demanded is sensitive to a change in price and increases by more (in percentage terms) than the price falls. This implies that, as you move to the right in this segment, total revenue rises. The increase in quantity sold more than compensates for the fall in price. However, when the mid-point is reached and demand becomes unit elastic, total revenue stops rising — it is at its maximum at this point. The remaining part of the curve is inelastic: that is, the increase in quantity demanded is no longer sufficient to compensate for the decrease in price, and total revenue falls. Table 5.1 summarises the situation.

Table 5.1 Total revenue, elasticity and a price change

Price elasticity of demand	For a price increase, total revenue...	For a price decrease, total revenue
Elastic	falls	rises
Unit elastic	does not change	does not change
Inelastic	rises	falls

Thus, if a firm is aware of the price elasticity of demand for its product, it can anticipate consumer response to its price changes, which may be a powerful strategic tool.

One very important point must be made here. If the price elasticity of demand varies along a straight-line demand curve, such a curve cannot be referred to as either elastic or inelastic. To do so is to confuse the elasticity with the *slope* of the demand curve. It is not only the steepness of the demand curve that determines the elasticity, but also the point on the curve at which the elasticity is measured.

Some other demand curves

Some special cases of the price elasticity of demand should also be mentioned. Demand may sometimes be totally insensitive to price, so that the same quantity will be demanded whatever price is set for it. In such a situation, demand is said to be *perfectly inelastic*. The demand curve in this case is vertical — as in D_i in Figure 5.17. In this situation, the numerical value of the price elasticity is zero, as quantity demanded does not change in response to a change in the price of the good.

Another extreme is shown on the same figure, where D_e is a horizontal demand curve and demand is *perfectly elastic*. The numerical value of the elasticity here is infinity. Consumers demand an unlimited quantity of the good at price P_e. No firm has any incentive to lower price below this level, but if price were to rise above P_e, demand would fall to zero.

The third demand curve plotted in Figure 5.17 ($D_{PED=1}$) is another special case. This is a demand curve which has unit elasticity along its entire length. Mathematically it is a *rectangular hyperbola*. The key feature of such a demand curve is that if price changes at any point along the curve, total revenue remains constant, as the percentage change in price is offset by an equal and opposite percentage change in the quantity demanded.

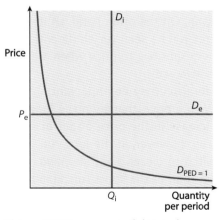

Figure 5.17 Some unusual demand curves

An example

A study by the Institute for Fiscal Studies for the UK found that the price elasticity of demand for wine was −1.69. This means that demand for wine is elastic. If the price of wine were to increase by 10% (ceteris paribus), there would be a fall of 16.9% in the quantity of wine demanded.

Influences on the price elasticity of demand

A number of important influences on the price elasticity of demand can now be identified. The most important is the availability of substitutes for the good or service under consideration. For example, think about the demand for cauliflower. Cauliflower and broccoli are often seen as being very similar, so if the price of cauliflower is high one week, people might quite readily switch to broccoli. The demand for cauliflower can be said to be price sensitive (elastic), as consumers can readily substitute an alternative product. On the other hand, if the price of all vegetables rises, demand will not change very much, as there are no substitutes for vegetables in the diet. Thus, goods that have close substitutes available will tend to exhibit elastic demand, whereas the demand for goods for which there are no substitutes will tend to be more inelastic.

Associated with this is the question of whether an individual regards a good or service as a necessity or as a luxury item. If a good is a necessity, then demand for it will tend to be inelastic, whereas if a good is regarded as a luxury, consumers will tend to be more price-sensitive. This is closely related to the question of substitutes, as by labelling a good as a necessity one is essentially saying that there are no substitutes for it.

A second influence on the price elasticity of demand is the relative share of the good or service in overall expenditure. You may tend not to notice small changes in the price of an inexpensive item that is a small part of overall expenditure, such as salt or sugar. This tends to mean that demand for that good is relatively inelastic. On the other hand, an item that figures large in the household budget will be seen very differently, and consumers will tend to be much more sensitive to price when a significant proportion of their income is involved.

Finally, the time period under consideration may be important. Consumers may respond more strongly to a price change in the long run than to one in the short run. An increase in the price of petrol may have limited effects in the short run; however, in the long run, consumers may buy smaller cars or switch to diesel. Thus, demand tends to be more elastic in the long run than in the short run. Habit or commitment to a certain pattern of consumption may dictate the short-run pattern of consumption, but people do eventually adjust to price changes.

Cauliflower and broccoli are easily substituted, so demand will be elastic

Study tip

Be ready to identify the four key influences on the *PED*:
- the availability of close substitutes for the good
- whether the good is perceived as a necessity
- the proportion of income or expenditure devoted to the good
- the time period over which elasticity is considered

Exercise 5.4

Examine Table 5.2, which shows the demand for a particular red wine at different prices.

Table 5.2 Demand for Château Econ

Price (£)	Quantity demanded (bottles per week)
10	20
8	40
6	60
4	80
2	100

a Draw the demand curve.
b Calculate the price elasticity of demand when the initial price is £8.
c Calculate the price elasticity of demand when the initial price is £6.
d Calculate the price elasticity of demand when the initial price is £4.

Summary

- The price elasticity of demand measures the sensitivity of the quantity of a good demanded to a change in its price.
- As there is an inverse relationship between quantity demanded and price, the price elasticity of demand is always negative.
- Where consumers are sensitive to a change in price, the percentage change in quantity demanded will exceed the percentage change in price. The elasticity of demand then takes on a value that is numerically greater than 1, and demand is said to be elastic.
- Where consumers are not very sensitive to a change in price, the percentage change in quantity demanded will be smaller than the percentage change in price. Elasticity of demand then takes on a value that is numerically smaller than 1, and demand is said to be inelastic.
- When demand is elastic, a fall (rise) in price leads to a rise (fall) in total revenue.
- When demand is inelastic, a fall (rise) in price leads to a fall (rise) in total revenue.
- The size of the price elasticity of demand is influenced by the availability of substitutes for a good, the relative share of expenditure on the good in the consumer's budget and the time that consumers have to adjust.

Key term

income elasticity of demand (YED) a measure of the sensitivity of quantity demanded to a change in consumer incomes

The income elasticity of demand

Elasticity is a measure of the sensitivity of a variable to changes in another variable. In the same way as the price elasticity of demand is determined, an elasticity measure can be calculated for any other influence on demand or supply. **Income elasticity of demand (YED)** is therefore defined as:

$$YED = \frac{\text{\% change in quantity demanded}}{\text{\% change in consumer income}}$$

Unlike the price elasticity of demand, the income elasticity of demand may be either positive or negative. Remember the distinction between normal and inferior goods? For normal goods the quantity demanded will increase as consumer income rises, whereas for inferior goods the quantity demanded will tend to fall as income rises. Thus, for normal goods the YED will be positive, whereas for inferior goods it will be negative.

Suppose you discover that the *YED* for wine is 0.7. How do you interpret this number? If consumer incomes were to increase by 10%, the demand for wine would increase by 10 × 0.7 = 7%. This example of a normal good may be helpful information for wine merchants, if they know that consumer incomes are rising over time.

On the other hand, if the *YED* for coach travel is −0.3, that means that a 10% increase in consumer incomes will lead to a 3% fall in the demand for coach travel — perhaps because more people are travelling by car. In this instance, coach travel would be regarded as an inferior good.

In some cases the *YED* may be very strongly positive. For example, suppose that the *YED* for digital cameras is +2. This implies that the quantity demanded of such cameras will increase by 20% for every 10% increase in incomes. An increase in income is encouraging people to devote more of their incomes to this product, which increases its share in total expenditure. Such goods are referred to as **superior or luxury goods**.

Cross elasticity of demand

Another useful measure is the **cross elasticity of demand (*XED*)**. This is helpful in revealing the interrelationships between goods. Again, this measure may be either positive or negative, depending on the relationship between the goods. It is defined as:

$$XED = \frac{\% \text{ change in quantity demanded of good X}}{\% \text{ change in price of good Y}}$$

If the *XED* is seen to be positive, it means that an increase in the price of good Y leads to an increase in the quantity demanded of good X. For example, an increase in the price of apples may lead to an increase in the demand for pears. Here apples and pears are regarded as substitutes for each other; if one becomes relatively more expensive, consumers will switch to the other. A high value for the *XED* indicates that two goods are very close substitutes. This information may be useful in helping a firm to identify its close competitors.

On the other hand, if an increase in the price of one good leads to a fall in the quantity demanded of another good, this suggests that they are likely to be complements. The *XED* in this case will be negative. An example of such a relationship would be that between coffee and sugar, which tend to be consumed together.

Examples

A study by the Institute for Fiscal Studies using data for the UK found that the cross elasticity of demand for wine with respect to a change in the price of beer was −0.60, whereas the cross elasticity with respect to the price of spirits was +0.77. The negative cross elasticity with beer suggests that wine and beer are complements: a 10% increase in the price of beer would lead to a 6% fall in the quantity demanded of wine. In contrast, the cross elasticity of demand for wine with respect to the price of spirits is positive, suggesting that wine and spirits are substitutes. An increase in the price of spirits leads to an increase in the quantity demanded of wine.

Key terms

superior good one for which the income elasticity of demand is positive, and greater than 1, such that as income rises, consumers spend proportionally more on the good

cross elasticity of demand (*XED*) a measure of the sensitivity of quantity demanded of a good or service to a change in the price of some other good or service

Price elasticity of supply

As elasticity is a measure of sensitivity, its use need not be confined to influences on demand, but can also be turned to evaluating the sensitivity of quantity *supplied* to a change in its determinants — in particular, price.

It was argued in Chapter 4 that the supply curve is likely to be upward sloping, so the price elasticity of supply can be expected to be positive. In other words, an increase in the market price will induce firms to supply more output to the market. The **price elasticity of supply (PES)** is defined as:

$$PES = \frac{\% \text{ change in the quantity supplied}}{\% \text{ change in price}}$$

So, if the price elasticity of supply is 0.8, an increase in price of 10% will encourage firms to supply 8% more. As with the price elasticity of demand, if the elasticity is greater than 1, supply is referred to as being elastic, whereas if the value is between 0 and 1, supply is considered inelastic. *Unit elasticity* occurs when the price elasticity of supply is exactly 1, so that a 10% increase in price induces a 10% increase in quantity supplied.

The value of the elasticity will depend on how willing and able firms are to increase their supply. For example, if firms are operating close to the capacity of their existing plant and machinery, they may be unable to respond to an increase in price, at least in the short run. So here again, supply can be expected to be more elastic in the long run than in the short run. Figure 5.18 illustrates this. In the short run, firms may be able to respond to an increase in price only in a limited way, and so supply may be relatively inelastic, as shown by S_s in the figure. However, firms can become more flexible in the long run by installing new machinery or building new factories, so supply can then become more elastic, moving to S_l.

There are two limiting cases of supply elasticity. For some reason, supply may be fixed such that, no matter how much price increases, firms will not be able to supply any more. For example, it could be that a certain amount of fish is available in a market, and however high the price goes, no more can be obtained. Equally, if the fishermen know that the fish they do not sell today cannot be stored for another day, they have an incentive to sell, however low the price goes. In these cases, supply is perfectly inelastic. At the other extreme is perfectly elastic supply, where firms would be prepared to supply any amount of the good at the going price.

These two possibilities are shown in Figure 5.19. Here S_i represents a perfectly inelastic supply curve: firms will supply Q_i whatever the price, perhaps because that is the amount available for sale. Supply here is vertical. At the opposite extreme, if supply is perfectly elastic then firms are prepared to supply any amount at the price P_e, and the supply curve is given by the horizontal line S_e.

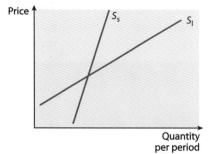

Figure 5.18 Short- and long-run supply

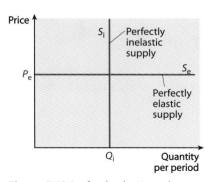

Figure 5.19 Perfectly elastic and inelastic supply

Imagine the following scenario. You are considering a pricing strategy for a bus company. The economy is heading into recession, and the company is running at a loss. Your local rail service provider has announced an increase in rail fares. How (if at all) do you use the following information concerning the elasticity of bus travel with respect to various variables to inform your decision on price? Would you raise or lower price?

- price elasticity of demand   −1.58
- income elasticity of demand   −2.43
- cross elasticity of demand with respect to rail fares   +2.21
- your price elasticity of supply   +1.15

Summary

- The income elasticity of demand (*YED*) measures the sensitivity of quantity demanded to a change in consumer incomes. It serves to distinguish between normal, luxury and inferior goods.
- The cross elasticity of demand (*XED*) measures the sensitivity of the quantity demanded of one good or service to a change in the price of some other good or service. It can serve to distinguish between substitutes and complements.
- The price elasticity of supply (*PES*) measures the sensitivity of the quantity supplied to a change in the price of a good or service. The price elasticity of supply can be expected to be greater in the long run than in the short run, as firms have more flexibility to adjust their production decisions in the long run.

Case study 5.2

Rice

In 2007/08, sudden and unexpected rises in food prices hit the headlines. There were riots on the streets of cities in many countries around the world, with protestors demonstrating against massive increases in the prices of some staple foods, especially wheat and rice.

The increases affected some countries especially severely. In much of South East Asia, rice is a staple commodity, forming a part of most people's daily diet. For some countries, such as the Philippines, much of the rice consumed has to be imported, so the price rises caused particular difficulties. The demonstrators wanted governments to intervene to control the prices and protect the poor.

It was reported that in some countries, poor households were coping with the price rises by changing their eating habits, by consuming less meat, or by finding other

ways of cutting down. The United Nations called for worldwide action to prevent hunger and malnutrition from spreading.

People in South East Asia were severely affected by the rise in the price of rice in 2007/08

Follow-up questions

a Would you expect the demand for rice to be price elastic or inelastic?

b Explain your answer to part (a), referring to the passage to provide evidence to support your explanation.

c Do you think that government intervention to control prices would be an effective answer to the problem?

Case study 5.3

Bicycles

If you had visited Shanghai in the early 1990s, one thing that would have struck you is that the roads were dominated by bicycles. Cars were relatively few in number, and in busy streets in the city centre, cars had to thread their way through the mass of bicycles.

Now, things are different. True, there are still many more bicycles on the streets than you would find in the UK, but they have their own part of the road. This still causes mayhem at junctions, when cars need to turn across the cycle tracks, but things are more orderly. The number of cars has increased significantly.

In the period since the early 1990s, China's economy has gone through a period of rapid economic growth and transformation. As part of this process, real incomes have risen, and many households have become much better off, especially in the urban areas where much of the change has been concentrated.

Follow-up questions

a What reasons might help to explain the change in the pattern of traffic between cars and bicycles in China over the period described in the passage?

b What would you expect to be the nature of the income elasticity of demand for bicycles in China?

c What would you expect to be the nature of the income elasticity of demand for cars in China?

Case study 5.4

Fish

Imagine a remote island in the South Seas. Some of the islanders own canoes which they use to go fishing, selling their catch on the beach when they return each day. Some islanders only go fishing occasionally, as they find it more worthwhile to spend their time on other activities. The island has no electricity, so there is no way of storing the fish that are caught — if they are not consumed on the day of the catch, they must be thrown away.

The market for fish on the island is limited by the size of the population. Fortunately for the fishermen, the islanders enjoy fish, and regard it as an important part of their diet, although they also grow vegetables and raise goats and chickens. Fruit and coconuts are also abundant.

Follow-up questions

a What would you expect to be the nature of the price elasticity of supply in the short run (that is, on any given day)?

b Suppose that, on one particular day, fishing conditions are so good that all fishermen return with record catches. How would this affect the price of fish?

c How might the situation in (b) affect the supply of fish on the following day?

d How would you expect the supply of fish to be affected by the invention of a new style of canoe that makes it easier to catch fish?

e How would the market be affected if this new-style canoe also enabled fish to be traded with a neighbouring island?

Prices and resource allocation

Now that you are familiar with the use of the demand and supply model, it is time to take a wider view of the process of resource allocation within society. An important question is whether markets can be relied upon to guide this process, or whether there are times when markets will fail. This chapter begins to address this by examining how prices can act as market signals to guide resource allocation, and by identifying circumstances in which this process may not work effectively. In this discussion, some new tools will be needed in order to identify what constitutes an efficient allocation of resources.

Learning objectives

After studying this chapter, you should:
- have an overview of how the price mechanism works to allocate resources
- be able to see how prices provide incentives to producers
- be aware of the effects of the entry and exit of firms into and out of a market
- understand the concepts of productive and allocative efficiency
- be familiar with the way in which resources are allocated in a free market economy
- appreciate the situations in which markets may fail to allocate resources effectively

Dealing with scarcity

As Chapter 1 indicated, all societies face the fundamental economic problem of scarcity. Because there are unlimited wants but finite resources, it is necessary to take decisions on which goods and services should be produced, how they should be produced and for whom they should be produced. For an economy the size of the UK, there is thus an immense coordination problem. Another way of looking at this is to ask how consumers can express their preferences between alternative goods so that producers can produce the best mix of goods and services.

Some alternative possibilities for handling this problem will now be considered. In a **free market economy**, market forces are allowed to allocate resources. At the other extreme, in a centrally planned economy the state plans and directs resources into a range of uses. In between there is the mixed economy. In order to evaluate these alternatives, it is necessary to explore how each of them operates.

Key term

free market economy one in which resource allocation is guided by market forces without intervention by the state

Consumer demand for laptops has risen over the last few years

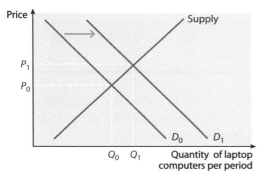

Figure 6.1 The market for laptop computers

In a free market economy, prices play the key role; this is sometimes referred to as the laissez-faire approach to resource allocation.

Prices and preferences

How can consumers signal their preferences to producers? Demand and supply analysis provides the clue. Figure 6.1 shows the demand and supply for laptop computers. These have become popular goods in recent years. That is to say, over time there has been a rightward shift in the demand curve — in the figure, from D_0 to D_1. This simply means that consumers are placing a higher value on these goods; they are prepared to demand more at any given price. The result, as you know from comparative static analysis, is that the market will move to a new equilibrium, with price rising from P_0 to P_1 and quantity traded from Q_0 to Q_1: there is a movement along the supply curve.

The shift in the demand curve is an expression of consumers' preferences; it embodies the fact that they value laptop computers more highly now than before. The price that consumers are willing to pay represents their valuation of laptop computers. This was discussed in Chapter 3: the demand curve represents the marginal social benefit derived from consuming the good.

Prices as signals and incentives

From the producers' perspective, the question is how they receive signals from consumers about their changing preferences. Price is the key. Figure 6.1 shows how an increase in demand for laptop computers leads to an increase in the equilibrium market price. The shift in the demand curve leads to an increase in the equilibrium price, which encourages producers to supply more computers — there is a movement *along* the supply curve. This is really saying that producers find it profitable to expand their output of laptop computers at that higher price. The price level is thus a signal to producers about consumer preferences.

Notice that the price signal works equally well when there is a decrease in the demand for a good or service. Figure 6.2, for example, shows the market for video recordings. With the advent of DVDs from 1997 and the Blu-ray Disc in 2006, there has been a large fall in the demand for video recordings, so the demand for them shifted to the left — consumers demanded fewer videos at any price. Thus, the demand curve shifted from D_0 to D_1. Producers of video recordings found that they could not sell as many videos at the original price as before, and had to reduce their price to avoid an increase in their unsold stocks. There was a movement along the supply curve to a lower equilibrium price at P_1, and a lower quantity traded at Q_1. You may like to think of this as a movement along the firm's production possibility curve for DVDs and videos.

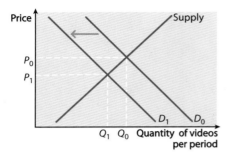

Figure 6.2 The market for video recordings

Extension material

As DVDs and Blu-ray Discs grew in popularity, the demand for video (VHS) recordings continued to fall, just as vinyl music records became a niche in the music market in earlier years. The changes in technology that allowed digital downloads of music and films have in turn affected the demand for DVDs and Blu-ray. This seems to be a dynamic market, in which technology leads to products going through a life cycle, with a surge in popularity followed by a consolidation phase before going into decline as yet more new and better products come onto the market. As the market for a product develops, there are likely to be changes in the PED, which can affect a firm's pricing strategy. Perhaps you can think of other markets in which this sort of life cycle has been apparent.

Thus, you can see how existing producers in a market receive signals from consumers in the form of changes in the equilibrium price, and respond to these signals by adjusting their output levels.

Entry and exit of firms

The discussion so far has focused on the reactions of existing firms in a market to changes in consumer preferences. However, this is only part of the picture. Think back to Figure 6.1, where there was an increase in demand for laptop computers following a change in consumer preferences. The equilibrium price rose, and existing firms expanded the quantity supplied in response. Those firms are now earning a higher producer surplus than before. Other firms not currently in the market will be attracted by these surpluses, perceiving this to be a profitable market in which to operate.

If there are no barriers to entry, more firms will join the market. This in turn will tend to shift the supply curve to the right, as there will then be more firms prepared to supply. As a result, the equilibrium market price will tend to drift down again, until the market reaches a position in which there is no further incentive for new firms to enter the market. This will occur when the rate of return for firms in the laptop market is no better than in other markets.

Figure 6.3 illustrates this situation. The original increase in demand leads, as before, to a new equilibrium with a higher price P_1. As new firms

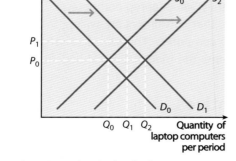

Figure 6.3 The market for laptop computers revisited

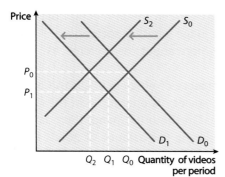

Figure 6.4 The market for video recordings

join the market in quest of producer surplus, the supply curve shifts to the right to S_2, pushing the price back down to P_0, but with the quantity traded now up at Q_2.

If the original movement in demand is in the opposite direction, as it was for video recordings in Figure 6.2, a similar long-run adjustment takes place. As the market price falls, some firms in the market may decide that they no longer wish to remain in production, and will exit from the market altogether. This will shift the supply curve to the left in Figure 6.4 (to S_2) until only firms that continue to find it profitable will remain in the market. In the final position price is back to P_0, and quantity traded has fallen to Q_2.

Summary

- If market forces are to allocate resources effectively, consumers need to be able to express their preferences for goods and services in such a way that producers can respond.
- Consumers express their preferences through prices, as prices will adjust to equilibrium levels following a change in consumer demand.
- Producers have an incentive to respond to changes in prices. In the short run this occurs through output adjustments of existing firms (movements along the supply curve), but in the long run firms will enter the market (or exit from it) until there are no further incentives for entry or exit.

Aspects of efficiency

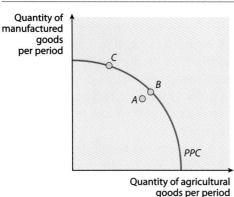

Figure 6.5 Productive efficiency

In tackling the fundamental economic problem of scarcity, a society needs to find a way of using its limited resources as effectively as possible. In normal parlance it might be natural to refer to this as a quest for *efficiency*. From an economist's point of view there are two key aspects of efficiency, both of which are important in evaluating whether markets in an economy are working effectively.

Chapter 1 introduced one of these aspects in relation to the production possibility curve (*PPC*). Figure 6.5 shows a country's production possibility curve. One of the choices to be made in allocating resources in this country is between producing agricultural or manufactured goods.

In Chapter 1 it was seen that at a production point such as *A* the economy would not be using its resources fully, since by moving to a point *on* the *PPC* it would be possible to produce more of both types of good. For example, if production took place at point *B*, then more of both agricultural and manufactured goods could be produced, so that society would be better off than at *A*.

A similar claim could be made for any point along the *PPC*: it is more efficient to be at a point *on* the frontier than at some points *within* it. However, if you compare point *B* with point *C*, you will notice that the economy produces more manufactured goods at *C* than at *B* — but only at the expense of producing fewer agricultural goods.

productive efficiency attained when a firm operates at minimum average total cost, choosing an appropriate combination of inputs (cost efficiency) and producing the maximum output possible from those inputs (technical efficiency)

allocative efficiency achieved when consumer satisfaction is maximised

economic efficiency a situation in which both productive efficiency and allocative efficiency have been reached

Pareto optimum an allocation of resources is said to be a Pareto optimum if no reallocation of resources can make an individual better off without making some other individual worse off

This draws attention to the trade-off between the production of the two sorts of goods. It is difficult to judge whether society is better off at *B* or at *C* without knowing more about the preferences of consumers.

This discussion highlights the two aspects of efficiency. On the one hand, there is the question of whether society is operating on the *PPC*, and thus using its resources effectively. On the other hand, there is the question of whether society is producing the balance of goods that consumers wish to consume. These two aspects of efficiency are known as **productive efficiency** and **allocative efficiency**, and are discussed in more detail below. The term **economic efficiency** is used to describe a situation in which both productive and allocative efficiency has been achieved — in other words, a situation in which society is producing the balance of goods that consumers wish to consume at minimum cost.

In terms of Figure 6.5, both *B* and *C* are on the *PPC*, so both are productively efficient points, but it is not possible to judge which of the two is better without knowing consumers' preferences.

An efficient point for a society would be one in which no redistribution of resources could make any individual better off without making some other individual worse off. This is known as the *Pareto criterion*, after the nineteenth-century economist Vilfredo Pareto, who first introduced the concept.

Notice, however, that *any* point along the *PPC* is a **Pareto optimum**: with a different distribution of income among individuals in a society, a different overall equilibrium will be reached.

Costs facing firms

total cost (*TC*) the sum of all costs that are incurred in producing a given level of output

average total cost (*ATC*) total cost divided by the quantity produced

marginal cost (*MC*) the cost of producing an additional unit of output

fixed costs costs incurred by a firm that do not vary with the level of output

sunk costs costs incurred by a firm that cannot be recovered if the firm ceases trading

In looking for productive efficiency, it is useful to begin by considering the costs faced by firms. As a firm expands its production, it incurs costs. In particular, it needs appropriate quantities of the factors of production that are used in producing output. In order to increase output, the firm may need to hire more workers, to rent more buildings and to obtain the required machinery and other capital goods.

In talking about costs, economists distinguish between total, marginal and average costs. **Total cost (*TC*)** is the sum of all costs that are incurred in order to produce a given level of output. Total cost will always increase as the firm increases its level of production, as this will require more inputs of factors of production, materials and so on.

Average total cost (*ATC* or *AC*) is simply the cost per unit of output — it is total cost divided by the level of output produced.

Equally important as these measures is the concept of **marginal cost (*MC*)**, which was introduced in Chapter 4. It is defined as the change in total cost associated with a small change in output. In other words, it is the additional cost incurred by the firm if it increases output by 1 unit.

Because the firm cannot vary some of its inputs in the short run, some costs may be regarded as fixed, and some as variable. In this short run, some **fixed costs** are **sunk costs**: that is, they are costs

Key term

variable costs costs that vary
with the level of output

that the firm cannot avoid paying even if it chooses to produce no output at all. However, the firm also incurs **variable costs**, which are directly related to the level of output. These arise as the firm takes on more labour or varies its use of other factors of production. The way in which the costs will vary depends on the required mix of the factors of production, and on whether the prices of labour or capital alter as output increases. Total costs are the sum of fixed and total variable costs.

total costs = total fixed costs + total variable costs

Extension material

Marginal cost is of particular significance in economic analysis. We have seen how existing producers in a market receive signals from consumers in the form of changes in the equilibrium price, and respond to these signals by adjusting their output levels. Notice that the threshold at which a firm will decide it is not profitable to supply is the point at which the price received by the firm reaches the cost to the firm of producing the last unit of the good — in other words, the marginal cost. If the price is higher than the cost of an extra unit, the firm will make a profit by producing it. In a competitive market the supply curve reflects that marginal cost.

Quantitative skills 6.1

Relationship between output and costs

Table 6.1 provides an arithmetic example to illustrate the relationship between these different aspects of costs. The firm represented here faces fixed costs of £225 per week. The table shows the costs of production for up to 6,000 units of the firm's product per week. Column 3 shows total variable costs of production: you can see that these rise quite steeply as the volume of production increases. Adding fixed and variable costs gives the total costs at each output level. This is shown in column 4, which is the sum of columns 2 and 3.

Table 6.1 The short-run relationship between output and costs (in £s)

(1) Output (000 units per week)	(2) Fixed costs (TFC)	(3) Total variable costs (TVC)	(4) Total costs (2) + (3) (TC)	(5) Average total cost (4)/(1) (ATC)	(6) Marginal cost $\Delta(4)/\Delta(1)$ (MC)	(7) Average variable cost (3)/(1) (AVC)	(8) Average fixed cost (2)/(1) (AFC)
1	225	85	310	310		85	225
					65		
2	225	150	375	187.5		75	112.5
					60		
3	225	210	435	145		70	75
					90		
4	225	300	525	131.25		75	56.25
					175		
5	225	475	700	140		95	45
					395		
6	225	870	1,095	182.5		145	37.5

Average total cost (*ATC*, column 5) is calculated as total cost divided by output. To calculate marginal cost, you need to work out the additional cost of producing an extra unit of output at each output level. This is calculated as the change in costs divided by the change in output (Δ column 4 divided by Δ column 1, where Δ means 'change in').

Finally, average variable costs $\left(AVC, \text{i.e.} \dfrac{\text{column 3}}{\text{column 1}}\right)$ and average fixed costs $\left(AFC, \text{i.e.} \dfrac{\text{column 2}}{\text{column 1}}\right)$ can be calculated.

Efficiency in a market

Aspects of efficiency can be explored further by considering an individual market. First, however, it is necessary to identify the conditions under which productive and allocative efficiency can be attained.

Productive efficiency

The production process entails combining a range of inputs of factors of production in order to produce output. Firms may find that there are benefits from large-scale production, so that efficiency may improve as firms expand production.

Economies of scale

Productive efficiency can be seen in terms of the average total cost of production. In this context, productive efficiency can be defined in terms of the minimum average cost at which output can be produced, noting that average cost is likely to vary at different scales of output. **Economies of scale** occur when an increase in the scale of production leads to production at lower long-run average cost.

Average cost may fall as the scale of output increases for various reasons. Some of these are to do with the way the firm operates as it expands. For example, as a firm expands, it may be able to use division of labour, or to utilise technology that is only suitable for large-scale production. Another possibility is that an expanding firm can set up specialist departments to handle finance or procurement more cost-effectively. These are known as **internal economies of scale**, as they are internal to the firm itself.

External economies of scale occur where average cost falls as the whole industry expands. For example, it might be that as an industry expands, a pool of skilled labour becomes available, so that a firm is able to hire labour more cost-effectively without having to spend out on training.

There may also be situations in which average cost rises as the scale of output increases. **Internal diseconomies of scale** arise where a firm faces higher average costs at higher levels of output. For example, a firm may reach the stage where it becomes more difficult to manage the firm because the size of the labour force, or the logistics of operation, become unwieldy. **External diseconomies of scale** could be present where the industry grows to such an extent that there is insufficient skilled labour, thus pushing wages and labour costs up.

Two aspects of productive efficiency

There are two aspects to productive efficiency. One entails making the best possible use of the inputs of factors of production: in other words, it is about producing as much output as possible from a given set of inputs. This is sometimes known as **technical efficiency**. However, there is also the question of whether the *best* set of inputs has been chosen. For example, there may be techniques of production that use mainly capital and not much labour, and alternative techniques that are more labour intensive. The firm's choice between these techniques will depend crucially on the relative prices of capital and labour. This is sometimes known as **cost efficiency**.

Key terms

economies of scale occur for a firm when an increase in the scale of production leads to production at lower long-run average cost

internal economies of scale economies of scale that arise from the expansion of a firm

external economies of scale economies of scale that arise from the expansion of the industry in which a firm is operating

internal diseconomies of scale diseconomies of scale that arise from the expansion of a firm

external diseconomies of scale diseconomies of scale that arise from the expansion of the industry in which a firm is operating

technical efficiency attaining the maximum possible output from a given set of inputs

cost efficiency the appropriate combination of inputs of factors of production, given the relative prices of those factors

Microeconomics Part 2

To attain productive efficiency, both technical efficiency and cost efficiency need to be achieved. In other words, productive efficiency is attained when a firm chooses the appropriate combination of inputs (cost efficiency) and produces the maximum output possible from those inputs (technical efficiency).

It is worth noting that the choice of technique of production may depend crucially upon the level of output that the firm wishes to produce. The balance of factors of production may well change according to the scale of activity. If the firm is producing very small amounts of output, it may well choose a different combination of capital and labour than if it were planning mass production on a large scale.

The firm's decision process

Thus, the firm's decision process is a three-stage procedure. First, the firm needs to decide how much output it wants to produce. Second, it has to choose an appropriate combination of factors of production, given that intended scale of production. Third, it needs to produce as much output as possible, given those inputs. Once the intended scale of output has been decided, the firm has to minimise its costs of production. These decisions are part of the response to the question of *how* output should be produced. Remember also the concept of *marginal cost*, which refers to the cost faced by a firm in changing the output level by a small amount. This becomes an important part of the discussion.

Allocative efficiency

Allocative efficiency is about whether an economy allocates its resources in such a way as to produce a balance of goods and services that matches consumer preferences. In a complex modern economy, it is clearly difficult to identify such an ideal result. How can an appropriate balance of goods and services be identified?

Take the market for an individual product, such as the market for laptop computers that was considered earlier in the chapter. It was then argued that, in the long run, the market could be expected to arrive at an equilibrium price and quantity at which there was no incentive for firms either to enter the market or to exit from it. Figure 6.6 will remind you of the market situation.

The sequence of events in the diagram shows that, from an initial equilibrium with price at P_0 and quantity traded at Q_0, there was an increase in demand, with the demand curve shifting to D_1. In response, existing firms expanded their supply, moving up the supply curve. However, the lure of the producer surplus (abnormal profits) that was being made by these firms then attracted more firms into the market, such that the supply curve shifted to S_2, a process that brought the price back down to the original level of P_0.

Now think about that price from the point of view of a firm. P_0 is at a level where there is no further incentive to attract new firms, but no firm wishes to leave the market. In other words, no surplus is being made on that marginal unit, and the marginal

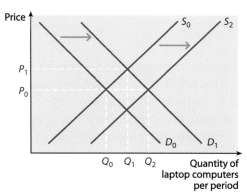

Figure 6.6 The market for laptop computers revisited again

firm is just breaking even on it. The price in this context would seem to be just covering the marginal cost of production.

However, it was also argued that from the consumers' point of view, any point along the demand curve could be regarded as the marginal benefit received from consuming a good or service.

Price and marginal cost

Where is all this leading? Putting together the arguments, it would seem that market forces can carry a market to a position in which, from the firms' point of view, the price is equal to marginal cost, and from the consumers' point of view, the price is equal to marginal benefit.

This is an important result. Suppose that the marginal benefit from consuming a good were higher than the marginal cost to society of producing it. It could then be argued that society would be better off producing more of the good because, by increasing production, more could be added to benefits than to costs. Equally, if the marginal cost were above the marginal benefit from consuming a good, society would be producing too much of the good and would benefit from producing less. The best possible position is thus where marginal benefit is equal to marginal cost — in other words, where *price is set equal to marginal cost*.

If all markets in an economy operated in this way, resources would be used so effectively that no reallocation of resources could generate an overall improvement. Allocative efficiency would be attained. The key question is whether the market mechanism will work sufficiently well to ensure that this happens — or whether it will fail. In other words, are there conditions that could arise in a market, in which price would not be set at marginal cost? This will be explored in the next chapter.

Efficiency and society

If a society could reach a position of economic efficiency — that is, achieving both productive and allocative efficiency — would that always be the ideal position? Thinking back to Samuelson's three economic questions introduced in Chapter 1, allocative and productive efficiency provide answers to *what* should be produced and to *how* it should be produced. After all, allocative efficiency is about producing the appropriate balance of goods and services that consumers wish to produce, and productive efficiency is about whether those goods and services are being produced at minimum cost. However, the third question remains: *for whom* are these goods and services being produced? In other words, there may also be issues surrounding *equity*.

A society could find itself in a position in which it had achieved a position of economic efficiency, but where the resources in society were heavily concentrated in the hands of a relatively small part of the population, with other groups being excluded and living in poverty. In such a situation the authorities may see the need for resources to be redistributed in order to protect the vulnerable. It is important to remember this, as it suggests that economic efficiency is not the *only* objective of a society. Furthermore, it will be seen that there are many situations in which a free market will fail to achieve economic efficiency.

Exercise 6.1

Consider Figure 6.7, which shows a production possibility curve (*PPC*) for an economy that produces consumer goods and investment goods.

Identify each of the following (*Hint*: in some cases more than one answer is possible):

a a point of productive inefficiency

b a point that is Pareto-superior to *B*

c a point of productive efficiency

d a point of allocative efficiency

e an unattainable point (*Hint*: think about what would need to happen for society to reach such a point)

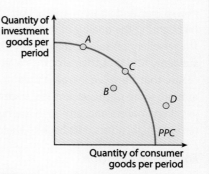

Figure 6.7 A production possibility curve

Summary

- A society needs to find a way of using its limited resources as efficiently as possible.
- Productive efficiency occurs when firms have chosen appropriate combinations of factors of production and produce the maximum output possible from those inputs.
- Allocative efficiency occurs when firms produce an appropriate bundle of goods and services, given consumer preferences.
- An allocation of resources is said to be a Pareto optimum if no reallocation of resources can make an individual better off without making some other individual worse off.
- An individual market exhibits aspects of allocative efficiency when the marginal benefit received by society from consuming a good or service matches the marginal cost of producing it — that is, when price is equal to marginal cost.
- A society may also need to consider the distribution of resources in society, balancing equity with efficiency.

Case study 6.1

Jewellery

A local craft market is populated by a variety of stalls selling a range of items — antiques, football memorabilia, second-hand books, hand-made jewellery and other items. The same sellers are present at the market every time it opens, each with their regular place, but there are some vacant stalls. The stall holders just make enough profit to make it worth their while.

One week, the craft market is featured in the local newspaper, and an item appears on local television highlighting the quality of design and value for money of the jewellery on sale at the market. The jewellery sellers suddenly find that their stock is moving very rapidly, and realise that they can increase their prices. As word gets around, some of the vacant stalls are taken up by new jewellery makers and, although the number of buyers remains high, prices drift back to their original level.

New jewellery stalls have come into the local craft market

Follow-up question

Sketch a demand and supply diagram to track these changes in the market for jewellery.

MICROECONOMICS

Part 3
Market failure and government intervention

Market failure and externalities

If markets are to be effective in guiding the allocation of resources in society, a precondition is that market prices reflect the full costs and benefits associated with market transactions. However, there are many situations in which this is not so, and there are costs or benefits that are external to the workings of the market mechanism. This chapter examines the circumstances in which this may happen, and provides a justification for government intervention to improve the workings of the market.

Learning objectives

After studying this chapter, you should:
- recognise situations in which the free market mechanism may fail to take account of costs or benefits associated with market transactions
- be familiar with situations in which there may be a divergence between private and social costs or benefits, such that price is not set equal to marginal cost
- be able to use diagrams to analyse positive and negative externalities in either production or consumption
- appreciate reasons why government may need to intervene in markets in which externalities are present
- be familiar with a wide range of examples of externalities
- recognise ways in which external costs or benefits may be valued

Market failure

The previous chapter discussed how the price mechanism leads to an allocation of resources that is good for society. This works through the process described by Adam Smith as the invisible hand, under which prices act as signals to both consumers and producers. They adjust their economic decisions in response to price and thus price affects how resources are used in the economy.

However, Adam Smith also sounded a word of warning. He felt that there were too many factors that interfered with the free market system, such as over-protectionism and restrictions on trade. At the same time, he was not convinced that a free market economy would be wholly effective, noting also that firms might at times collude to prevent the free operation of the market mechanism:

People of the same trade seldom meet together, even for merriment and diversion, but the conversation ends in a conspiracy against the public, or in some contrivance to raise prices...

(Adam Smith, *The Wealth of Nations*, Vol. I)

So there may be situations in which consumer interests need to be protected, if there is some sort of **market failure** that prevents the best outcome from being achieved.

Causes of market failure

There are several situations in which market failure may arise. In each case, the failure occurs because a market settles in a position in which **marginal social cost** diverges from **marginal social benefit**. This chapter introduces the most important reasons for market failure, and explores one of the most common.

Imperfect competition

The discussion of market adjustment in the previous chapter argued that the entry and exit of firms ensures that a market will evolve towards a situation in which price is equal to marginal cost. However, this rested on the assumption that markets are competitive. Firms were fairly passive actors in these markets, responding perhaps rather tamely to changes in consumer preferences. The real world is not necessarily like that, and in many markets, firms have more power over their actions than has so far been suggested.

In the extreme, there are markets in which production is dominated by a single firm. In 1998 Microsoft was taken to court in the USA, accused of abusing its dominant position. At the time, Microsoft was said to control 95% of the market for operating systems for PCs — and not just in the USA. This was 95% of the *world* market. When a firm achieves such dominance, there is no guarantee that it will not try to exploit its position at the expense of consumers.

The very fact that there was a court case against Microsoft bears witness to the need to protect consumers against dominant firms. In the UK, the Competition and Markets Authority (CMA) has a brief to monitor the way in which markets operate and to guard against anti-competitive acts by firms.

This is one example of how imperfect competition can lead to a distortion in the allocation of resources. Firms with a dominant position in a market may be able to restrict output and charge higher prices to consumers.

Externalities

If market forces are to guide the allocation of resources, it is crucial that the costs that firms face and the prices to which they respond reflect the actual costs and benefits associated with the production and consumption of goods. There are a number of situations and markets where some costs or benefits are not reflected in market prices. Such a situation is known as an **externality**. This causes a divergence between marginal social cost and marginal social benefit in a market equilibrium situation. In the presence of such externalities, a price will emerge that is not equal to the 'true' marginal cost.

There are many examples of such externalities. An obvious one is pollution. A firm that causes pollution in the course of its production process imposes costs on others, but does not have to pay these costs. As a result, these costs are not reflected in market prices. This causes a distortion in the allocation of resources.

Pollution is an example of an externality

Not all externalities are negative. There may be situations in which a firm takes an action that benefits others. For example, if a firm chooses to upgrade the road that runs past its factory, this benefits other users of the road, even though they did not have to contribute to the cost of the upgrading.

Not all externalities are on the supply side of the market. There may also be externalities in consumption, which may be positive or negative. If your neighbours mount an excellent firework display on 5 November, you can benefit without having to pay. Externalities are discussed later in this chapter.

Information failure

If markets are to perform a role in allocating resources, it is important that all relevant economic agents (buyers and sellers) have good information about market conditions, otherwise they may not be able to take rational decisions.

In order to determine their own willingness to pay, consumers must be able to perceive the benefits to be gained by their consuming particular goods or services. Such benefits may not always be clear. For example, people may not fully perceive the benefits to be gained from education — or they may fail to appreciate the harmfulness of smoking tobacco.

In other market situations, economic agents on one side of the market may have different information from those on the other side: for example, sellers may have information about the goods that they are providing that buyers cannot discern. Chapter 8 explains that such information failure can also lead to a suboptimal allocation of resources.

Public goods

There is a category of goods known as public goods, which because of their characteristics cannot be provided by a purely free market. Street lighting is one example: there is no obvious way in which a private firm could charge all the users of street lighting for the benefits they receive from it. Such goods are also discussed in Chapter 8.

Merit and demerit goods

The government believes that some goods will be underconsumed in a free market. If people do not fully perceive the benefits to be gained from consuming a good, they will demand less than is socially desirable. In some developing countries, education may show aspects of a merit good, if parents do not fully perceive the benefits that their children could gain from it. This helps to explain low school enrolment in such countries.

There are also some goods that the government believes will be overconsumed in a free market. An obvious example is addictive recreational drugs, where consumers may misperceive the benefits from consumption. Chapter 8 examines these goods in more detail.

Income distribution

Chapter 9 discusses equity. It is commonly accepted that safeguards need to be in place in any economy to ensure that the distribution of income does not become so skewed that poverty escalates. If there is substantial poverty in a society, the allocation of resources is unlikely to be optimal. Chapter 9 examines the extent to which inequality in the distribution of income can be considered a form of market failure that requires some intervention by government. In addition, Chapter 9 examines some ways in which government intervention may have unintended effects — in other words, situations in which there may be *government failure*.

Summary

- Free markets do not always lead to the best possible allocation of resources: there may be market failure.
- Markets may fail when there is imperfect competition, so that firms are able to utilise market power to disadvantage consumers.
- When there are costs or benefits that are external to the price mechanism, the economy will not reach allocative efficiency.
- Markets can operate effectively only when participants in the market have full information about market conditions.
- Public goods have characteristics that prevent markets from supplying the appropriate quantity.
- Goods that the government believes will be underconsumed (overconsumed) in a free market are known as merit goods (demerit goods).
- Most societies are concerned to some extent with notions of equity.

Study tip

Market failure is often used as a justification for government intervention in markets, so it is important to be aware of its various causes and to be able to recognise situations in which market failure may occur.

Externalities

Externality is one of those ugly words invented by economists, which says exactly what it means. It simply describes a cost or a benefit that is external to the market mechanism.

An externality will lead to a form of market failure because, if the cost or benefit is not reflected in market prices, it cannot be taken into consideration by all parties to a transaction. In other words, there may be costs or benefits resulting from a transaction that are borne (or enjoyed) by some third party not directly involved in that transaction. This in turn implies that decisions will not be aligned with the best interests of society.

For example, if there is an element of costs that is not borne by producers, it is likely that 'too much' of the good will be produced. Where there are benefits that are not included, it is likely that too little will be produced. Later in the chapter, you will see that this is exactly what happens. Externalities can affect either demand or supply in a market: that is to say, they may arise either in **consumption** or in **production**.

In approaching this topic, begin by tackling Exercise 7.1, which offers an example of each type of externality.

Exercise 7.1

Each of the following situations describes a type of externality. Do each of these externalities affect production or consumption?

a A factory in the centre of a town, and close to a residential district, emits toxic fumes through a chimney during its production process. Residents living nearby have to wash their clothes more frequently because of the pollution, and incur higher medical bills as a result of breathing in the fumes.

b Residents living along a main road festoon their houses with lavish Christmas lights and decorations during the month of December, helping passers-by to capture the festive spirit.

Toxic fumes

Example (a) in Exercise 7.1 is a negative production externality. The factory emits toxic fumes. These impose costs on the residents (third parties) living nearby, who incur high washing and medical bills. The households face costs as a result of the production activities of the firm, so the firm does not face the full costs of its activity.

Thus, the **private costs** faced by the producer are lower than the social costs: that is, the costs faced by society as a whole. The producer will take decisions based only on its private costs, ignoring the **external costs** it imposes on society.

Figure 7.1 illustrates this situation under the assumption that firms operate in a competitive market (i.e. there is not a monopoly). Here, D (MSB) represents the demand curve, which was characterised in Chapter 3 as representing the marginal social benefit derived from consuming a good. In other words, the demand curve represents consumers' willingness to pay for the good, and thus reflects their marginal valuation of the product.

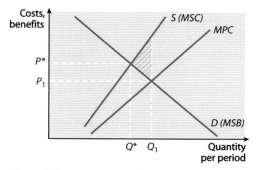

Figure 7.1 A negative production externality

Producers face marginal private costs given by the line *MPC*, but in fact impose higher costs than this on society. Thus *S* represents the supply curve that includes these additional costs imposed on society. This may be regarded as being the marginal social cost (*MSC*) of the firms' production.

If the market is unregulated by the government, firms will choose how much to supply on the basis of the marginal (private) cost they face, shown by *MPC* in Figure 7.1. The market equilibrium will thus be at quantity traded Q_1, where firms just break even on the marginal unit sold. Price will be set at P_1.

This is not a good outcome for society, as it is clear that there is a divergence between the price in the market and the 'true' marginal cost — in other words, a divergence between marginal social benefit and marginal social cost. It is this divergence that is at the heart of the market failure. The last unit of this good sold imposes higher costs on society than the marginal benefit derived from consuming it. Too much is being produced.

In fact, the optimum position is at Q^*, where marginal social benefit is equal to marginal social cost. This will be reached if the price is set equal to (social) marginal cost at P^*. Less of the good will be consumed, but also less pollution will be created, and society will be better off than at Q_1.

> **Quantitative skills 7.1**
>
> **Identifying welfare loss in a diagram**
> Figure 7.1 can be used to identify the extent of the welfare loss that society suffers. When the market outcome is at Q_1 instead of at Q^*, each unit of output that is produced above Q^* imposes a cost equal to the vertical distance between *MSC* and *MPC*. The total of this is the shaded area, which therefore represents the difference between marginal social cost and marginal benefit over the range of output between the optimum output and the free market level of output.

Christmas lights

Situation (b) in Exercise 7.1 is an example of a positive consumption externality. Residents of this street decorate their homes in order to share the Christmas spirit with passers-by. The benefit they gain from the decorations spills over and adds to the enjoyment of others. In other words, the social benefits from the residents' decision to provide Christmas decorations go beyond the private enjoyment that they receive.

Figure 7.2 illustrates this situation. *MPB* represents the marginal private benefits gained by residents from the Christmas lights; but *MSB* represents the full marginal social benefit that the community gains, which is higher than the *MPB*. Residents will provide decorations up to the point Q_2, where their marginal private benefit is just balanced by the marginal cost of the lights. However, if the full social benefits received are taken into account, Q^* would be the optimum point: the residents do not provide enough décor for the community to reach the optimum. The shaded triangle in Figure 7.2 shows the welfare loss: that is, the amount of social benefit forgone if the outcome is at Q_2 instead of Q^*.

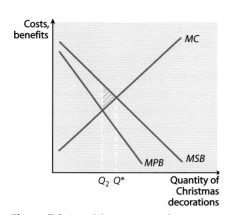

Figure 7.2 A positive consumption externality

Positive and normative revisited

Situation (b) in Exercise 7.1 is a reminder of the distinction between positive and normative analysis, which was introduced in Chapter 1. Economists would agree that Figure 7.2 shows the effects of a beneficial consumption externality. However, probably not everyone would agree that the lavish Christmas decorations are providing such benefits. This is where a *normative judgement* comes into play. It could equally be argued that the lavish Christmas decorations are unsightly and inappropriate, or that they constitute a distraction for drivers and are therefore likely to cause accidents. After all, not everyone enjoys the garish.

Exercise 7.1 (continued)

Discussion so far has focused on two examples of externalities: a production externality that had negative effects, and a consumption externality that was beneficial to society. In fact, there are two other possibilities.

c A factory that produces chemicals, located on the banks of a river, installs a new water purification plant that improves the quality of water discharged into the river. A trout farm located downstream finds that its productivity increases, and that it has to spend less on filtering the water.

d Liz, a 'metal' enthusiast, enjoys playing her music at high volume late at night, in spite of the fact that she lives in a flat with inadequate sound insulation. The neighbours prefer rock, but cannot escape the metal.

Water purification

Example (c) is a production externality that has *positive* effects. The action taken by the chemical firm to purify its waste water has beneficial effects on the trout farm, which finds that its costs have been reduced without it having taken any action whatsoever.

Figure 7.3 shows the position facing the chemicals firm. It has relatively high marginal private costs, given by MPC. However, its actions have reduced the costs of the trout farm, so the 'social' cost of the firm's production activities is lower than its private cost. Thus, in this case marginal social cost, shown by MSC in the figure, is lower than marginal private cost. The firm will produce up to the point where MPC equals marginal social benefit: that is, at Q_3.

In this market position, notice that the marginal benefit society receives from consuming the product is higher than the marginal social cost of producing it, so too little of the product is being consumed for society's good. Society would be better off at Q^*, where marginal social benefit is equal to marginal social cost.

Again, the shaded triangle in Figure 7.3 represents the extent of the inefficiency: it is given by the excess of marginal social benefit over marginal social cost, over the range of output between the market outcome and society's optimum position.

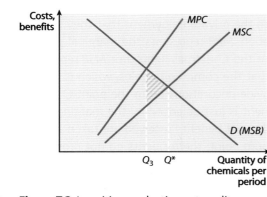

Figure 7.3 A positive production externality

Rock and metal

Example (d) is a *negative* consumption externality. Liz, the metal fan, gains benefit from listening to her music at high volume, but the neighbours also hear her music and suffer as a result. Indeed, it may be that when they try to listen to rock, the metal interferes with their enjoyment. Their benefit is reduced by having to hear the metal.

Figure 7.4 illustrates this. The situation can be interpreted in terms of the benefits that accrue as a result of Liz's consumption of loud metal music. Liz gains benefit as shown by the line *MPB*, which represents marginal private benefit. However, the social benefit is lower than this if the vexation suffered by the neighbours is taken into account, so *MSB* in Figure 7.4 represents the marginal social benefits from Liz's metal.

Liz will listen to metal up to the point where her marginal private benefit is just equal to the marginal cost of playing it, at Q_4. However, the optimal position that takes the neighbours into consideration is where marginal social benefit is equal to marginal cost — at Q^*. Thus, Liz plays too much metal for the good of society.

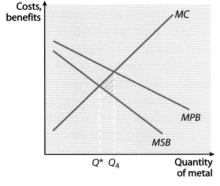

Figure 7.4 A negative consumption externality

Summary
- Markets can operate effectively only if all relevant costs and benefits are taken into account in decision making.
- Some costs and benefits are external to the market mechanism, and are thus neglected, causing a distortion in resource allocation.
- Such external costs and benefits are known as 'externalities'.
- Externalities may occur in either production or consumption, thereby affecting either demand or supply.
- Externalities may be either positive or negative, but either way resources will not be optimally allocated if they are present.

Externalities occur in a wide variety of market situations, and constitute an important source of market failure. This means that externalities may hinder the achievement of good resource allocation from society's perspective.

Exercise 7.2

Discuss examples of some externalities that you meet in everyday situations, and classify them as affecting either production or consumption.

Study tip

Make sure that you understand the four varieties of externalities:
- negative production externality
- negative consumption externality
- positive production externality
- positive consumption externality

Be ready with examples of each.

Externalities and the environment

Concern for the environment has been growing in recent years, with 'green' lobbyist groups demanding attention, sometimes through demonstrations and protests. There are so many different facets to this question that it is sometimes difficult to isolate the core issues. Externalities lie at the heart of much of the debate.

Global warming

Some of the issues are international in nature, such as the debate over global warming. The key concern here is the way in which emissions of greenhouse gases are said to be warming up the planet. Sea levels are rising and major climate change seems imminent.

One reason why this question is especially difficult to tackle is that actions taken by one country can have effects on other countries. Scientists argue that the problem is caused mainly by pollution created by transport and industry, especially in the richer countries of the world. However, poorer countries suffer the consequences as well, especially countries such as Bangladesh. Here much of the land is low lying and prone to severe flooding almost every year. In some years up to three-quarters of the land area is under water at the height of the flooding.

In principle, this is similar to example (a) in Exercise 7.1: it is an example of a negative production externality, in which the nations causing most of the damage face only part of the costs caused by their lifestyles and production processes. The inevitable result in an unregulated market is that too much pollution is produced.

When externalities cross international borders in this way, the problem can be tackled only through international cooperation. For example, at the Kyoto World Climate Summit held in Japan in 1997, almost every developed nation agreed to cut greenhouse gas emissions by 6% by 2010. However, the USA, the largest emitter of carbon dioxide, withdrew from the agreement in early 2001, fearing the consequences of such a restriction on the US economy. Canada also withdrew, and it proved difficult to find an agreement for the future that was acceptable to all parties.

Acid rain and water resources

Global warming is not the only example of international externality effects. Scandinavian countries have suffered from acid rain caused by pollution in other European countries, including the UK. Forest fires left to burn in Indonesia have caused air pollution in neighbouring Singapore.

Another environmental issue concerns rivers. Some of the big rivers of the world, such as the Nile in Africa, pass through several countries on their way to the sea. The Nile runs through Egypt at the end of its journey, and is crucial for the economy. If countries further upstream were to increase their usage of the river, perhaps through new irrigation projects, this could have disastrous effects on Egypt. Again, the actions of one set of economic agents would be having damaging effects on others, and these effects would not be reflected in market prices, in the sense that the upstream countries would not have to face the full cost of their actions.

Part of the problem here can be traced back to the difficulty of enforcing property rights. If the countries imposing the costs could be forced to make appropriate payment for their actions, this would help to bring the costs back within the market mechanism. Such a process is known in economics as 'internalising the externality', and will be examined later in this chapter.

Biodiversity

Concern has also been expressed about the loss of *biodiversity*, a word that is shorthand for 'biological diversity'. The issue here is that when a section of rainforest is cleared to plant soya beans, or for timber, it is possible that species of plants, insects or animals whose existence is not even known at present may be wiped out. Many modern medicines are based on chemicals that occur naturally in the wild. By eradicating species before they have been discovered, possible scientific advances will be forgone. Notice that when it comes to measuring the value of what is being destroyed, biodiversity offers particular challenges — namely, the problem of putting a value on something that might not even be there.

Externalities and transport

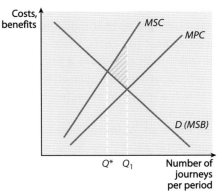

Figure 7.5 Traffic congestion

The London authorities have attempted to tackle traffic congestion in the city using the congestion charge. When traffic on the roads reaches a certain volume, congestion imposes heavy costs on road users. This is another example of an externality.

Figure 7.5 illustrates the situation. Suppose that D (MSB) represents the demand curve for car journeys along a particular stretch of road. When deciding whether or not to undertake a journey, drivers will balance the marginal benefit gained from making the journey against the marginal cost that they face. This is given by MPC — the marginal private cost of undertaking journeys. When the road is congested, a motorist who decides to undertake the journey adds to the congestion, and slows the traffic. The MPC curve incorporates the cost to the motorist of joining a congested road, and the chosen number of journeys will be at Q_1.

However, in adding to the congestion the motorist not only suffers the costs of congestion, but also imposes some marginal increase in costs on all other users of the road. Thus, the marginal social costs (MSC) of undertaking journeys are higher than the cost faced by any individual motorist. MSC is therefore higher than MPC. Society would be better off with lower congestion: that is, with the number of journeys undertaken being limited to Q^*, where marginal social benefit equals marginal social cost. By imposing a charge on motorists entering central London, the authorities are trying to ensure that drivers face at least part of the social costs they impose on others by using congested roads.

The congestion charge in London is an attempt to make drivers face some of the social costs of their journeys

Externalities and health

Healthcare is a sector in which there is often public provision, or at least some state intervention in support of the health services. In the UK, the National Health Service is the prime provider of healthcare, but private healthcare is also available, and the use of private health insurance schemes is on the increase. Again, externalities can help to explain why there should be a need for government to intervene.

Consider the case of vaccination against a disease such as measles. Suppose an individual is considering whether or not to be vaccinated. Being vaccinated reduces the probability of that individual contracting the disease, so there are palpable potential benefits to that individual. However, these benefits must be balanced against the costs. There may be a direct charge for the vaccine, some individuals may have a phobia against needles, or they may be concerned about possible side-effects. Individuals will opt to be vaccinated only if the marginal expected benefit to them is at least as large as the marginal cost.

From society's point of view, however, there are potential benefits that individuals will not take into account. After all, if they do contract measles, there is a chance of their passing it on to others. Indeed, if lots of people decide not to be vaccinated, there is the possibility of a widespread epidemic, which would be costly and damaging to many.

Figure 7.6 illustrates this point. The previous paragraph argues that the social benefits to society of having people vaccinated against measles exceed the private benefits that will be perceived by individuals, so marginal social benefits exceed marginal private benefits. Private individuals will choose to balance marginal private benefit against marginal private cost at Q_1, whereas society would prefer more people to be vaccinated at Q^*. This parallels the discussion of a positive consumption externality. Chapter 8 considers another aspect of healthcare provision.

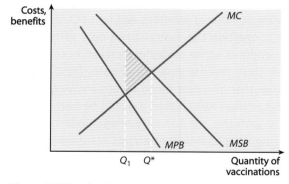

Figure 7.6 Vaccination

Externalities and education

You are reading this textbook, so it is reasonably safe to assume that you are following a course in economics. You have decided to demand education. This is yet another area in which externalities may be important.

When you decided to take AS/A Levels (including economics), there were probably a number of factors that influenced your decision. Perhaps you intend to demand even more education in the future, by going on to study at university. Part of your decision process probably takes into account the fact that education improves your future earnings potential. Your expected lifetime earnings depend in part upon your level of qualifications. Research has shown that, on average, graduates earn more during their lifetimes than non-graduates. This is partly because there is a productivity effect: by becoming educated, you cultivate a range of skills that in later life will make you more productive, and this helps to explain why you can expect higher lifetime earnings than someone who chooses not to demand education. There is also a signalling effect, as having a degree signals to potential employers that you have the ability to cope with university study and have gained a range of skills.

What does society get out of this? Evidence suggests that, not only does education improve productivity, but a *group* of educated workers cooperating with each other become even more productive. This is an externality effect, as it depends upon interaction between educated workers — but each individual perceives only the individual benefit, and not the benefits of cooperation.

In other words, when you decide to undertake education, you do so on the basis of the expected private benefits that you hope to gain from education. However, you do not take into account the additional benefits through cooperation that society will reap. So here is another example of a positive consumption externality. As with healthcare, some other aspects of education will be discussed in Chapter 8.

Externalities and tourism

As international transport has become easier and cheaper, more people want to travel to new and different destinations. For less developed countries, this offers an opportunity to earn much-needed foreign exchange.

There has been some criticism of this. The building of luxury hotels in the midst of the poverty that characterises many less developed countries is said to have damaging effects on the local population by emphasising differences in living standards.

However, constructing the infrastructure that tourists need may have beneficial effects on the domestic economy. Improved roads and communication systems can benefit local businesses. This effect can be interpreted as an externality, in the sense that the local firms will face lower costs as a result of the facilities provided for the tourist sector.

Summary

- Externalities arise in many aspects of economic life.
- Environmental issues are especially prone to externality effects, as market prices do not always incorporate environmental issues, especially where property rights are not assigned.
- Congestion on the roads can also be seen as a form of externality.
- Externalities also arise in the areas of healthcare provision and education, where individuals do not always perceive the full social benefits that arise.
- A number of approaches have been proposed to measure externalities. Measurement may enable a social cost–benefit analysis to be made of projects involving a substantial externality element.

Exercise 7.3

Table 7.1 shows the situation in a market where pollution is generated by the production process.

a At what level of output would marginal social benefit be equal to marginal private cost? (*Note*: this is the quantity of output that would be produced by firms in an unregulated competitive market.)

b By how much would marginal social cost exceed marginal private cost at this level of output?

c At what level of output would marginal social benefit be equal to marginal social cost?

d What amount of tax would induce firms to supply this quantity of output?

Table 7.1 A market with pollution

Quantity produced (thousands per week)	Marginal social benefit	Marginal private cost	Marginal social cost
10	80	5	10
20	75	10	20
30	70	20	35
40	60	32	60
50	48	48	90
60	30	75	125
70	8	110	175

Dealing with externalities

Externalities arise in situations where there are items of cost or benefit associated with transactions, and these are not reflected in market prices. In these circumstances a free market will not lead to an optimum allocation of resources. One approach to dealing with such market situations is to bring those externalities into the market mechanism — a process known as **internalising an externality**.

The London congestion charge may be seen as an attempt to internalise the externality effects of traffic congestion by forcing motorists to face the full marginal cost of their decisions. In the case of pollution this principle would entail forcing the polluting firms to face the full social cost of their production activities. This is sometimes known as the *polluter pays* principle.

Pollution

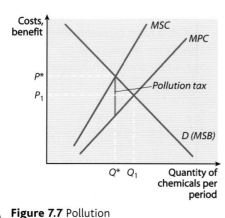

Figure 7.7 Pollution

Figure 7.7 illustrates a negative production externality: pollution. Suppose that firms in the market for chemicals use a production process that emits toxic fumes, thereby imposing costs on society that the firms themselves do not face. In other words, the marginal private costs faced by these firms are less than the marginal social costs that are inflicted on society. As explained earlier in the chapter, firms in this market will choose to produce up to point Q_1 and charge a price of P_1 to consumers. At this point, marginal social benefit is below the marginal cost of producing the chemicals, so it can be claimed that 'too much' of the product is being produced — that society would be better off if production were at Q^*, with a price charged at P^*.

Note that this optimum position is not characterised by *zero* pollution. In other words, from society's point of view it pays to abate pollution only up to the level where the marginal benefit of reducing pollution is matched by the marginal cost of doing so. Reducing pollution to zero would be too costly.

How can society reach the optimum output of chemicals at Q*? In line with the principle that the polluter should pay, one approach would be to impose a tax on firms such that polluters face the full cost of their actions. In Figure 7.7, if firms were required to pay a tax equivalent to the vertical distance between marginal private cost (*MPC*) and marginal social cost (*MSC*), they would choose to produce at Q*, paying a tax equal to the green line on the figure.

An alternative way of looking at this question is via a diagram showing the marginal benefit and marginal cost of emissions reduction. In Figure 7.8, *MB* represents the marginal social benefits from reducing emissions of some pollutant and *MC* is the marginal costs of reducing emissions. The optimum amount of reduction is found where marginal benefit equals marginal cost, at e*. Up to this point, the marginal benefit to society of reducing emissions exceeds the marginal cost of the reduction, so it is in the interest of society to reduce pollution. However, beyond that point the marginal cost of reducing the amount of pollution exceeds the benefits that accrue, so society will be worse off. Setting a tax equal to t* in Figure 7.8 will induce firms to undertake the appropriate amount of emission reduction.

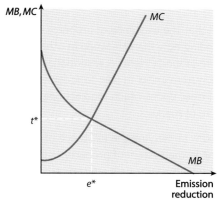

Figure 7.8 Reducing the emission of toxic fumes

This is not the only way of reaching the objective, however. Figure 7.8 suggests that there is another possibility — namely, to impose environmental standards, and to prohibit emissions beyond e*. This amounts to controlling quantity rather than price and, if the government has full information about marginal costs and marginal benefits, the two policies will produce the equivalent result.

Measuring benefits and costs

Either of the approaches outlined above will be effective — *if* the authorities have full information about the marginal costs and benefits. But how likely is this? There are many problems with this proviso. The measurement of both marginal benefits and marginal costs is fraught with difficulties.

The marginal social benefits of reducing pollution cannot be measured with great precision, for many reasons. It may be argued that there are significant gains to be made in terms of improved health and lower death rates if pollution can be reduced, but quantifying this is not straightforward. Even if it were possible to evaluate the saving in resources that would need to be devoted to future medical care resulting from the pollution, there are other considerations: quantification of the direct improvements to quality of life, whether or not to take international effects into account when formulating domestic policy, and the appropriate discount rate for evaluating benefits that will be received in the future. Moreover, the environmentalist and the industrialist may well arrive at different evaluations of the benefits of pollution control, reflecting their different viewpoints.

Exercise 7.4

You discover that your local authority has chosen to locate a new landfill site for waste disposal close to your home. What costs and benefits for society would result? Would these differ from your private costs and benefits? Would you object?

The measurement of costs may also be problematic. For example, it is likely that there will be differences in efficiency between firms. Those using modern technology may face lower costs than those using relatively old capital equipment. Do the authorities try to set a tax that is specific to each firm to take such differences into account? If they do not, but instead set a flat-rate tax, then the incentives may be inappropriate. This would mean that a firm using modern technology would face the same tax as one using old capital. The firm using new capital would then tend to produce too little output relative to those using older, less efficient capital.

Extension material

Property rights

Nobel prize winner Ronald Coase argued that the existence of property rights and transaction costs is key to understanding how markets work. In other words, the existence of a system of secure property rights is essential as an underpinning for the economy. The legal system exists in part to enforce property rights, and to provide the set of rules under which markets operate. When property rights fail, there is a failure of markets.

In this view of the world, one of the reasons underlying the existence of some externalities is that there is a failing in the system of property rights. For example, think about the situation in which a factory is emitting toxic fumes into a residential district. One way of viewing this is that the firm is interfering with local residents' clean air. If those residents could be given property rights over clean air, they could require the firm to compensate them for the costs it was inflicting. However, the problem is that, with such a wide range of people being affected to varying degrees (according to prevailing winds and how close they live to the factory), it is impossible in practical terms to use the assignment of property rights to internalise the pollution externality. This is because the problem of coordination requires high transaction costs in order for property rights to be individually enforced. Therefore, the government effectively takes over the property rights on behalf of the residents, and acts as a collective enforcer.

Ronald Coase thus argued that externality effects could be internalised in conditions where property rights could be enforced, and where the transaction costs of doing so were not too large.

Summary

- In seeking to counter the harmful effects of externalities, governments look for ways of internalising the externality, by bringing external costs and benefits within the market mechanism.
- For example, the 'polluter pays' principle argues that the best way of dealing with a pollution externality is to force the polluter to face the full costs of its actions.
- Attempts have been made to tackle pollution through taxation or through the regulation of environmental standards.
- In some cases the allocation of property rights can be effective in curbing the effects of externalities — so long as the transaction costs of implementing it are not too high.

Exercise 7.5

Each of the Figures 7.9–7.12 shows a particular type of externality.

For each figure, identify the sort of externality, and state whether the result is too much or too little output being traded in a free market.

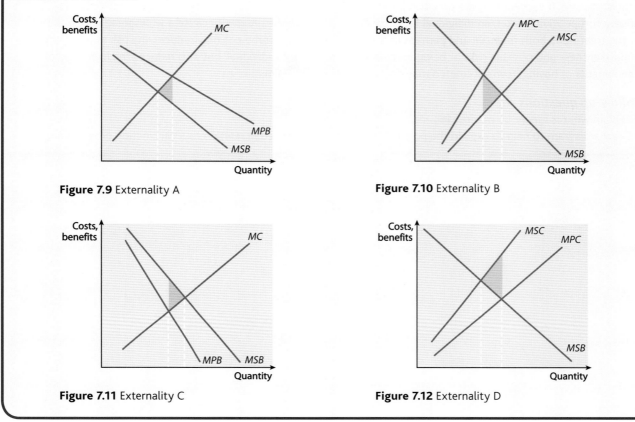

Figure 7.9 Externality A

Figure 7.10 Externality B

Figure 7.11 Externality C

Figure 7.12 Externality D

Case study 7.1

Healthcare: public or market?

In July 2013, the NHS celebrated its 65th anniversary amid continuing debate about whether healthcare should be state-provided, or whether market forces should be given a greater role. In the UK, market forces have played an increasing part in allocating resources within the public health sector through the operation of internal markets, but the debate over public vs private provision continues. So far, the proportion of health expenditure that is undertaken by the public sector has changed little.

What does economic analysis have to say about the matter? The justification for public provision of healthcare rests on the existence of **market failure**. There may be a number of reasons why there might be some form of market failure in the provision of healthcare, whether we consider the provision of preventative or curative measures.

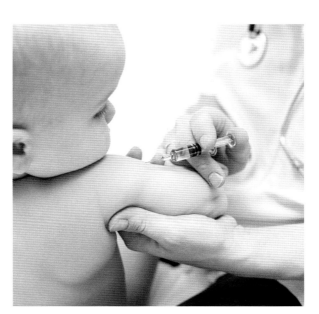

A vaccination programme has palpable benefits for society

Case study 7.1 (continued)

In the case of preventative healthcare, there may be other factors at work. Take the case of vaccination against disease. If vaccinations are provided by a private competitive market, an individual faces costs of the treatment, both financial and perhaps in the unpleasantness and possible risks of being vaccinated. The benefits of having been vaccinated may be perceived as relatively low, if the individual sees a low probability of being infected. However, the benefits of vaccination from the point of view of society may be greater, because a widespread vaccination programme not only reduces the risk of infection for each individual, but also reduces the likelihood of an epidemic.

Follow-up questions

a Explain what is meant by **market failure**.

b Draw a diagram to help to explain the possible market failure outlined in relation to a vaccination programme.

Chapter 8

Other forms of market failure

Externalities are not the only form of market failure. There are also situations where the characteristics of a good or service can affect the effective operation of a market. This chapter explores goods with unusual economic characteristics and markets that may fail as a result of problems with information.

Learning objectives

After studying this chapter, you should:
- understand the nature of public goods and problems that arise in their provision
- be able to identify examples of public goods
- be aware of the characteristics of merit and demerit goods
- be able to give examples of possible merit and demerit goods
- appreciate the significance of asymmetric information as a source of market failure

---

Public goods

Key terms

private good a good that, once consumed by one person, cannot be consumed by somebody else; such a good has excludability and is rivalrous

public good a good that is non-exclusive and non-rivalrous — consumers cannot be excluded from consuming the good, and consumption by one person does not affect the amount of the good available for others to consume

Most of the goods that individuals consume are **private goods**. You buy a can of Diet Coke, you drink it, and it's gone. You may choose to share it with a friend, but you do not have to: by drinking it you can prevent anyone else from doing so. Furthermore, once it is gone, it's gone: nobody else can subsequently consume that Coke.

The two features that characterise a private good are:
- other people can be excluded from consuming it
- once consumed by one person, it cannot be consumed by another

The first feature can be described as *excludability*, whereas the second feature might be described by saying that consumption of a private good is *rivalrous*: the act of consumption uses up the good.

Not all goods and services have these two characteristics. There are goods that, once provided, are available to all. In other words, people cannot be excluded from consuming such goods. There are other goods that do not diminish through consumption, so they are non-rivalrous in consumption. Goods that have the characteristics of *non-excludability* and *non-rivalry* are known as **public goods**.

Examples of public goods that are often cited include street lighting, a lighthouse and a nuclear deterrent. For example, once street lighting has been provided in a particular street, anyone who walks along that street at night benefits from the lighting — no one can be excluded from consuming it. So street lighting is non-exclusive. In addition, the fact that one person has walked along the street does not mean that there is less street lighting left for later walkers. So street lighting is also non-rivalrous.

The key feature of such a market is that, once the good has been provided, there is no incentive for anyone to pay for it — so the market will fail, as no firm will have an incentive to supply the good in the first place. This is often referred to as the **free-rider problem**, as individual consumers can free-ride and avoid having to pay for the good if it is provided.

The free-rider problem makes it difficult to charge for a public good, so the private sector will be reluctant to supply such goods. In fact, pure public goods are relatively rare, but there are many goods that have some but not all of the required characteristics. On the face of it, the lighthouse service seems to be a good example of a public good. Once

Extension material

A key question is how well the market for a public good is likely to operate. In particular, will a free market reach a position where there is allocative efficiency, with price equal to marginal social cost?

Think about the supply and demand curves for a public good such as street lighting. To simplify matters, suppose there are just two potential demanders of the good, a and b. Consider Figure 8.1. If it is assumed that the supply is provided in a competitive market, S represents the supply curve, reflecting the marginal cost of providing street lighting. The curves d_a and d_b represent the demand curves of the two potential demanders. For a given quantity Q_1, a would be prepared to pay P_a and b would pay P_b.

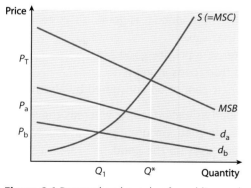

Figure 8.1 Demand and supply of a public good

If these prices are taken to be the value that each individual places on this amount of the good, then $P_a + P_b = P_T$ represents the social benefit derived from consuming Q_1 units of street lighting. Similarly, for

any given quantity of street lighting, the marginal social benefit derived from consumption can be calculated as the vertical sum of the two demand curves. This is shown by the curve *MSB*. So the optimal provision of street lighting is given by Q^*, at which point the marginal social benefit is equated with the marginal cost of supplying the good.

However, if person a were to agree to pay P_a for the good, person b could then consume Q_1 of the good free of charge, but would not be prepared to pay in order for the supply to be expanded beyond this point — as person b's willingness to pay is below the marginal cost of provision beyond this point. So the social optimum at Q^* cannot be reached. Indeed, when there are many potential consumers, the likely outcome is that *none* of this good will be produced: why should any individual agree to pay if he or she can free-ride on others?

The free-rider problem helps to explain why these sorts of goods have typically been provided through state intervention. This begs the question of how the state can identify the optimal quantity of the good to be provided — in other words, how the government determines Q^*. The extent to which individuals value a particular good cannot be directly observed. However, by including statements about the provision of public goods in their election manifestos, politicians can collect views about public goods provision via the medium of the ballot box. This is an indirect method, but it provides some mandate for the government to take decisions.

Note that public goods are called 'public goods' not because they are publicly provided, but because of their characteristics.

the lighthouse has been constructed and is sending out its signal, all boats and ships that pass within the range of its light can benefit from the service: that is, it is non-excludable. Moreover, the fact that one ship has seen the lighthouse signal does not reduce the amount of light available to the next ship, so it is also non-rivalrous.

However, this does not mean that ships cannot be charged for their use of lighthouse services. In 2002 an article in the *Guardian* reported that ships were complaining about the high charges to which they were subjected for lighthouse services. Ships of a certain size must pay 'light dues' every time they enter or leave UK ports, and the fees collected are used to fund lighthouses, buoys and beacons around the coast. In principle, it could be argued that this renders lighthouses excludable, as ships can be prevented from sailing if they have not paid their dues, and so could not consume the lighthouse services. At the heart of the complaints from the shipping companies was the fact that leisure craft below a certain threshold did not have to pay the charges, and they made more use of the lighthouses than the larger vessels. This is one example of the way in which it becomes necessary to design a charging system to try to overcome the free-rider problem associated with the provision of public goods.

Extension material

There are many goods that are either non-rivalrous or non-excludable, but not both. One example of this is a football match. If I go to watch a Premiership football match, my 'consumption' of the match does not prevent the person sitting next to me from also consuming it, so it is non-rivalrous. However, if I go along without my season ticket (or do not have a ticket), I can clearly be excluded from consuming the match, so it is *not* non-exclusive.

A stretch of road may be considered non-exclusive, as road users are free to drive along it. However, it is not non-rivalrous, in the sense that as congestion builds up consumption is affected. This example is also imperfect as a public good because, by installing toll barriers, users can be excluded from consuming it. These goods, which have some but not all of the characteristics of public goods, are known as quasi-public goods.

A particular set of problems arise with goods that have strong non-excludability characteristics, but are rivalrous. A famous example is where land in a village is communally owned, and where local farmers are free to graze their cattle on that common land. Each individual farmer has the incentive to use the common land for grazing, but as the number of cows increases, the land suffers, and eventually may not be useful for anything. In this instance, the nature of the land leads to its degradation. This situation arises in some developing countries, but similar arguments can be used in the case of over-fishing in stretches of ocean. This is known as the *Tragedy of the Commons*.

Charging ships for lighthouse services when they enter or leave ports is one way to overcome the free-rider problem

Where goods have some features of a public good, the free market may fail to produce an ideal outcome for society. Exercise 8.1 provides some examples of goods: to what extent may each of these be considered to be non-rivalrous or non-excludable?

Exercise 8.1

For each of the following goods, think about whether they have elements of non-rivalry, non-excludability, both or neither:

a a national park

b a playground

c a theatre performance

d an apple

e a television programme

f a firework display

g police protection

h a lecture

i a DVD recording of a film

j the national defence

Tackling the public goods problem

For some public goods, the failure of the free market to ensure provision may be regarded as a serious problem — for example, in such cases as street lighting or law and order. Some government intervention may thus be needed to make sure that a sufficient quantity of the good or service is provided. Notice that this does not necessarily mean that the government has to provide the good itself. It may be that the government will raise funds through taxation in order to ensure that street lighting is provided, but could still make use of private firms to supply the good through some sort of subcontracting arrangement. In the UK, it may be that the government delegates the responsibility for provision of public goods to local authorities, which in turn may subcontract to private firms.

In some other cases, it may be that changes in technology may alter the economic characteristics of a good. For example, in the case of television programmes, originally provision was entirely through the BBC, funded by the licence fee. Subsequently, ITV set up in competition, using advertising as a way of funding its supply. More recently, the advent of satellite and digital broadcasting has reduced the degree to which television programmes are non-excludable, allowing private firms to charge for transmissions.

Summary

- A private good is one that, once consumed by one person, cannot be consumed by anyone else — it has characteristics of excludability and rivalry.
- A public good is non-exclusive and non-rivalrous.
- Because of these characteristics, public goods tend to be underprovided by a free market.
- One reason for this is the free-rider problem, whereby an individual cannot be excluded from consuming a public good, and thus has no incentive to pay for it.
- Public goods, or goods with some of the characteristics of public goods, must be provided with the assistance of the government or its agents.

Merit goods

> **Key term**
>
> **merit good** a good that brings unanticipated benefits to consumers, such that society believes it will be underconsumed in a free market

There are some goods that the government believes will be undervalued by consumers, so that too little will be consumed in a free market. In other words, individuals do not fully perceive the benefits that they will gain from consuming such goods. These are known as **merit goods**.

One situation in which the merit good phenomenon arises is where the government is in a better position than individuals to take a long-term view of what is good for society. In particular, governments may need to take decisions on behalf of future generations as well as the present. Resources need to be used wisely in the present in order to protect the interests of tomorrow's citizens. Notice that this may require decision-makers to make normative judgements about the appropriate weighting to be given to the present as opposed to the future.

There is a strong political element involved in identifying the goods that should be regarded as merit goods: this is because there is a subjective or normative judgement involved, since declaring a good to be a merit good requires the decision-maker to make a choice on behalf of the population, which may be seen as being paternalistic.

At the heart of the notion of a merit good, therefore, is the decision-maker's perception that there is a divergence between the marginal benefit that individuals perceive to arise from consuming a good, and the social benefit that actually accrues from its consumption. This is reminiscent of the arguments in Chapter 7 about consumption externalities, where a positive consumption externality arises when the marginal social benefit from consuming a good is greater than the marginal private benefit.

Education as a merit good?

Figure 8.2 shows how this situation can be analysed. The example used here is education. In the UK everyone is required to attend school, at least up to age 16. Part of this requirement may be attributed to a merit good argument. It can be argued that education provides benefits to society in excess of those that are perceived by individuals. In other words, society believes that individuals will derive a benefit from education that they will not realise until after they have acquired that education. Thus, the government decrees that everyone must consume education up to the age of 16, whether they want to or not and whether they have the means to do so or not. This is a merit good argument. In Figure 8.2 marginal social benefit (*MSB*) is shown as being higher than marginal private benefit (*MPB*). Thus, society would like to provide Q^* education, where $MSB = MC$ (marginal social cost), but individuals would choose to consume only Q_1 education, where $MPB = MC$, because they do not expect the future benefits to be as high as the government does.

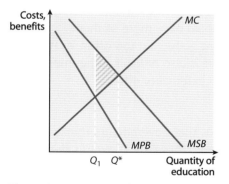

Figure 8.2 A merit good

In this case there may be other issues affecting the market for education. Chapter 7 argued that there would also be positive externality effects if educated workers were better able to cooperate with each other. There may be a further argument that individuals may fail to demand sufficient education because of information failure: in other words, they may not perceive the full benefits that will arise from education. The situation may be aggravated if parents have the responsibility of financing their children's education, because they are taking decisions *on behalf of* their children. In the case of tertiary education, there is no guarantee that parents will agree with their children about the benefits of a university education — it could go either way.

Higher education

Another important issue that arises in the context of education concerns equity in access to higher education. Research has shown that graduates tend to enjoy higher lifetime earnings than non-graduates. However, if some groups have better access to credit markets than others, then those groups may be more able to take advantage of a university education. Specifically, it has been argued that people from low-income households may be discouraged from taking up university places because of failure in credit markets. In other words, the difficulty of raising funds in the present to pay for a university education may prevent people from gaining the longer-term benefits of having received a university education — hence the launching of student loan schemes, which should help to address this particular form of market failure.

Drop-out in less developed countries

In some societies it has been suggested that the merits of education are better perceived by some groups in society than others. Thus in some less developed countries, individuals in relatively well-off households demand high levels of education, as they realise the long-run benefits that they can receive in terms of higher earnings — and, perhaps, political influence. In contrast, low-income households in remote rural areas may not see the value of education. As a result, drop-out from secondary — and even primary — education tends to be high. This is clearly a merit good argument that may need to be addressed by government, perhaps by making primary education compulsory or free — or both.

Other merit goods

Other examples of merit goods are museums, libraries and art galleries. These are goods that are provided or subsidised because someone somewhere thinks that communities should have more of them. Economists are wary of playing the merit good card too often, as it entails such a high normative element. It is also difficult sometimes to disentangle merit good arguments from externality effects.

Demerit goods

There is also a category of goods that governments think will be overconsumed in a free market. These are known as **demerit goods** — or sometimes as 'merit bads'. Obvious examples are hard drugs and tobacco. Here the argument is that individual consumers overvalue the benefits from consuming such a good.

Figure 8.3 shows the market for cocaine. Marginal private benefits (*MPB*) are shown as being much higher than marginal social benefits (*MSB*), so that in a free market too much cocaine is consumed. Society would like to be at Q^*, but ends up at Q_1. In this particular market, the government may see the marginal social benefit from consuming cocaine to be so low (e.g. at *MSB** in the figure) that consumption should be driven to zero.

Be ready with examples of merit goods, for use if called upon to discuss the concept. Remember that using examples is an excellent way of showing that you understand key economic ideas — as long as they are good examples, of course.

Key term

demerit good a good that brings less benefit to consumers than they expect, such that too much will be consumed by individuals in a free market

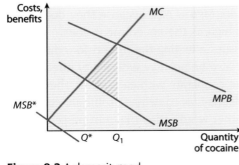

Figure 8.3 A demerit good

Again, this could be interpreted as partly an information problem, in the sense that individual consumers may not perceive the dangers of addiction and thus may overvalue cocaine. In addition, addiction would have the effect of making an individual's demand for the good highly inelastic in the long run. However, it is paternalistic of the government to intervene directly for this reason, although it might wish to correct other externalities — for instance, those imposed on others when addicts steal to fund their habit.

An alternative approach is to try to remove the information failure; clearly, the government has adopted this approach in seeking to educate people about the dangers of tobacco smoking.

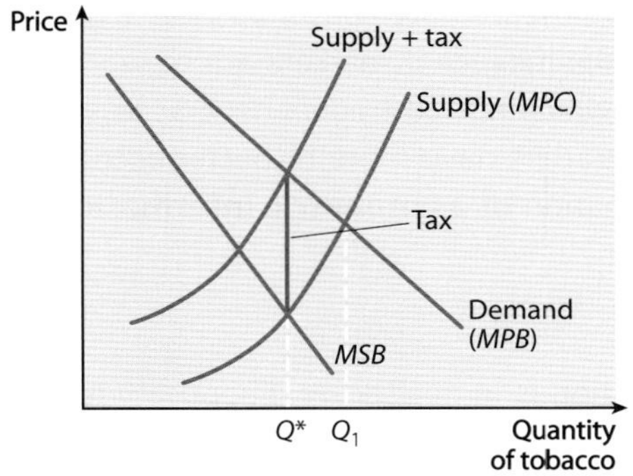

Taxing tobacco

The market for tobacco is characterised in Figure 8.4. Demand (*MPB*) represents the marginal private benefit that consumers gain from smoking tobacco. However, the government believes that consumers underestimate the damaging effects of smoking, so that the true benefits are given by *MSB* (marginal social benefit). Given the marginal cost (supply) curve, in an unregulated market consumers will choose to smoke up to Q_1 tobacco. The optimum for society, however, is at Q^*.

One way of tackling this problem is through taxation. If the government imposes a tax shown by the red line in Figure 8.4, this effectively shifts the supply curve to the market, as shown in the figure. This raises the price in the market, so consumers are persuaded to reduce their consumption to the optimal level at Q^*. Notice that because the demand curve (*MPB*) is quite steep (relatively inelastic), a substantial tax is needed in order to reach Q^*. Empirical evidence suggests that the demand for tobacco is relatively inelastic — and therefore tobacco taxes have risen to comprise a large portion of the price of a packet of cigarettes.

Figure 8.4 Taxing tobacco

Quantitative skills 8.1

Identifying a tax on a graph

The tax in Figure 8.4 is given by the length of the vertical red line. If Q^* is the desired level of output at which marginal social benefit is equal to marginal social cost, then this is the level of tax needed to induce smokers to choose Q^*, as long as the 'supply + tax' curve appropriately represents the extent to which marginal social cost exceeds marginal social benefit at this point. In practice, this may be difficult to ascertain.

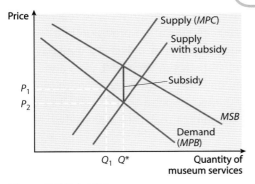

Figure 8.5 Subsidising museums

Subsidising a merit good

Conversely, if the government wishes to encourage the consumption of a merit good, it may do so through subsidies. Thus, the museum service is subsidised, and the ballet and opera have enjoyed subsidies in the past. Figure 8.5 shows how such a subsidy might be used to affect the quantity of museum services provided. Demand (*MPB*) again shows the demand for museum services from the public, which is below the marginal social benefit (*MSB*) that the authorities perceive to be the true value of museum services. Thus the free-market equilibrium position is at Q_1, although the government believes that Q^* is the socially optimum position. By providing a subsidy, the supply curve is shifted to the right, and consumers will choose to demand the optimum quantity at the subsidised price P_2.

Information failures

Key term

asymmetric information
a situation in which some participants in a market have better information about market conditions than others.

If markets are to be effective in guiding resource allocation, it is important that economic decision-makers receive full and accurate information about market conditions. Consumers need information about the prices at which they can buy and the quality of the products for sale. Producers need to be able to observe how consumers react to prices. Information is thus of crucial significance if markets are to work. However, there are some markets in which not all traders have access to good information, or in which some traders have more or better access to it than others. This is known as a situation of **asymmetric information**, and can be a source of market failure.

Healthcare

One example of asymmetric information is in healthcare. Suppose you go to your dentist for a check-up. He tells you that you have a filling that needs to be replaced, although you have had no pain or problems with it. In this situation the seller in a market has much better information about the product than the buyer. You as the buyer have no idea whether or not the recommended treatment is needed, and without going to another dentist for a second opinion you have no way of finding out. You might think this is an unsatisfactory situation, as it seems to give a lot of power to the seller relative to the consumer. The situation is even worse where the dentist does not even publish the prices for treatment until after it has been carried out! The Office of Fair Trading criticised private dentists for exactly this sort of practice when they reported on this market in March 2003. Indeed, dentists are now required by law to publish prices for treatment.

The same argument applies in the case of other areas of healthcare, where doctors have better information than their patients about the sort of treatment that is needed.

Exercise 8.2

Ethel, an old-age pensioner, is sitting quietly at home when the doorbell rings. At the door is a stranger called Frank, who tells her that he has noticed that her roof is in desperate need of repair, and if she does not get something done about it very soon, there will be problems in the next rainstorm. Fortunately, he can help — for a price. Discuss whether there is a market failure in this situation, and what Ethel (or others) could do about it.

Education

The market for education is similar. Teachers or government inspectors may know more about the subjects and topics that students need to study than the students do themselves. This is partly because teachers are able to take a longer view and can see education provision in a broader perspective. Students taking economics at university may have to take a course in mathematics and statistics in their first year, and some will always complain that they have come to study economics, not maths. It is only later that they come to realise that competence in maths is crucial these days for the economics that they will study later in their course.

How could this problem be tackled? The answer would seem to be obvious — if the problem arises from an information failure, then the answer should be to improve the information flow, in this case to students.

Dentists have better information than their patients about what treatments are needed

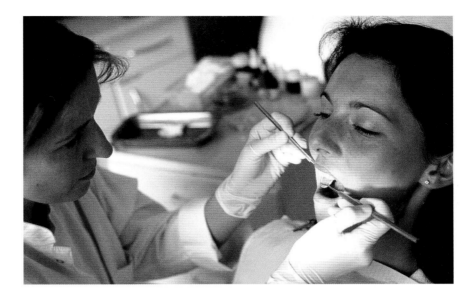

This might be achieved by providing a convincing explanation of why the curriculum has been designed in a particular way. It may also be necessary to provide incentives for students to study particular unpopular subjects, perhaps by making success a requirement for progression to the next stage of the course. By understanding the economic cause of a problem, it is possible to devise a strategy that should go some way towards removing the market failure.

Second-hand cars

One of the most famous examples of asymmetric information relates to the second-hand (or 'pre-owned', by the latest terminology) car market. This is because the first paper that drew attention to the problem of asymmetric information, by Nobel laureate George Akerlof, focused on this market.

Akerlof argued that there are two types of car. Some cars are good runners and are totally reliable, whereas some are continually breaking down and needing parts and servicing; the latter are known as 'lemons' in the USA (allegedly from fruit machines, where lemons offer the lowest prize). The problem in the second-hand car market arises because the owners of cars (potential sellers) have better information about their cars than the potential buyers. In other words, when a car owner decides to sell a car, he or she knows whether it is a lemon or a good-quality car — but a buyer cannot tell.

In this sort of market, car dealers can adopt one of two possible strategies. One is to offer a high price and buy up all the cars in the market, knowing that the lemons will be sold on at a loss. The problem is that, if the lemons make up a large proportion of the cars in the market, this could generate overall losses for the dealers. The alternative is to offer a low price, and just buy up all the lemons to sell for scrap. In this situation, the market for good-quality used cars is effectively destroyed because owners of good-quality cars will not accept the low price — an extreme form of market failure!

The insurance market

People take out insurance to cover themselves against the risk of uncertain future events. Asymmetric information can cause problems with this market in two different ways. Suppose an individual approaches an insurance company wanting health insurance. The individual knows more about his or her health and health history than the insurance company. After all, the individual knows whether they are prone to illness or if they are accident-prone. This could mean that the people most likely to take out health insurance are the ones most likely to fall ill or be involved in accidents. This is known as **adverse selection**. A second form of information failure in terms of insurance is known as **moral hazard**. An individual who has taken out insurance may be more likely to take risks, knowing that he or she is covered by insurance. For example, if someone has taken out insurance against the loss of their mobile phone, they may be less careful about leaving it around.

These issues are not unique to the insurance market, but can arise in other situations as well. For example, an individual goes to a bank wanting to borrow money to undertake a project. The bank needs to know about the likelihood that the borrower will default on the loan, either because the project may fail, or because the person turns out to be unreliable. The potential borrower has much better information about these things than does the bank. Adverse selection may mean that the individuals most likely to want to borrow could be those who are unreliable or wanting to finance risky projects. In this situation, the bank may insist on charging a high rate of interest on the loan in order to cover itself. The market is then likely to fail, because potential borrowers who are reliable, or who are proposing safe projects, may find that they face higher interest charges than are justified, so may not borrow.

Moral hazard will arise here if borrowers take more risk with their projects once they have received loans, thus increasing the probability of default.

Summary

- A merit good is one that society believes should be consumed by individuals, whether or not they have the means or the willingness to do so.
- There is a strong normative element in the identification of merit goods.
- Demerit goods (or 'merit bads') are goods that society believes should not be consumed by individuals even if they wish to do so.
- In the case of merit and demerit goods, 'society' (as represented by government) believes that it has better information than consumers about these goods, and about what is good (or bad) for consumers.
- Information deficiency can lead to market failure in other situations: for example, where some participants in a market have better information about some aspect(s) of the market than others.
- Examples of this include healthcare, education and second-hand cars.
- Asymmetric information can also result in problems of adverse selection and moral hazard.

Exercise 8.3

The *Guardian* reported on 27 August 2004 that the pharmaceutical company GlaxoSmithKline had been forced to publish details of a clinical trial of one of its leading anti-depressant drugs, following a lawsuit that had accused the company of concealing evidence that the drug could be harmful to children. Discuss the extent to which this situation may have led to a market failure because of information problems.

Case study 8.1

Television in a digital world

In the UK, we spend an average of just under 3 hours a day, every day, watching television. That amounts to 20 hours a week; or over 43 days a year; or over 9 years in the life of an average person. Watching television comes behind only work and sleep as a pastime. It accounts for about half of our leisure time.

The BBC is publicly funded by the television licence fee

From an early stage, government has been intimately involved in television broadcasting. At several points, there were calls for the government to take over the BBC (notably during the General Strike of 1926 and the Suez Crisis of 1956).

The major part of the BBC's income comes through a mandatory licence, which comes to just under £3 billion per annum, or not far off one day's gross domestic product for the UK. The government grants licences (via its regulator) to broadcasters. In exchange for the right to broadcast, these companies have to fulfil a number of obligations.

Why should the government be so involved in broadcasting? The basic reason is the existence of market failure: the idea that a freely functioning market in broadcasting will not produce the socially desirable outcome. The issue is: why won't the free market, left unregulated, inform, educate and entertain? There are three main types of market failure relevant for broadcasting:

- broadcasting is a *public good*
- the broadcasting market is inherently concentrated, leading to *market power*
- consumption of broadcasting is subject to *externalities*

Source: Adapted from Robin Mason, 'Television in the digital world', *Economic Review*, Vol. 22, No. 3 (February 2005), pp. 2–6.

Follow-up questions

a Discuss the three forms of market failure mentioned, and discuss why they are potentially relevant to broadcasting.

b Given that the article was written in 2005, to what extent do you think that further developments in the technology of broadcasting since then have affected these forms of market failure?

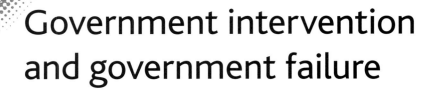

Government intervention and government failure

Previous chapters have identified various ways in which markets can fail to bring about an efficient allocation of resources in a society. This chapter investigates how governments may intervene in an attempt to correct market failure. The chapter also explores how some well-intentioned interventions by government can sometimes produce unintended results, leading to government failure.

> **Learning objectives**
>
> After studying this chapter, you should:
> - be familiar with ways in which governments intervene in an attempt to address market failure
> - be able to analyse the effects of sales taxes and subsidies
> - appreciate the role of government expenditure and state provision of goods and services
> - be familiar with the effects of price controls such as minimum wage legislation and rent controls
> - recognise ways of dealing with information failures
> - be able to identify areas in which government actions may have unintended distortionary effects
> - be aware of some sources of government failure

Correcting market failure

As explained in previous chapters, markets fail when the price mechanism causes an inefficient allocation of resources within a society. This can occur when price is not set equal to marginal cost, or where marginal social benefit is not set equal to marginal social cost. In such circumstances, it seems apparent that by improving the way in which resources are allocated, the society could become better off. In other words, market failure is often viewed as a valid reason for governments to intervene in the economy.

Most governments see it as their responsibility to try to correct some of the failures of markets to allocate resources efficiently. This has led to a wide variety of policies being devised to address issues of market failure. However, the following discussion will show that some policies have unintended effects that may not culminate in successful elimination of market failure. Indeed, in some cases government intervention may introduce new market distortions, leading to a phenomenon known as **government failure**. This chapter examines some examples of government intervention and examines how this may sometimes lead to government failure.

> **Key term**
>
> **government failure** a misallocation of resources arising from government intervention

Taxes and subsidies

In the case of some of the forms of market failure that have been outlined, taxes and subsidies may seem an obvious way of tackling market failure. If the government perceives some goods to be merit goods, it may wish to encourage consumption, whereas in the case of demerit goods or goods whose production causes pollution (a negative externality), the government may wish to discourage consumption. In such a situation, the use of taxes and subsidies may seem a possible solution. Of course, governments also need to raise funds to finance the expenditure that they undertake, and the imposition of taxes is a way of raising revenue. One way of doing this is through expenditure taxes such as value added tax (VAT), which is levied on a wide range of goods and services. Consider the effect of excise duties on such items as alcohol or tobacco. These can be seen to be intended to affect consumption of particular goods perceived to be demerit goods.

The effects of a sales tax can be seen in a demand and supply diagram. An **indirect tax** is paid by the seller, so it affects the supply curve for a product. Figure 9.1 illustrates the case of a *fixed rate* or **specific tax** — a tax that is set at a constant amount per pack of cigarettes. Without the tax, the market equilibrium is at the intersection of demand and supply with a price of P_0 and a quantity traded of Q_0. The effect of the tax is to reduce the quantity that firms are prepared to supply at any given price — or, to put it another way, for any given quantity of cigarettes, firms need to receive the amount of the tax over and above the price at which they would have been prepared to supply that quantity. The effect is thus to move the supply curve upwards by the amount of the tax, as shown in the figure. We get a new equilibrium with a higher price at P_1 and a lower quantity traded at Q_1.

An important question is: who bears the burden of the tax? If you look at the diagram, you will see that the price difference between the with-tax and without-tax situations (i.e. $P_1 - P_0$) is *less* than the amount of the tax, which is the vertical distance between the with-tax and without-tax supply curves. Although the seller may be responsible for the mechanics of paying the tax, part of the tax is effectively passed on to the buyer in the form of the higher price. In Figure 9.1, the **incidence of the tax** falls partly upon the seller, but most of the tax is borne by the buyer.

The price elasticity of demand determines the incidence of the tax. If demand were perfectly inelastic, then the sellers would be able to pass the whole burden of the tax on to the buyers through an increase in price equal to the value of the tax, knowing that this would not affect demand. However, if demand were perfectly elastic, then the sellers would not be able to raise the price at all, so they would have to bear the entire burden of the tax.

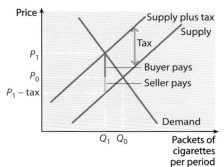

Figure 9.1 The effects of an indirect tax on cigarettes

Key terms

indirect tax a tax levied on expenditure on goods or services (as opposed to a direct tax, which is a tax charged directly to an individual based on a component of income)

specific tax a tax of a fixed amount imposed on purchases of a commodity

incidence of a tax the way in which the burden of paying a sales tax is divided between buyers and sellers

Exercise 9.1

Sketch demand and supply diagrams to confirm that the statements in the previous paragraph are correct — that is, that if demand is perfectly inelastic, then the tax falls entirely on the buyers, whereas if demand is perfectly elastic, it is the sellers who have to bear the burden of the tax.

Key terms

ad valorem tax a tax levied on a commodity set as a percentage of the selling price

subsidy a grant given by the government to producers to encourage production of a good or service

If the tax is not a constant amount, but a percentage of the price (known as an **ad valorem tax**), the effect is still on the supply curve, but the tax steepens the supply curve, as shown in Figure 9.2. Here, the free market equilibrium would be where demand equals supply, with price at P_0 and the quantity traded at Q_0. With an ad valorem tax in place, the price rises to P_1, with quantity falling to Q_1.

In some situations, the government may wish to encourage production of a particular good or service, perhaps because it views the good as having strategic significance to the country or because it perceives it to be a merit good. One way it can do this is by giving **subsidies**.

Subsidies were discussed in the previous chapter in the context of merit goods. Here, subsidies are used to encourage producers to increase their output of particular goods. Subsidies have been especially common in agriculture, which is often seen as being of strategic significance. In recent years, the USA has come under pressure to reduce the subsidies that it grants to cotton producers. Analytically, we can regard a subsidy as a sort of negative indirect tax that shifts the supply curve down — as shown in Figure 9.3. Without the subsidy, market equilibrium is at price P_0 and the quantity traded is Q_0. With the subsidy in place, the equilibrium price falls to P_1 and quantity traded increases to Q_1.

Again, notice that because the price falls by less than the amount of the subsidy, the benefits of the subsidy are shared between the buyers and sellers — depending on the elasticity of demand. If the aim of the subsidy is to increase production, it is only partially successful; the degree of success also depends upon the elasticity of demand.

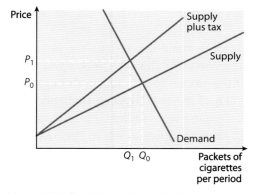

Figure 9.2 The effects of an ad valorem tax on cigarettes

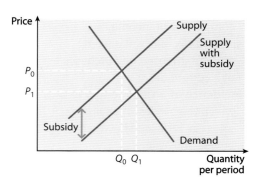

Figure 9.3 The effects of a subsidy

Extension material

An important question is how a sales tax will affect total welfare in society. Consider Figure 9.4, which shows the market for DVDs. Suppose that the government imposes a specific tax on DVDs. This would have the effect of taking market equilibrium from the free market position at P^* with quantity traded at Q^* to a new position, with price now at P_t and quantity traded at Q_t. Remember that the price rises by less than the amount of the tax, implying that the incidence of the tax falls partly on buyers and partly on sellers. In Figure 9.4 consumers pay more of the tax (the area P^*P_tBE) than the producers (who pay FP^*EG). The effect on society's overall welfare will now be examined.

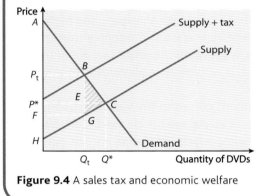

Figure 9.4 A sales tax and economic welfare

Remember that the total welfare that society receives from consuming a product is the sum of consumer and producer surplus. The situation before and after the sales tax is as follows. Before the tax, consumer surplus is given by the area AP^*C and producer surplus is given by the triangle P^*CH. How about afterwards? Consumer surplus is now the smaller triangle AP_tB, and producer surplus is FGH. The area P_tBGF is the revenue raised by the government from the tax, which should be included in total welfare on the assumption that the government uses this wisely. The total amount of welfare is now $ABGH$. If you compare these total welfare areas before and after the tax, you will realise that they differ by the area BCG. This triangle represents a deadweight loss that arises from the imposition of the tax. It is sometimes referred to as the **excess burden** of the tax.

So, even where the government intervenes to raise funding for its expenditure — and spends wisely — a distortion is introduced to resource allocation, and society must bear a loss of welfare.

Key term

excess burden of a sales tax the deadweight loss to society following the imposition of a sales tax

Government expenditure and state provision

Government plans to invest in the HS2 rail link have sparked large-scale protests

Expenditure taxes are not only imposed to address perceived market failure, but also in order to help finance the government's expenditure. This includes expenditure on the administration of government, but also to enable transfer payments to be made in order to affect the distribution of income in a society — protecting the vulnerable and addressing poverty that may exist. Expenditure may also be needed to encourage the provision of public goods, even if the government does not itself provide these directly.

Maintaining an appropriate balance between the public and private sectors is one of the fundamental dilemmas of government. For private firms to operate effectively and to compete in international markets, they need access to public goods such as a good transport and communications infrastructure. If the government does not put sufficient resources into road maintenance, or the development of the rail network, then firms may face higher costs, and be disadvantaged relative to their international competitors. On the other hand, if the government over-invests, then there is an opportunity cost, because more resources used for infrastructure implies that fewer resources are available for private sector investment. The debate about the HS2 rail link provides an example of the tension that can arise when the government seeks to invest heavily in specific projects.

In some markets, governments have been seen to intervene to regulate price directly. This could be viewed as a response to market failure — for example, if it were apparent that price was not being set equal to marginal cost. Some governments in developing countries have at times intervened to control food prices in urban areas in response to civil unrest. This can create a form of government failure if it provides weak incentives for farmers to raise production or improve their crops. Regulation of prices has also been introduced in order to protect vulnerable members of society, one example being the introduction of a minimum wage.

The UK National Minimum Wage

In 1999 the UK National **Minimum Wage** came into force, designed to protect workers on low pay. To illustrate how this works, Figure 9.5 represents the labour market for office cleaners. Employers demand labour according to the wage rate — the lower the wage, the higher the demand for the labour of office cleaners. On the supply side, more workers will offer themselves for work when the wage rate is relatively high. If the market is unregulated, it will reach equilibrium with a wage rate W^* and quantity of labour L^*.

Suppose now that the government comes to the view that W^* is not sufficiently high to provide a reasonable wage for cleaners. One response is to impose a minimum wage, below which employers are not permitted to offer employment — say, W_{min} on the figure. This will have two effects on the market situation.

> ### Key term
>
> **minimum wage** a system designed to protect the low paid by setting a minimum wage rate that employers are permitted to offer workers

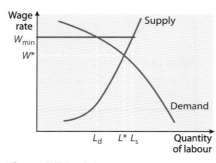

Figure 9.5 A minimum wage

Quantitative skills 9.1

Interpreting quantities on a graph

You should now be getting adept at interpreting the various diagrams that are used by economists. Figure 9.5 shows a market in disequilibrium, and you need to be clear about how to read off the relevant quantities. When the wage is at W_{min}, workers and employers have different aspirations. With the wage at this level, employers do not find it profitable to hire many workers, so that the demand for labour is only at L_d, whereas more workers (L_s) are prepared to offer themselves for work. The horizontal distance between these two quantities is thus the number of workers who would like to have jobs at that wage, but who will not be hired. In other words, this is unemployment.

What is happening here is that, with the minimum wage in effect, *some* workers (those who manage to remain in employment) are better off, and now receive a better wage. However, those who are now unemployed are worse off. It is not then clear whether the effect of the minimum wage is to make society as a whole better off — some people will be better off, but others will be worse off.

Notice that this analysis rests on some assumptions that have not been made explicit. In particular, it rests on the assumption that the labour market is competitive. Where there are labour markets in which the employers have some market power, and are able to offer lower wages to workers than would be obtained in a free market equilibrium situation, it is possible that the imposition of a minimum wage will increase employment.

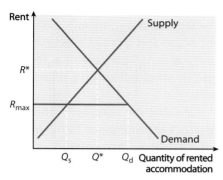

Rent ↑

R^*

R_{max}

Supply

Demand

Q_s Q^* Q_d Quantity of rented
accommodation

Figure 9.6 Rent controls

Rent controls

Another market in which governments have been tempted to intervene to affect prices is the housing market. Figure 9.6 represents the market for rented accommodation. The free market equilibrium would be where demand and supply intersect, with the equilibrium rent being R^* and the quantity of accommodation traded being Q^*.

If the government regards the level of rent as excessive, to the point where households on low incomes may be unable to afford rented accommodation, then, given that housing is one of life's necessities, it may regard this as unacceptable.

The temptation for the government is to move this market away from its equilibrium by imposing a maximum level of rent that landlords are allowed to charge their tenants. Suppose that this level of rent is denoted by R_{max} in Figure 9.6. Again, there are two effects that follow. First, landlords will no longer find it profitable to supply as much rental accommodation, and so will reduce supply to Q_s. Second, at this lower rent there will be more people looking for accommodation, so that demand for rented accommodation will move to Q_d. The upshot of the rent controls, therefore, is that there is less accommodation available, and more homeless people.

It can be seen that the well-meaning rent control policy, intended to protect low-income households from being exploited by landlords, merely has the effect of reducing the amount of accommodation available. This is not what was supposed to happen.

Price stabilisation

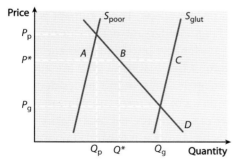

Price ↑

P_p

P^*

P_g

S_{poor} S_{glut}

A   B

C

D

Q_p Q^* Q_g Quantity

Figure 9.7 A buffer stock

In some commodity markets, prices can exhibit volatility over time. This could arise, for example, when the supply of a good varies from period to period because of the varying state of the harvest. In such a market, the supply curve will shift to the right when the harvest is good, but shift to the left in a period when the weather is poor or where crops are affected by some disease or blight. It may also be that the demand curve tends to shift around through time, with demand for some goods reflecting fluctuations in the performance of economies. In other words, demand may shift to the left when recession bites, but to the right in times of boom and prosperity. This was discussed in Chapter 5 in relation to the market for cocoa.

Suppose that Figure 9.7 represents a market in which demand is relatively stable between periods, but in which supply varies between S_{poor} when the harvest is poor and S_{glut} when the harvest is good. The price varies between P_p and P_g. This creates a high level of uncertainty for producers, who find it difficult to form accurate expectations about the future prospects for the commodity. This means that they are less likely to invest in ways of improving productivity because of uncertain future returns. If a way could be found of stabilising the price of the good, then this could encourage producers.

A **buffer stock** is a way of attempting to do this. A scheme is set up whereby excess supply is bought up by the buffer stock in glut years to prevent the price from falling too low. In periods when the harvest is poor, stocks of the commodity are released on to the market in order to maintain the price at the agreed level. In terms of Figure 9.7, suppose that it is agreed to maintain the price at P^*. When there is a glut year, with the supply curve located at S_{glut}, there is excess supply at the agreed price of the amount BC, so this amount is bought up by the buffer stock and stored. If the supply is at S_{poor} because of a poor harvest, there is excess demand, so the buffer stock releases the quantity AB on to the market, maintaining the price.

Although this does have the effect of stabilising the price at P^*, there is a downside. If the members of the buffer stock scheme agree to maintain the price at too high a level, relative to the actual average equilibrium price over time, then it will run into difficulties. Notice in Figure 9.7 that to maintain price at P^*, the buffer stock buys up more in the glut year than it has to sell in the poor harvest year. If this pattern is repeated, then the size of stocks to be stored will rise over time. This is costly and will eventually become unsustainable.

Legislation and regulation

In some markets, the government chooses to intervene directly through legislation and regulation, rather than by influencing prices. For example, it may limit the market power of large firms to protect consumers, or place direct controls on the emission of pollution.

Prohibition

An extreme form of this is to declare some goods illegal. This may also have unintended effects. Consider the situation in which action is taken to prohibit the consumption of a demerit good. Consider the case of a hard drug, such as cocaine. It can be argued that there are substantial social disbenefits arising from the consumption of hard drugs, and that addicts and potential addicts are in no position to make informed decisions about their consumption of them. One response to such a situation is to consider making the drug illegal — that is, to impose **prohibition**.

Figure 9.8 shows how the market for cocaine might look. You may wonder why the demand curve takes on this shape. The argument is that there are two types of cocaine user. There are the recreational users, who will take cocaine if it is available at a reasonable price, but who are not addicts. In addition, there is a hard core of habitual users who are addicts, whose demand for cocaine is highly inelastic. Thus, at low prices demand is relatively elastic because of the presence of the recreational users, who are relatively price-sensitive. At higher prices the recreational users drop away, and demand from the addicts is highly price-inelastic. Suppose that the supply in free market equilibrium is given by S_0; the equilibrium will be with price P_0 and quantity traded Q_0. If the drug is made illegal, this will affect supply. Some dealers will leave the market to trade in something else, and the police will succeed in confiscating a certain proportion of the drugs in the market. However, they are unlikely to be totally successful, so supply could move to, say, S_1.

In the new market situation, price rises substantially to P_1, and quantity traded falls to Q_1. However, what has happened is that the recreational users have dropped out of the market, leaving a hard core of addicts who will pay any price for the drug, and who may resort to muggings and

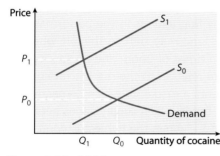

Figure 9.8 Prohibition

robberies in order to finance their habit. This behaviour clearly imposes a new sort of externality on society. And the more successful the police are in confiscating supplies, the higher the price will be driven. There may thus be disadvantages in using prohibition as a way of discouraging consumption of a demerit good.

Tackling information failure

Market failure can arise from information failure, especially where there is asymmetric information or where economic agents lack information or the capacity to process the information available. In such circumstances, the solution would seem to be to find a way of providing the information to remedy the situation.

One example discussed in Chapter 8 was that of second-hand cars, where car dealers may find that they cannot find buyers for good-quality cars at a fair price if potential buyers cannot distinguish quality. The solution here may be to tackle the problem at its root, by finding a way to provide information about quality. In the case of second-hand cars, AA inspection schemes or the offering of warranties may be a way of improving the flow of information about the quality of cars for sale. Buyers may then have confidence that they are not buying a lemon.

Similarly, in the case of the insurance market, the asymmetric information problem helps to explain why insurance companies try to cover themselves by insisting on comprehensive health histories of those who take out health insurance, and include exclusion clauses that entitle them to refuse to pay out if past illnesses have not been disclosed. It also helps to explain why banks may insist on collateral to back up loans.

Information problems may also be present in respect of some demerit goods. Think back to the tobacco example discussed in Chapter 8. Tobacco is seen by government as a demerit good on the grounds that smokers underestimate the damaging effects of smoking. There may also be negative externalities caused by passive smoking. At first, taxes were used to try to discourage smoking, but given the inelastic demand for tobacco, this proved ineffective. The taxes were reinforced by extensive campaigns to spread information about the damaging effects of smoking. When even this did not solve the problem, the government had to introduce regulation by prohibiting smoking in public buildings.

The negative externalities caused by passive smoking led the government to introduce a no-smoking ban in public places

Costs of intervention

Some roles are critical for a government to perform if a mixed economy is to function effectively. A vital role is the provision by the government of an environment in which markets can operate effectively. There must be stability in the political system if firms and consumers are to take decisions with confidence about the future. And there must be a secure system of property rights, without which markets could not be expected to work.

In addition, there are sources of market failure that require intervention. This does not necessarily mean that governments need to substitute markets with direct action. However, it does mean that they need to be more active in markets that cannot operate effectively, while at the same time performing an enabling role to encourage markets to work well whenever this is feasible.

Such intervention entails costs. There are costs of administering, and costs of monitoring the policy to ensure that it is working as intended. This includes the need to look out for the unintended distortionary effects that some policies can have on resource allocation in a society. It is therefore important to check that the marginal costs of implementing and monitoring policies do not exceed their marginal benefits.

Study tip

When thinking about government intervention and government failure, notice that governments intervene in markets in a variety of ways, and that you may need to look back at earlier chapters to draw together the material on these interventions. Do not forget that you may be called upon to evaluate such interventions as well as explaining them.

Summary

- Government failure can occur when well-meaning intervention by governments has unintended effects.
- Taxes and subsidies may be used to correct some forms of market failure and also to raise revenue to finance government expenditure.
- In some circumstances a minimum wage intended to protect the low paid may aggravate their situation by increasing unemployment.
- Rent controls may have the effect of reducing the amount of accommodation available.
- Schemes such as a buffer stock can help to stabilise prices, but may prove costly if not implemented carefully.
- Regulation can be used to tackle market failure, but such measures as prohibition may have unintended effects.
- Information failure can be tackled by ensuring that economic agents have access to the information that they need.

Case study 9.1

Who pays taxes?

This may sound like a simple question, but many politicians do not seem to know the answer. Nor do a great many journalists. In fact, if there is one important economic concept that almost no one in the general public seems to understand, it is tax incidence — the economic study of who really pays taxes.

You might think it is easy to work out who pays tax — just look at who is handing over the money. Beer drinkers pay alcohol duties when they buy a pint, businesses pay corporation tax when they file their accounts (unless they can find a way of avoiding doing so, as highlighted by the media). This aside, it all seems so straightforward. But this is where an economist has

to dig a little deeper. Consider the case of indirect taxes like VAT or the tax on alcohol. Who pays this tax?

To understand who is really paying a tax, we have to understand that both sides of the market (producers and consumers, or employers and employees) are trying to shift the burden of the tax on to the other side.

Suppose the government is worried about drunkenness in society, and introduces a new tax on vodka, intended to be paid by the consumer when they buy their bottle of Smirnoff at the off-licence. Will the vodka drinker have to bear the whole burden of the tax?

Source: Adapted from Antoine Bozio, 'Who pays taxes?', *Economic Review*, Vol. 25, No. 4 (April 2008), pp. 17–19.

Follow-up question

Draw a demand and supply diagram to examine how much of the new tax will be paid by the consumer, and how much by the producer. How would your answer differ if the demand for vodka were perfectly inelastic?

Case study 9.2

The Common Agricultural Policy

The European Union (EU) attracts a lot of criticism — arguably more than its fair share — but one policy where criticism is justified is its Common Agricultural Policy (CAP). Even among farmers and their extended families, support is not universal. One suspects that for the majority of EU governments, only the threat of violent actions by some farmers prevents a rapid phasing out of what is now a highly complex system of payments and protections for the EU's farm businesses. Back in 1957, when the treaty incorporating the CAP was signed, things were very different.

The six founding members had suffered food shortages during the war and their governments were determined to become self-sufficient; moreover, they feared that a fall in agricultural incomes would drive people off the land and into urban areas, threatening a rise in urban unemployment. Thus, at its inception, the CAP had two prime objectives: to increase agricultural production of basic commodities, such as cereals, milk and beef; and to support agricultural incomes. In 1950, agricultural employment accounted for 25% of total employment in Europe; hence, the founding fathers could legitimately claim that the CAP would, by protecting rural incomes, create a balance between urban and rural living standards.

The CAP guarantees farmers a price for each unit of output

The policy instrument selected to achieve the CAP's objectives was open-ended price support. In essence, farmers would be guaranteed a price for each unit of output, such as a tonne of wheat, regardless of the amount produced. If a farm could double or treble its output of say, cereals, it doubled or trebled its revenue. However, the CAP could not achieve its objectives by merely announcing a target price. Two additional instruments were needed: namely, tariff barriers and intervention.

Case study 9.2 (continued)

Compared to their counterparts in other parts of the world, western European farms are high cost. Setting a price to cover average unit production costs and leave sufficient for a profit necessitated protecting the prices of agricultural commodities produced within the EU from being undercut by cheaper imports from other parts of the world. The appropriate policy instrument here is a tariff or, to be strictly correct in the case of the CAP, a variable levy.

Source: Adapted from Séan Rickard,
'The Common Agriculture Policy', *Economic Review*,
Vol. 24, No. 3 (February 2007), pp. 17–21.

Follow-up question

Discuss the economic arguments surrounding the continuance of the CAP, and the possible presence of government failure. Do you think that the original arguments that led to the establishment of the CAP remain valid in the twenty-first century?

Key terms

Microeconomics key terms

ad valorem tax a tax levied on a commodity set as a percentage of the selling price

adverse selection a situation in which a person at risk is more likely to take out insurance

allocative efficiency achieved when consumer satisfaction is maximised

asymmetric information a situation in which some participants in a market have better information about market conditions than others

average total cost (ATC) total cost divided by the quantity produced

buffer stock a scheme intended to stabilise the price of a commodity by buying excess supply in periods when supply is high, and selling when supply is low

capitalism a system of production in which there is private ownership of productive resources, and individuals are free to pursue their objectives with minimal interference from government

centrally planned economy decisions on resource allocation are guided by the state

ceteris paribus a Latin phrase meaning 'other things being equal'; it is used in economics when we focus on changes in one variable while holding other influences constant

comparative static analysis examines the effect on equilibrium of a change in the external conditions affecting a market

competitive demand demand for goods that are in competition with each other

competitive market a market in which individual firms cannot influence the price of the good or service they are selling, because of competition from other firms

competitive supply a situation in which a firm can use its factors of production to produce alternative products

complements two goods are said to be complements if people tend to consume them jointly, so that an increase in the price of one good causes the demand for the other good to fall

composite demand demand for a good that has multiple uses

composite supply where a product produced by a firm serves more than one market

consumer surplus the value that consumers gain from consuming a good or service over and above the price paid

consumption externality an externality that affects the consumption side of a market, which may be either positive or negative

cost efficiency the appropriate combination of inputs of factors of production, given the relative prices of those factors

cross elasticity of demand (XED) a measure of the sensitivity of quantity demanded of a good or service to a change in the price of some other good or service

demand the quantity of a good or service that consumers are willing and able to buy at any possible price in a given period

demand curve a graph showing how much of a good will be demanded by consumers at any given price

demerit good a good that brings less benefit to consumers than they expect, such that too much will be consumed by individuals in a free market

derived demand demand for a factor of production or a good which derives not from the factor or the good itself, but from the goods it produces

division of labour a process whereby the production procedure is broken down into a sequence of stages, and workers are assigned to particular stages

economic efficiency a situation in which both productive efficiency and allocative efficiency have been reached

economic growth an expansion in the productive capacity of the economy

economies of scale occur for a firm when an increase in the scale of production leads to production at lower long-run average cost

elasticity a measure of the sensitivity of one variable to changes in another variable

excess burden of a sales tax the deadweight loss to society following the imposition of a sales tax

external cost a cost that is associated with an individual's (a firm or household's) production or other economic activities, which is borne by a third party

externality a cost or a benefit that is external to a market transaction, and is thus not reflected in market prices

factors of production resources used in the production process; *inputs* into production, including labour, capital, land and entrepreneurship

firm an organisation that brings together factors of production in order to produce output

fixed costs costs incurred by a firm that do not vary with the level of output

free market economy one in which resource allocation is guided by market forces without intervention by the state

free-rider problem when an individual cannot be excluded from consuming a good, and thus has no incentive to pay for its provision

government failure a misallocation of resources arising from government intervention

gross domestic product (GDP) a measure of the economic activity carried out in an economy during a period

incidence of a tax the way in which the burden of paying a sales tax is divided between buyers and sellers

income elasticity of demand (YED) a measure of the sensitivity of quantity demanded to a change in consumer incomes

indirect tax a tax levied on expenditure on goods or services (as opposed to a direct tax, which is a tax charged directly to an individual based on a component of income)

inferior good one where the quantity demanded decreases in response to an increase in consumer incomes

internalising an externality an attempt to deal with an externality by bringing an external cost or benefit into the price system

invisible hand term used by Adam Smith to describe the way in which resources are allocated in a market economy

joint demand demand for goods which are interdependent, such that they are demanded together

joint supply where a firm produces more than one product together

law of demand a law that states that there is an inverse relationship between quantity demanded and the price of a good or service, ceteris paribus

macroeconomics the study of the interrelationships between economic variables at an aggregate (economy-wide) level

marginal cost (MC) the cost of producing an additional unit of output

marginal social benefit (MSB) the additional benefit that society gains from consuming an extra unit of a good

marginal social cost (MSC) the cost to society of producing an extra unit of a good

market a set of arrangements that allows transactions to take place

market economy market forces are allowed to guide the allocation of resources within a society

market equilibrium a situation that occurs in a market when the price is such that the quantity that consumers wish to buy is exactly balanced by the quantity that firms wish to supply

market failure a situation in which the free market mechanism does not lead to an optimal allocation of resources, e.g. where there is a divergence between marginal social benefit and marginal social cost.

merit good a good that brings unanticipated benefits to consumers, such that society believes it will be underconsumed in a free market

microeconomics the study of economic decisions taken by individual economic agents, including households and firms

minimum wage a system designed to protect the low paid by setting a minimum wage rate that employers are permitted to offer workers

mixed economy resources are allocated partly through price signals and partly on the basis of direction by government

model a simplified representation of reality used to provide insight into economic decisions and events

moral hazard a situation in which a person who has taken out insurance is prone to taking more risk

normal good one where the quantity demanded increases in response to an increase in consumer incomes

normative statement a statement involving a value judgement that is about what *ought to be*

opportunity cost in decision making, the value of the next-best alternative forgone

Pareto optimum an allocation of resources is said to be a Pareto optimum if no reallocation of resources can make an individual better off without making some other individual worse off

positive statement a statement about what *is*, i.e. about *facts*

price elasticity of demand (PED) a measure of the sensitivity of quantity demanded to a change in the price of a good or service. It is measured as: % change in quantity demanded / % change in price

price elasticity of supply (PES) a measure of the sensitivity of quantity supplied of a good or service to a change in the price of that good or service

private cost a cost incurred by an individual (firm or consumer) as part of its production or other economic activities

private good a good that, once consumed by one person, cannot be consumed by somebody else; such a good has excludability and is rivalrous

producer surplus the difference between the price received by firms for a good or service and the price at which they would have been prepared to supply that good or service

production externality an externality that affects the production side of a market, which may be either positive or negative

production possibility curve a curve showing the maximum combinations of goods or services that can be produced in a set period of time given available resources

productive efficiency attained when a firm operates at minimum average total cost, choosing an appropriate combination of inputs (cost efficiency) and producing the maximum output possible from those inputs (technical efficiency)

prohibition an attempt to prevent the consumption of a demerit good by declaring it illegal

public good a good that is non-exclusive and non-rivalrous — consumers cannot be excluded from consuming the good, and consumption by one person does not affect the amount of the good available for others to consume

resource allocation the way in which a society's productive assets are used amongst their alternative uses

Microeconomics

scarcity a situation that arises because people have unlimited wants in the face of limited resources

specific tax a tax of a fixed amount imposed on purchases of a commodity

subsidy a grant given by the government to producers to encourage production of a good or service

substitutes two goods are said to be substitutes if consumers regard them as alternatives, so that the demand for one good is likely to rise if the price of the other good rises

sunk costs costs incurred by a firm that cannot be recovered if the firm ceases trading

superior good one for which the income elasticity of demand is positive, and greater than 1, such that as income rises, consumers spend proportionally more on the good

supply curve a graph showing the quantity supplied at any given price

technical efficiency attaining the maximum possible output from a given set of inputs

total cost (*TC*) the sum of all costs that are incurred in producing a given level of output

unemployment results when people seeking work at the going wage cannot find a job

variable costs costs that vary with the level of output

Questions

Microeconomics practice questions

Part 1: Scarcity and choice

1 'Wants are unlimited but resources are finite.' This illustrates:

  A That all needs may be satisfied
  B The problem of scarcity
  C That a centrally planned economy is the best means of allocating resources
  D That resources are free

2 Figure 1 illustrates two production possibility curves.

Which of the following would involve an opportunity cost? A movement from:

  A *X* to *B*
  B *B* to *Y*
  C *X* to *A*
  D *B* to *C*

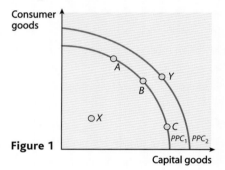

Figure 1

3 Which of the following is a sustainable source of energy?

  A Electricity generated from coal
  B Oil from the North Sea
  C Gas from shale sands
  D Electricity generated from wind farms

4 Statement 1: The UK economy has had a double dip recession.

Statement 2: The government should reduce taxes to increase the rate of economic growth.

Which of the following is correct about the above statements?

	Statement 1	Statement 2
A	Normative	Normative
B	Normative	Positive
C	Positive	Normative
D	Positive	Positive

5 Suppose that a local garage introduces division of labour for car servicing. A disadvantage of such division of labour in this process could be that:

  A Workers may find it more difficult to get a job in another industry
  B Labour productivity will increase
  C The training required will be reduced
  D Workers spend more time moving from one activity to another

Part 2: How competitive markets work

1 Which of the following would cause a rightward *shift* of the demand curve for cars?

  A An increase in VAT on cars

  B A decrease in the cost of components used in cars

  C An increase in the price of petrol

  D An increase in real incomes of consumers

2 Which of the following would cause a movement *along* a given demand curve for wheat?

  A A subsidy given to wheat farmers

  B An increase in the population

  C A decrease in the demand for bread

  D An increase in the popularity of rice, a substitute for wheat

3 Which of the following would cause a rightward *shift* of the supply curve for sweetcorn?

  A A severe drought in areas where sweetcorn is grown

  B An increased preference for sweetcorn among consumers

  C A fall in the price of other vegetables

  D An increase in productivity caused by increased use of fertilisers

4 Which of the following would cause a movement *along* the supply curve for beef?

  A A decrease in consumption of beef following a health scare

  B A government subsidy for beef farmers

  C A rise in the cost of animal feed

  D An increase in the number of cows

5 An increase in value added tax on petrol would cause:

  A A shift in the supply curve to the right and its gradient to get steeper

  B A shift in the demand curve to the left

  C A shift in the supply curve to the left and its gradient to get steeper

  D A movement along the supply curve

6 A subsidy to bee-keepers would cause:

  A The demand curve for honey to shift to the left

  B A fall in the price of honey

  C A decrease in the quantity of honey supplied

  D The supply curve of honey to shift to the left

7

Product	Price elasticity of demand	Income elasticity of demand
Rice	−0.3	−1.2
Beef steak	−1.7	+2.8
Carrots	−0.4	+0.8

Given the above information, it can be deduced that:

  A The demand for rice is more price elastic than the demand for beef steak

  B Rice is an inferior good whereas carrots are a normal good

  C The demand for rice is more income elastic than the demand for beef steak

  D The demand for carrots is price elastic and income elastic

8 Demand for a product will become more price elastic if:

  A Stocks of the product increase

  B The product becomes more durable

  C More consumers regard the product as being essential

  D A new substitute becomes available

9 If the cross-price elasticity of demand between two products is negative then it may be deduced that they are:

A Complements
B Inferior goods
C Substitutes
D Normal goods

10 When demand is price elastic, a reduction in price will lead to:

A A decrease in total revenue
B An increase in total revenue
C A more than proportionate fall in quantity demanded
D A decrease in the profits of the firm selling the product

11 The supply of a product is likely to be very price inelastic if:

A There are close substitutes for it
B It is perishable
C Large stocks are available
D It forms a large percentage of consumer incomes

12 If a 10% rise in price of copper causes a 10% increase in the quantity supplied then supply is:

A Price inelastic
B Perfectly inelastic
C Perfect elastic
D Unitary elastic

13 Which of the following is **not** a function of the price mechanism in a free market economy?

A To provide signals to producers to increase or decrease output when price changes
B To indicate changes in consumer wants
C To keep prices stable
D To allocate resources

14 In a free market economy, if the current market price is above the equilibrium price then:

A There will be an extension of supply and a contraction in demand
B The price will rise
C There will be an extension of demand and a contraction in supply
D There will be a rightward shift of the demand curve

Questions 15 and 16 are based on Figure 2.

15 An increase in supply would cause:

A A contraction in demand and an increase in price
B An extension of demand and a decrease in price
C A contraction in supply and an increase in price
D An extension of supply and a decrease in price

16 An increase in demand would cause:

A Consumer surplus to decrease
B Producer surplus to decrease
C Both consumer surplus and producer surplus to increase
D Both consumer surplus and producer surplus to decrease

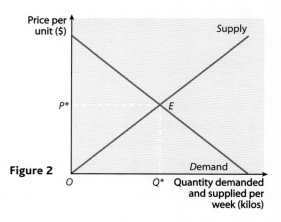

Figure 2

17 For an economy as a whole, efficiency in production would be achieved:

   A At any point along a production possibility curve
   B When there are unemployed resources
   C At a point to the right of an existing production possibility curve
   D When resources are shared equally

18 Illustrating your answer with a supply and demand diagram, explain the effect of an increase in VAT on sweets and crisps.

19 The price of coffee has fluctuated considerably over the last 5 years.

   a Analyse reasons which might explain why the price of coffee fluctuates. Illustrate your answer with a supply and demand diagram.
   b Assess the effects on consumers and producers of fluctuations in the price of coffee.

20 The UK housing market

Home ownership dropped from 68% in 2001 to 64% in 2011 partly because of the difficulties in securing mortgages from banks and building societies and the need to provide large deposits to secure the lowest interest rates. Consequently, more people are renting accommodation, causing rents to increase significantly.

Given the UK's rising and ageing population, more homes are needed. However, house builders are unwilling to build new houses when economic growth prospects are weak. Furthermore, it takes considerable time to obtain planning permission and then to build new houses.

Some economists have suggested that the government should offer subsidies to house builders to encourage them to increase the rate of house building. However, this would involve an increase in public expenditure at a time when the government is trying to reduce its expenditure in order to reduce the budget deficit.

   a Illustrating your answer with a supply and demand diagram, explain why rents have increased.
   b Analyse the factors influencing the demand for houses to buy.
   c Assess the factors influencing the elasticity of supply of houses.
   d Evaluate the effects of a decision by the government to subsidise the building of new houses.

Part 3: Market failure and government intervention

1 Market failure might occur in a free market economy when:

   A Firms enter the market in response to higher prices
   B A net welfare loss results from intervention by the government
   C Prices rise when there is excess demand
   D There is underprovision of public goods

2 From Figure 3, it can be deduced that:

   A The free market level of output is *OY*
   B The welfare loss is *EAC*
   C The welfare gain from increasing output from *OY* to *OX* is *YACX*
   D A reduction in the quantity produced below *OX* would reduce the welfare loss

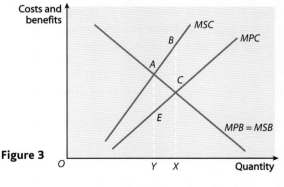

Figure 3

3 New vaccine

A new vaccine is developed to prevent the spread of coughs and colds, which are the main cause of around 130 million working days lost through absenteeism in the UK. The government decides to make this vaccine freely available to anyone who wants it, much to the delight of the pharmaceutical company that developed it.

   a   What are the private benefits of the production and consumption of this new vaccine?
   b   Explain the opportunity cost of providing the vaccine free to individuals.
   c   Assess the external benefits of the new vaccine, illustrating your answer with an externalities diagram.

4 The free-rider problem arises because:

   A   Producers charge a price for private goods
   B   There is no opportunity cost in providing a public good
   C   Private goods are always free
   D   Public goods are non-excludable

5 Public goods differ from private goods because:

   A   Public goods are excludable
   B   It is impossible to charge for private goods
   C   Private goods are always underprovided in a market economy
   D   Public goods are non-excludable and non-rivalrous

6 Without government intervention, it is unlikely that workers will make adequate provision for their pensions. The most likely reason is:

   A   Workers have inadequate information
   B   Pensions are a public good
   C   Life expectancy is falling
   D   There is no tax on pension contributions

7 Which of the following is likely to cause a decrease in the occupational mobility of labour?

   A   A decrease in stamp duty on buying a property
   B   A decrease in house price differentials between different parts of the country
   C   A reduction in government-funded training programmes
   D   A reduction in transport costs

8 Between 2009 and 2012, the price of maize fluctuated between $144 per tonne and $330 per tonne. The most likely explanation is that:

   A   Demand and supply of maize are price elastic
   B   The supply of maize is unaffected by changes in weather conditions
   C   Demand and supply of maize are price inelastic
   D   The demand for maize is continuously decreasing

9 Tax on tobacco

Many governments tax tobacco as a means of raising revenue. Indeed the UK government raised £12.1 billion from the tax on tobacco in 2011/12. The effect of the tax increases in the 2012 Budget was to increase the price of a packet of cigarettes by 37p. However, there is evidence that this has led to a significant increase in smuggling as people try to avoid the taxes, which account for a large proportion of the cost of a packet of cigarettes.

Similarly, heavy taxes on alcohol have led to an increase in sales on the black market. Further, it has been found that in some years, when taxes on alcohol have been increased, tax revenue has actually decreased. A different approach has been adopted by the Scottish Government, which has introduced a minimum price for alcohol.

a Giving examples, distinguish between the private costs and external costs of cigarette consumption.
b Illustrating your answer with a supply and demand diagram, analyse the effect of an increase in tax on tobacco.
c To what extent does taxation of tobacco result in government failure?
d Assess the likely economic effects of a minimum price being set for alcoholic drinks.
e Examine **two** other ways in which the government might discourage the consumption of alcohol and tobacco.

SECTION
2

MACROECONOMICS

Part 4
Economic policy
objectives and indicators
of macroeconomic
performance

Chapter 10

Macroeconomic performance: inflation

This part of the book switches attention to macroeconomics. Macroeconomics has much in common with microeconomics, but focuses on the whole economy, rather than on individual markets and how they operate. Although the way of thinking about issues is similar, and although similar tools are used, now it is interactions between economic variables at the level of the whole economy that are studied. This chapter introduces some key aspects of macroeconomic performance and how to use data. It will also discuss inflation, which is one of the key indicators of macroeconomic performance. The following chapters will explore unemployment and economic growth, which are also major concerns for governments in macroeconomics.

> ### Learning objectives
>
> After studying this chapter, you should:
> - be aware of the main economic aggregates in a modern economy
> - understand the distinction between real and nominal variables
> - be familiar with the use of index numbers and the calculation of percentage rates of change
> - appreciate the significance of alternative measurements of inflation in the context of the UK economy
> - be aware of the causes and consequences of inflation

Economic performance

Key term

macroeconomics the study of the interrelationships between economic variables at an aggregate (macroeconomic) level

Microeconomics highlights the importance of individual markets in achieving allocative and productive efficiency. In a modern economy, there are so many separate markets that it is difficult to get an overall picture of how well the economy is working. When it comes to monitoring its overall performance, the focus thus tends to be on the macroeconomic aggregates. 'Aggregates' here means 'totals' — for example, total unemployment in an economy, or total spending on goods and services — rather than, say, unemployed workers in a particular occupation, or spending on a particular good.

There are a number of dimensions in which the economy as a whole can be monitored. One prime focus of economic policy in recent years has been the inflation rate, as it has been argued that maintaining a stable economic environment is crucial to enabling markets to operate effectively. A second focus has been unemployment, which has been seen as an indicator of whether the economy is using its resources to the full — in other words, whether there are factors of production that are not being fully utilised. In addition, of course, there may be concern that the people who are unemployed are being disadvantaged.

Perhaps more fundamentally, there is an interest in economic growth. Is the economy expanding its potential capacity as time goes by, thereby making more resources available for members of society? In fact, it might be argued that this is the most fundamental objective for the economy, and the most important indicator of the economy's performance.

Other concerns may also need to be kept in mind. In particular, there is the question of how the economy interacts with the rest of the world. The UK is an 'open' economy — one that actively engages in international trade — and this aspect of UK economic performance needs to be monitored too. This is done through the balance of payments accounts, which will be examined in Chapter 17.

The importance of data

To monitor the performance of the economy, it is crucial to be able to observe how the economy is functioning, and for this you need data. Remember that economics, especially macroeconomics, is mainly a non-experimental discipline. It is not possible to conduct experiments to see how the economy reacts to various stimuli in order to learn how it works. Instead, it is necessary to observe the economy, and to come to a judgement about whether or not its performance is satisfactory, and whether macroeconomic theories about how the economy works are supported by the evidence.

So, a reliable measure is needed for tracking each of the variables mentioned above, in order to observe how the economy is evolving through time. The key indicators of the economy's performance will be introduced as this chapter unfolds.

Sources of data

Most of the economic statistics used by economists are collected and published by various government agencies. Such data in the UK are published mainly by the Office for National Statistics (ONS). Data on other countries are published by the International Monetary Fund (IMF), the World Bank and the United Nations, as well as national sources. There is little alternative to relying on such sources because the accurate collection of data is an expensive and time-consuming business.

Care needs to be taken in the interpretation of economic data. It is important to be aware of how the data are compiled, and the extent to which they are indicators of what economists are trying to measure. It is also important to remember that the economic environment is ever changing, and that single causes can rarely be ascribed to the economic events that are observed. This is because the ceteris paribus condition that underlies so much economic analysis is rarely fulfilled in reality. In other words, you cannot rely on 'other things remaining constant' when using data about the real world.

It is also important to realise that even the ONS cannot observe with absolute accuracy. Indeed, some data take so long to be assembled that early estimates are provisional in nature and subject to later revision as more information becomes available. Data used in international comparisons must be treated with even greater caution.

Real and nominal measurements

The measurement of economic variables poses many dilemmas for statisticians. Not least is the fundamental problem of what to use as units of measurement. Suppose economists wish to measure the total output produced in an economy during successive years. In the first place, they cannot use volume measures. They may be able to count how many computers, passenger cars, tins of paint and cauliflowers the economy produces — but how do they add all these different items together to produce a total?

An obvious solution is to use the money values. Given prices for all the items, it is possible to calculate the money values of all these goods and thus produce a measurement of the total output produced in an economy during a year in terms of pounds sterling. However, this is just the beginning of the problem because, in order to monitor changes in total output between 2 years, it is important to be aware that not only do the volumes of goods produced change, but so too do their prices. In effect, this means that, if pounds sterling are used as the unit of measurement, the unit of measurement will change from one year to the next as prices change.

This is a problem that is not faced by most of the physical sciences. After all, the length of a metre does not alter from one year to the next, so if the length of something is being measured, the unit is fixed. Economists, however, have to make allowance for changing prices when measuring in pounds sterling.

Measurements made using prices that are current at the time a transaction takes place are known as measurements of **nominal values**. When prices are rising, these nominal measurements will always overstate the extent to which an economic variable is growing through time. Clearly, to analyse performance, economists will be more interested in **'real' values** — that is, the quantities produced after having removed the effects of price changes. One way in which these real measures can be obtained is by taking the volumes produced in each year and valuing these quantities at the prices that prevailed in some base year. This then enables allowance to be made for the changes in prices that take place, permitting a focus on the real values. These can be thought of as being measured at *constant prices*.

How can we add together all the different items an economy produces?

For example, suppose that last year you bought a tub of ice cream for £2, but that prices have risen, so that this year you had to pay £2.20 for the same tub. Your *real* consumption of the item has not changed, but your spending has increased. If you were to use the value of your spending to measure changes in consumption through time, it would be misleading, as you know that your *real* consumption has not changed at all (so is still £2), although its *nominal* value has increased to £2.20.

Quantitative skills 10.1

Converting nominal measurements to real

It is worth being aware that the ratio of the current (nominal) value of a variable to its constant price (real) value (multiplied by 100) is a price index. For example:

$$100 \times \frac{\text{nominal GDP}}{\text{real GDP}} \text{ is a price index}$$

So, if we know GDP at current prices and we know the relevant price index, we can calculate the real value of GDP.

For example, in 2013, GDP for the UK in current prices was estimated to be £1.613 billion, and the underlying price index was 105.2 (based on 2010 = 100). The real value of GDP can thus be calculated as:

$$100 \times \frac{1.613}{105.2} = £1.533 \text{ billion.}$$

Quantitative skills 10.2

Calculating a percentage change

In macroeconomics it is often important to be able to calculate the percentage change in a variable. For example, it may be that there is interest in knowing how rapidly prices are changing, or in calculating the rate of economic growth. In the previous paragraph, the price of a tub of ice cream was supposed to have increased from £2 to £2.20. To calculate the percentage change in the price, calculate the change in price (2.20 − 2 = 0.20) and express that as a percentage of the original value. In other words, the percentage change is:

$$100 \times (2.20 - 2) \div 2 = 10\%$$

Notice that the change in the variable is always expressed as a percentage of the initial value, not the final value.

Index numbers

Key term

index number a device for comparing the value of a variable in one period or location with a base observation (e.g. the retail price index measures the average level of prices relative to a base period)

In some cases there is no apparent unit of measurement that is meaningful. For example, if you wished to measure the general level of prices in an economy, there is no meaningful unit of measurement that could be used. In such cases the solution is to use **index numbers**, which is a form of ratio that compares the value of a variable with some base point.

For example, suppose the price of a 250 g pack of butter last year was 80p, and this year it is 84p. How can the price between the two periods be compared? One way of doing it is to calculate the percentage change using the formula introduced above:

$$100 \times (84 - 80) \div 80 = 5\%$$

An alternative way of doing this is to calculate an index number. In the above example, the current value of the index could be calculated as the current value divided by the base value, multiplied by 100. In other words, this would be $100 \times 84 \div 80 = 105$. The resulting number gives the current value relative to the base value. This turns out to be a useful way of expressing a range of economic variables where you want to show the value relative to a base period. Index numbers can also be used to compare between regions or to compare variables measured in different units — anything where you want to compare with some base level.

One particular use for this technique is when you want to show the average level of prices at different points in time. For such a general price index, one procedure is to define a typical basket of commodities that reflects the spending pattern of a representative household. The cost of that bundle can be calculated in a base year, and then in subsequent years. The cost in the base year is set to equal 100, and in subsequent years the index is measured relative to that base date, thereby reflecting the change in prices since then. For example, if in the second year the weighted average increase in prices were 2.5%, then the index in year 2 would take on the value 102.5 (based on year 1 = 100). Such a general index of prices could be seen as an index of the *cost of living* for the representative household, as it would give the level of prices faced by the average household relative to the base year.

Exercise 10.1

Table 10.1 contains data on oil and petrol prices.

Table 10.1 Prices of oil and petrol

Date	Oil price ($ per barrel)	Average petrol price, London (£ per litre)	Average supermarket petrol price (£ per litre)
June 2011	112	1.361	1.346
June 2012	97	1.340	1.309
June 2013	104	1.342	1.330
June 2014	113	1.305	1.285

Source: The AA

a Construct index numbers based on June 2011 = 100 and compare the movements in the price of petrol in London with the price of oil during this period.
b Construct index numbers to compare petrol prices in London with the average supermarket price for each of the periods.

Summary

- Macroeconomics is the study of the interrelationships between economic variables at the level of the whole economy.
- Some variables are of particular interest when monitoring the performance of an economy — for example, inflation, unemployment and economic growth.
- As economists cannot easily conduct experiments in order to test economic theory, they rely on the use of economic data: that is, observations of the world around them.
- Data measured in money terms need to be handled carefully, as prices change over time, thereby affecting the units in which many economic variables are measured.
- Index numbers are helpful in comparing the value of a variable with a base date or unit.

The consumer price index and inflation

The most important general price index in the UK is the **consumer price index (CPI)**, which has been used by the government in setting its inflation target since the beginning of 2004. This index is based on the prices of a bundle of goods and services measured at different points in time. A total of 180,000 individual price quotes on 680 different products are collected by the ONS each month, by visits to shops and using the telephone and internet. Data on spending from *Household Final Monetary Consumption Expenditure* are used to compile the weights for the items included in the index. These weights are updated each year, as changes in the consumption patterns of households need to be accommodated if the index is to remain representative. A criticism of the index has been that it excludes housing costs of owner occupiers, and a new index (the CPIH) was launched in March 2013 to remedy this. This is published alongside the CPI.

It is important to remember that the CPI provides a measurement of the *level* of prices in the economy. This is not inflation: **inflation** is the *rate of change* of prices, and the percentage change in the CPI provides one estimate of the inflation rate.

Key terms

consumer price index (CPI) a measure of the general level of prices in the UK, adopted as the government's inflation target since December 2003

inflation the rate of change of the average price level: for example, the percentage annual rate of change of the CPI

Exercise 10.2

Table 10.2 provides data on consumer prices for the UK, USA and Italy.

Table 10.2 Consumer prices

	UK consumer price index	USA consumer price index	Italy consumer price index
2003	84.5	84.4	87.3
2004	85.6	86.6	89.2
2005	87.3	89.6	91.0
2006	89.4	92.4	92.9
2007	91.5	95.1	94.6
2008	94.8	98.7	97.7
2009	96.8	98.4	98.5
2010	100.0	100.0	100.0
2011	104.5	103.2	102.8
2012	107.4	105.3	105.9
2013	110.2	106.8	107.2

Source: OECD

a Calculate the annual inflation rates for each of the countries from 2004 to 2013.

b Plot these three inflation series on a graph against time.

c By what percentage did prices increase in each country over the whole period — that is, between 2003 and 2013?

d Which economy do you judge to have experienced most stability in the inflation rate?

Alternative measurements of inflation

The traditional measure of inflation in the UK for many years was the **retail price index (RPI)**, which was first calculated (under another name) in the early twentieth century to evaluate the extent to which workers were affected by price changes during the First World War. When the Blair government first set an explicit inflation target, it chose the RPIX, which is the RPI excluding mortgage interest payments. This was felt to be a better measure of the effectiveness of macroeconomic policy. It was argued that if interest rates are used to curb inflation, then including mortgage interest payments in the inflation measure will be misleading.

The CPI replaced RPIX partly because it is believed to be a more appropriate indicator for evaluating policy effectiveness. In addition, it has the advantage of being calculated using the same methodology as is used in other countries within the European Union, so that it is more useful than the RPIX for making international comparisons of inflation.

The CPI and RPI are based on a similar approach, although there are some significant differences in the detail of the calculation. Both measures set out to calculate the overall price level at different points in time. Each is based on calculating the overall cost of a representative basket of goods and services at different points in time relative to a base period. The result of these calculations is an index that shows how the general

Key term

retail price index (RPI) a measure of the average level of prices in the UK level of prices has changed relative to the base year. The rate of inflation is then calculated as the percentage rate of change of the price index, whether it be the CPI or RPI.

The indexes share a common failing, arising from the fixed weights used in calculating the overall index. Suppose the price of a particular item rises more rapidly than other prices during the year. One response by consumers is to substitute an alternative, cheaper, product. As the indexes are based on fixed weights, they do not pick up this substitution effect, and therefore tend to overstate the price level in terms of the cost of living. Some attempt is made to overcome this problem by changing the weights on an annual basis in order to limit the impact of major changes. This includes incorporating new items when appropriate — for example, 14 new items were included in the CPI in 2014, including interchangeable lens digital cameras and fresh fruit snacking pots, reflecting changes in consumer spending patterns.

Differences between the CPI and RPI

The CPI and RPI differ for a number of reasons, partly because of differences in the content of the basket of goods and services that are included, and partly in terms of the population of people who are covered by the index. For example, in calculating the weights, the RPI excludes pensioner households and the highest-income households, whereas the CPI does not. There are also some other differences in the ways that the calculations are carried out. RPIX removes mortgage payments from the RPI.

Figure 10.1 shows data for the rates of change of the RPI and the CPI since 2002. These rates have been calculated on a monthly basis, computing the percentage rate of change of each index relative to the value 12 months previously.

A noticeable characteristic of Figure 10.1 is that for much of the period the CPI has shown a lower rate of change than the RPI (except in 2009). In part this reflects the way in which the prices are combined, but it also reflects the fact that different items and households are covered. Since its introduction, the CPIH has stayed quite close to the CPI.

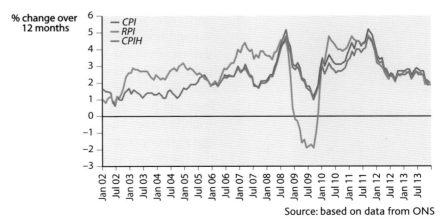

Source: based on data from ONS

Figure 10.1 Alternative inflation measures in the UK, 2002–13

Until the end of 2003, the government's target for inflation was set at 2.5% per annum in the RPIX. After that date, the target for the CPI was set at 2% per annum. Since 1997, the Bank of England has had the responsibility of ensuring that inflation remains within one percentage point of this target. You can see from Figure 10.1 that inflation accelerated (on both measures) after March 2006, and in March 2007 the rate of change of CPI went above 3%, thus moving out of the permissible target range for the first time since the inflation target was introduced. Inflation then accelerated again during 2008, partly because of rising food prices in world markets, before plummeting in the global financial crisis that hit in late 2009. Notice how RPI inflation actually went negative at this time. This partly reflected the fact that interest rates were at an all-time low, which affected mortgage interest payments, causing RPI to fall for a period.

Causes of inflation

Inflation occurs when there is a rise in the general price level. However, it is important to distinguish between a one-off increase in the price level and a sustained rise over a long period of time. For example, a one-off rise in the price of oil may have an effect on the price level, but why should prices continue to rise after an initial period of adjustment?

Nonetheless, this is one reason why prices may begin to increase. Inflation thus may be initiated by an increase in the costs faced by firms. This is sometimes referred to as **cost-push inflation**, as the increase in the overall level of prices is cost-driven.

An alternative explanation for a rise in the general price level could come from the demand side, where an increase in aggregate demand leads to a rise in prices, especially if the economy is close to its full capacity. An increase in the price level emanating from the demand side of the macroeconomy is sometimes referred to as **demand-pull inflation**.

Why should there be *persistent* increases in prices over time? One-off movements in either aggregate demand or aggregate supply may lead to one-off changes in the overall price level, but unless the movements continue in subsequent periods there is no reason to suppose that inflation will continue. One explanation is provided by changes in the supply of money circulating in an economy.

Persistent inflation can take place only when the **money stock** grows more rapidly than real output. This can be shown in terms of aggregate demand and aggregate supply. If the money supply increases, firms and households in the economy find they have excess cash balances: that is, for a given price level they have more purchasing power than they expected to have. Their impulse will thus be to increase their spending. They will probably also save some of the excess, which will tend to result in lower interest rates — which will then reinforce the increase in aggregate demand.

If the money supply continues to increase, the process repeats itself, with prices then rising persistently. One danger of this is that people will get so accustomed to the process that they speed up their spending decisions, which simply accelerates the whole process.

To summarise, the analysis suggests that, although a price rise can be triggered on either the supply side or the demand side of the macroeconomy, persistent inflation can arise only through persistent excessive growth in the money stock.

Key terms

cost-push inflation inflation initiated by an increase in the costs faced by firms, arising on the supply side of the economy
demand-pull inflation inflation initiated by an increase in aggregate demand
money stock the quantity of money in the economy

Costs of inflation

A crucial question is why it matters if an economy experiences inflation. The answer is that very high inflation gives rise to a number of costs.

The fact that firms have to keep amending their price lists raises the costs of undertaking transactions. These costs are often known as the *menu costs* of inflation; however, these should not be expected to be significant unless inflation really is very high. A second cost of very high inflation is that it discourages people from holding money because, at the very high nominal interest rates that occur when inflation is high, the opportunity cost of holding money becomes great. People therefore try to keep their money in interest-bearing accounts for as long as possible, even if it means making frequent trips to the bank — for which reason these are known as the *shoe leather costs* of inflation.

This reluctance to use money for transactions may inhibit the effectiveness of markets. For example, there was a period in the early 1980s when inflation in Argentina was so high that some city parking fines had to be paid in litres of petrol rather than in cash. Markets will not work effectively when people do not use money and the economy begins to slip back towards a barter economy. The situation may be worsened if taxes or pensions are not properly indexed so that they do not keep up with inflation.

However, these costs are felt mainly when inflation reaches the *hyperinflation* stage. This has been rare in developed countries in recent years, although many Latin American economies were prone to hyperinflation for a period in the 1980s, and some of the transition economies also went through very high inflation periods as they began to introduce market reforms; one example of this was the Ukraine, where inflation reached 10,000% per year in the early 1990s. Another example is the African country of Zimbabwe, where *The Economist* in April 2013 claimed that inflation had reached 230,000,000% in 2008.

However, there may be costs associated with inflation even when it does not reach these heights, especially if inflation is volatile. If the rate of change of prices cannot be confidently predicted by firms, the increase in uncertainty may be damaging, and firms may become reluctant to undertake the investment that would expand the economy's productive capacity.

Furthermore, as Chapter 6 emphasised, prices are very important in allocating resources in a market economy. Inflation may consequently inhibit the ability of prices to act as reliable signals in this process, leading to a wastage of resources and lost business opportunities.

It is these last reasons that have elevated the control of inflation to one of the central planks of UK government macroeconomic policy. However, it should be noticed that the target for inflation has not been set at zero. During the period when the inflation target was set in terms of RPIX, the inflation target was 2.5%; from 2004 the target for CPI inflation was 2%. The reasoning here is twofold. One argument is that it has to be accepted that measured inflation will overstate actual inflation, partly because it is so difficult to take account of quality changes in products such as PCs, where it is impossible to distinguish accurately between a price change and a quality change.

A Zimbabwean looks at a new 50 billion dollar bank note issued in 2009

Second, wages and prices tend to be sticky in a downward direction: in other words, firms may be reluctant to lower prices and wages. A modest rate of inflation (e.g. 2%) thus allows relative prices to change more readily, with prices rising by more in some sectors than in others. This may help price signals to be more effective in guiding resource allocation.

Deflation

The recession that began to affect many advanced countries in the late 2000s raised the possibility that the overall level of prices in an economy might fall. This situation of negative inflation is known as **deflation**. Figure 10.1 showed that the UK experienced falling prices according to the RPI for a period.

Deflation is sometimes perceived to be bad for the economy on the grounds that economic agents will see this as a sign that the economy is in terminal decline. Indeed, if people expect prices to continue to fall, they may postpone purchases in the expectation of being able to buy at a lower price in the future. This would then mean a fall in demand in the economy, perpetuating the recession. However, central banks have ways of intervening to prevent deflation being long-lived, and it is not clear that consumers would actually act in the way described.

Inflation in the UK and throughout the world

Figure 10.2 shows a time path for the rate of change in price levels since 1949. RPI has been used for this purpose, as the CPI was introduced only in 1997, so there is no consistent long-run series for it. The figure provides the backdrop to understanding the way the UK economy evolved during this period. Apart from the period of the Korean War, which generated inflation in 1951–52, the 1950s and early 1960s were typified by a low rate of inflation, with some acceleration becoming apparent in the early 1970s.

The instability of the 1970s was due to a combination of factors. Oil prices rose dramatically in 1973–74 and again in 1979–80, which certainly contributed to rising prices, not only in the UK but worldwide. However, inflation was further fuelled by the abandonment of the fixed exchange rate system, under which sterling had been tied to the US dollar until 1972. Under a fixed exchange rate system, the government must dedicate the use of monetary policy to maintaining the value of the currency. However, the transition to a floating exchange rate system freed up monetary policy in a way that was perhaps not fully understood by the government of the day. As you can see in Figure 10.2, prices were allowed to rise rapidly — by nearly 25% in 1974/75. The diagram also shows how inflation was gradually reined in during the 1980s, and underlines the relative stability that has now been achieved, with inflation keeping well within the target range set by the government until the late 2000s, as noted above. The significance of the exchange rate will be explained more fully in Chapter 17.

Figure 10.3 shows something of the extent to which the UK's experience is typical of the pattern of inflation worldwide. You can see from this how inflation in the advanced countries followed a similar general pattern in the early 1970s, with a period of gradual control after 1980. However, you can also see that the emerging and developing

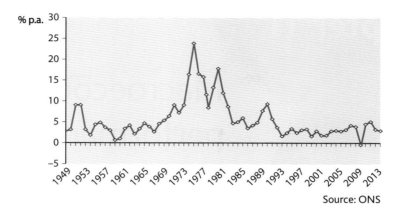

Figure 10.2 RPI inflation, 1949–2013 (% change over previous year)

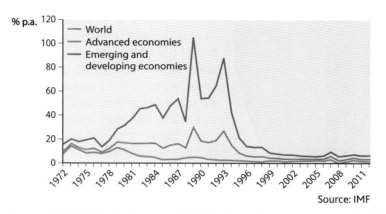
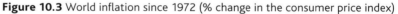

Figure 10.3 World inflation since 1972 (% change in the consumer price index)

economies in the world experienced inflation at a much higher average
level after 1974 because they proved to be less able to bring prices under
control after the oil price shocks. Much of this reflects events in Latin
America, which suffered especially high rates of inflation in the 1980s and
1990s. This instability in the macroeconomic environment has almost
certainly hindered development in the countries affected, and makes it
important to understand how inflation is generated and how to curb it.

Summary

- The control of inflation has been the major focus of macroeconomic
  policy in the UK since about 1976.
- Inflation can be initiated on either the supply side of an economy or
  the demand side.
- However, sustained inflation can take place only if there is also a
  sustained increase in money supply.
- High inflation imposes costs on society and reduces the effectiveness
  with which markets can work.
- Low inflation reduces uncertainty, and may encourage investment
  by firms.
- Deflation is negative inflation, and may need corrective action by the
  central bank to avoid perpetuating a recession.

Chapter 11

Macroeconomic performance: employment and unemployment

This chapter turns attention to two other important indicators of the performance of the macroeconomy: employment and unemployment. Labour is a key factor of production used in the production process, so employment is important in this context. Full employment is one of the key macroeconomic objectives. The existence of high unemployment suggests that the economy is not operating at full capacity, but some kinds of unemployment will always be present in a dynamic economy. This chapter explores the nature of employment and unemployment, and examines some of the problems in measuring unemployment as well as setting out the causes and consequences of this important indicator.

Learning objectives

After studying this chapter, you should:
- be aware of the composition of the UK population in terms of employed, unemployed and economically inactive
- understand the notion of full employment as an objective of macroeconomic policy
- be familiar with alternative measurements of unemployment in the UK
- understand the causes and consequences of unemployment

Employment and the UK workforce

Key terms

in employment people who are either working for firms or other organisations, or self-employed
economically inactive those people of working age who are not looking for work, for a variety of reasons
discouraged workers people who have been unable to find employment and who are no longer looking for work

In 2013, there were 40.3 million people living in the UK aged between the ages of 16 and 64. These are those considered to be of working age, although 65 is no longer seen as the normal retirement age. Figure 11.1 shows how they were distributed between three key economic categories: the employed, the unemployed and the economically inactive. Those **in employment** in this context include both those who are employed by firms or other organisations (such as government) and also the self-employed. The **economically inactive** include students, and those who have retired, are sick or are looking after family members. Also included are **discouraged workers** — people who have failed to find work and have given up looking. In other words, the economically inactive category includes all those people in the age range who are not considered to be

workforce people who are economically active — either in employment or unemployed

unemployed people who are economically active but not in employment

full employment a situation where people who are economically active in the workforce and are willing and able to work (at going wage rates) are able to find employment

active in the workforce. The unemployed are those who are in the workforce, but who are without jobs (a more precise definition will be provided soon).

The number of those employed is an important indicator, given that they contribute to the production process in their role as the factor of production: labour. Figure 11.2 shows the number of those in employment in each year since 1971. You can see that the number employed has increased substantially over this period, from just over 24 million in 1971 to nearly 29 million in 2013. It is also interesting to note that, although the number employed fell in 2009 as recession began to bite, the number employed recovered quite quickly, with employment in 2013 being slightly higher than it had been in 2008.

Full employment is seen as one of the core macroeconomic policy objectives. Having large numbers of people without jobs means that the economy is not making the best use of its labour resources, and is thus sacrificing potential output that could be produced. It is also undesirable from the perspective of the individuals who find themselves unemployed.

However, does this mean that everyone should have a job or be self-employed? Setting aside those who are economically inactive, there will always be some unemployment in a society, if only because there will be some people between jobs, or engaging in job search. Furthermore, if the economy were to be operating very close to full capacity, this would be likely to put upward pressure on wages and thus prices. In other words, there may be a conflict between achieving full employment and maintaining the stability of prices.

So full employment does not mean that unemployment will be zero. But it is difficult to specify a particular percentage that would constitute full employment. This may vary in different periods, and in different countries, partly reflecting the degree of flexibility in the labour market.

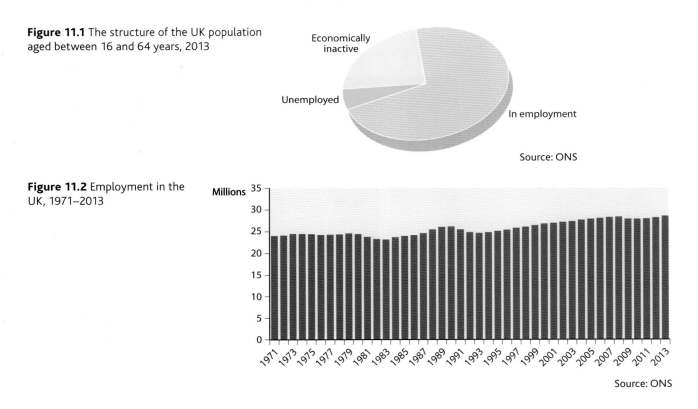

Figure 11.1 The structure of the UK population aged between 16 and 64 years, 2013

Source: ONS

Figure 11.2 Employment in the UK, 1971–2013

Source: ONS

The measurement of unemployment in the UK has also been contentious over the years, and the standard definition used to monitor performance has altered several times, especially during the 1980s, when a number of rationalisations were introduced.

Historically, unemployment was measured by the number of people registered as unemployed and claiming unemployment benefit (the Jobseeker's Allowance (JSA)). This measure of employment is known as the **claimant count of unemployment**. People claiming the JSA must declare that they are out of work, and capable of, available for and actively seeking work, during the week in which their claim is made.

One of the problems with the claimant count is that although people claiming the JSA must declare that they are available for work, it nonetheless includes some people who are claiming benefit, but are not actually available or prepared for work. It also excludes some people who would like to work, and who are looking for work, but who are not eligible for unemployment benefit, such as women returning to the labour force after childbirth.

Because of these problems, the claimant count has been superseded for official purposes by the so-called **ILO unemployment rate**, a measure based on the *Labour Force Survey*. This identifies the number of people available for work, and seeking work, but without a job. This definition corresponds to that used by the International Labour Organisation (ILO), and is closer to what economists would like unemployment to measure. It defines as being unemployed those people who are:

– without a job, want a job, have actively sought work in the last four weeks and are available to start work in the next two weeks; or

– out of work, have found a job and are waiting to start it in the next two weeks

Labour Market Statistics

The ILO employment rate is higher than the claimant count

Calculating the percentage rate of unemployment

When calculating the percentage rate of unemployment, the key question concerns the portion of the active workforce who are unemployed at any point in time. This is calculated by expressing the number of unemployed as a percentage of the active workforce (i.e. employed plus unemployed). In March 2014 it was estimated that there were 29.437 million people in employment and 2.135 people unemployed. The percentage rate was thus:

$100 \times 2.135 \div (29.437 + 2.135) = 6.76\%$.

Study tip

If you are confronted with a graph such as Figure 11.3, showing unemployment over an extended period and you need to describe the trends over that period, do not think that you have to work through picking out every observation, but focus on the main periods in which there were divergences from the norm.

Figure 11.3 shows the ILO unemployment rate since 1971, expressed as a percentage of the workforce. The surge in unemployment in the early 1980s stands out on the graph, when the percentage of the workforce registered as unemployed more than doubled in a relatively short period. Although this seemed to be coming under control towards the end of the 1980s, unemployment rose again in the early 1990s before a steady decline into the new millennium, rising again in the financial crisis and recession of the late 2000s.

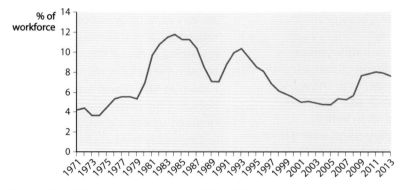

Figure 11.3 ILO unemployment rate, 1971–2013

Problems of measurement

It is important to be aware of the difficulties in measuring unemployment accurately. The claimant count is unreliable because it only captures those people who are eligible for the Jobseeker's Allowance, so it excludes some people who might be validly recognised as being unemployed. For example, it excludes people returning to the workforce after raising children or for other reasons of absence. It also excludes those who are on government training schemes and a range of other categories of people. The ILO unemployment data are based on sample evidence, and extrapolated up to give the picture for the UK as a whole. The sample cannot be guaranteed to be fully representative. From the perspective of economic analysis, it would also be helpful to know how many people are unemployed in the sense of not being able to find employment at their desired wage, but this is not covered in the definition.

Measuring unemployment in developing countries becomes even more difficult. If there is no social security system, then unemployed workers have no incentive to register as being unemployed. Furthermore, there may be people who cannot find jobs for which they are qualified, and who take jobs in second-choice occupations. This is a form of *underemployment*: for example, where qualified lawyers or doctors find themselves working as taxi drivers.

Causes of unemployment

There will always be some unemployment in a dynamic economy. At any point in time, there will be workers transferring between jobs. Indeed, this needs to happen if the pattern of production is to keep up with changing patterns of consumer demand and relative opportunity cost. In other words, in a typical period of time there will be some sectors of an economy that are expanding and others that are in decline. It is crucial that workers are able to transfer from those activities that are in decline to those that are booming. Accordingly, there will be some unemployment while this transfer takes place, and this is known as **frictional unemployment**.

In some cases, this transfer of workers between sectors may be quite difficult to accomplish. For example, coal mining may be on the decline in an economy, but international banking may be booming. It is clearly unreasonable to expect coal miners to turn themselves into international bankers overnight. In this sort of situation there may be some longer-term unemployment while workers retrain for new occupations and new sectors of activity. Indeed, there may be workers who find themselves redundant at a relatively late stage in their career and for whom the retraining is not worthwhile, or who cannot find firms that are prepared to train them for a relatively short pay-back time. Such unemployment is known as **structural unemployment**. It arises because of the mismatch between the skills of workers leaving contracting sectors and the skills required by expanding sectors in the economy.

Unemployment could also arise in a period of recession, when the demand for workers is low. This is sometimes referred to as **cyclical unemployment**. In addition, there may be periods when the economy is in equilibrium below full employment because of a deficiency in aggregate demand, which is known as **demand-deficient unemployment**. A solution to this might be to boost aggregate demand, but not all economists believe that this is appropriate, as will be discussed later. There may also be times of the year when the demand for labour varies because of seasonal effects: for example, the tourist sector experiences quiet periods during the winter. This may give rise to **seasonal unemployment**.

Key terms

frictional unemployment unemployment associated with job search: that is, people who are between jobs

structural unemployment unemployment arising because of changes in the pattern of economic activity within an economy

cyclical unemployment unemployment that arises during the downturn of the economic cycle, such as a recession

demand-deficient unemployment unemployment that arises because of a deficiency of aggregate demand in the economy, so that the equilibrium level of output is below full employment

seasonal unemployment unemployment that arises in seasons of the year when demand is relatively low

Beach lifeguards work seasonally, usually between May and September when the beaches are busy

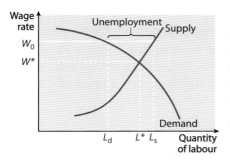

Figure 11.4 Unemployment in a labour market

A further reason for unemployment concerns the level of wages. Figure 11.4 shows a labour market in which a free market equilibrium would have wage W^* and quantity of labour L^*. If for some reason wages were set at W_0, there would be disequilibrium between labour supply (at L_s) and labour demand (at L_d). Expressing this in a different way, here is a situation in which there are more workers seeking employment at the going wage (L_s) than there are firms prepared to hire at that wage (L_d). The difference is unemployment.

There are a number of reasons why this situation might arise. Trade unions may have been able to use their power and influence to raise wages above the equilibrium level, thereby ensuring higher wages for their members who remain in employment, but denying jobs to others. Alternatively, it could be argued that wages will be inflexible downwards. Thus, a supply shock that reduced firms' demand for labour could leave wages above the equilibrium, and they may adjust downwards only slowly. Chapter 9 mentioned that in some situations the imposition of a minimum wage in a low-wage competitive labour market could also have the effect of institutionally setting the wage rate above its equilibrium level.

Finally, if unemployment benefits are set at a relatively high level compared with wages in low-paid occupations, some people may choose not to work, thereby creating some **voluntary unemployment**. From the point of view of those individuals, they are making a rational choice on the basis of the options open to them. From society's point of view, however, there needs to be a balance between providing appropriate social protection for those unable to obtain jobs and trying to make the best use of available resources for the benefit of society as a whole.

Key term

voluntary unemployment
   situation arising when an individual chooses not to accept a job at the going wage rate

---

Exercise 11.1

Classify each of the following types of unemployment as arising from frictional, structural, demand-deficient or other causes, and decide whether they are voluntary or involuntary:
a unemployment arising from a decline of the coal mining sector and the expansion of financial services
b a worker leaving one job to search for a better one
c unemployment that arises because the real wage rate is held above the labour market equilibrium
d unemployment arising from slow adjustment to a fall in aggregate demand
e unemployment arising because workers find that low-paid jobs are paying less than can be obtained in unemployment benefit

Consequences of unemployment

The costs of unemployment were mentioned earlier. From society's perspective, if the economy is operating below full capacity, then it is operating within the production possibility curve, and therefore is not making the best possible use of society's resources. In other words, if those unemployed workers were in employment, society would be producing more aggregate output; the economy would be operating more efficiently overall.

Furthermore, there may be costs from the perspective of prospective workers, in the sense that involuntary unemployment carries a cost to each such individual in terms of forgone earnings and the need to rely on social security support. At the same time, the inability to find work and to contribute to the family budget may impose a cost in terms of personal worth and dignity.

Exercise 11.2

Visit the website of the Office for National Statistics (at **www.statistics.gov.uk**) and find out the latest data for inflation and unemployment. Has the performance of the economy in respect of these two variables improved or deteriorated in the last year?

Summary

- The population of working age is made up of the employed, the unemployed and the economically inactive.
- Full employment is an objective of macroeconomic policy, as unemployment is costly to those who are unemployed and to society as a whole.
- Unemployment is measured in two ways. The claimant count is based on the number of people claiming Jobseeker's Allowance. The ILO measure is based on a sample of the population through the *Labour Force Survey.*
- Unemployment arises for a variety of reasons, and there will always be some unemployment in the economy, even when the economy is in equilibrium.

Case study 11.1

The UK economy in mid-2008

Figures 11.5 and 11.6 respectively show monthly inflation and unemployment in the UK between the beginning of 2004 and March 2008. Imagine that you are the chancellor of the exchequer considering the state of the economy.

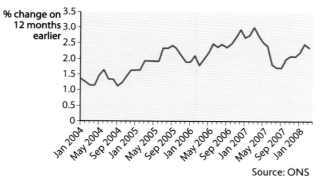

Figure 11.5 Inflation in the UK, 2004–08

Source: ONS

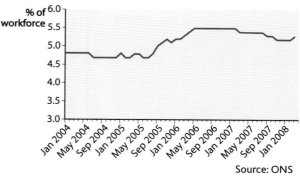

Figure 11.6 Unemployment in the UK, 2004–08

Source: ONS

Follow-up questions

a Discuss whether these two indicators give cause for concern about the performance of the economy. What other information would you need in order to come to a judgement?

b After you have thought about this, look back at Figures 10.1 and 11.3 to see what happened next.

Chapter 12

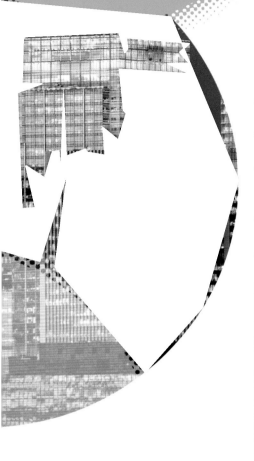

Measuring economic performance: economic growth

One of society's prime responsibilities is to provide a reasonable standard of living for its citizens and to promote their well-being. Hence one of the major objectives for economic policy in the long run is to enable improvements in well-being, and in order to do this it is first necessary to expand the resources available within society. A key element in this process is to achieve economic growth, which is the subject of this chapter. However, there may be more to well-being than just growth, and the chapter also explores some of the limitations of a strategy that aims to maximise GDP growth.

Learning objectives

After studying this chapter, you should:
- understand the meaning of economic growth and productivity
- be familiar with factors that can affect the rate of economic growth, particularly the role of investment
- appreciate the strengths and weaknesses of GDP as a measure of the standard of living in comparisons across time and between countries
- be aware of differences in growth rates between countries and of the explanations that have been advanced to explain them
- evaluate the importance to a society of economic growth and the costs that such growth may impose
- understand the meaning and significance of sustainable growth

What is economic growth?

It was noted in Chapter 1 that the total output of an economy can be measured by gross domestic product (GDP). Economic growth is the process by which real GDP increases over time. Remember from Chapter 10 that it is important to distinguish between *real* and *nominal* values. Real GDP is a measurement of total output in an economy that takes account of changing prices over time, so it is measured at constant prices. In considering economic growth, it is these real values that are relevant.

Long-run economic growth can be thought of as an expansion of the productive capacity of an economy. If you like, it is an expansion of the potential output of the economy. However, aggregate output can also rise in the short run in response to an increase in aggregate demand or an improvement in utilisation of the factors of production — for example, when unemployment falls. This is known as **short-run economic growth**.

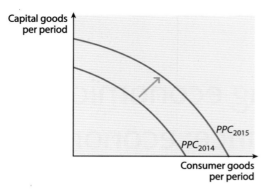

Figure 12.1 Economic growth

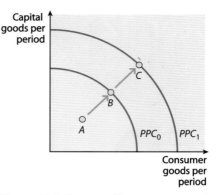

Figure 12.2 Short- and long-run economic growth

Chapter 1 discussed economic growth in terms of the production possibility curve (*PPC*). Figure 12.1 is a reminder, and reproduces Figure 1.4, where economic growth was characterised as an outward movement of the production possibility curve from PPC_0 to PPC_1. In other words, economic growth enables a society to produce more goods and services in any given period as a result of an expansion in its resources. This is long-run economic growth. Short-run economic growth takes place when an economy moves towards the production possibility curve from a point *within* it. Remember that if the economy is operating inside its *PPC*, it is failing to use all of its factors of production effectively, so a move towards the *PPC* is possible when employment rises and output increases as a result.

If economists try to measure economic growth using the rate of change of GDP as an indicator, they are not necessarily measuring long-run economic growth. GDP growth measures the *actual* rate of change of output rather than growth in the *potential* output capacity of the economy.

In Figure 12.2, a movement from *A* to *B* represents a move to the *PPC*. This is an increase in actual output resulting from using up surplus capacity in the economy, and represents short-run (actual) economic growth; notice that moving from *A* to *B* does not entail an increase in productive capacity. On the other hand, a movement of the *PPC* itself, enabling the move from *B* to *C*, represents long-run economic growth. When economists observe a change in GDP, they cannot easily distinguish between the two sorts of effect, especially if the economy is subject to a business cycle — in other words, if the economy is not always operating at full capacity. Long-run economic growth can also be seen in terms of the underlying trend rate of growth of real GDP.

Figure 12.3 helps to illustrate this. It shows the annual growth rate of real GDP in the UK since 1950. You can see that it is quite difficult to determine the underlying trend because the year-to-year movements are so volatile. Figure 12.4

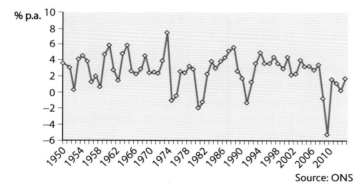

Source: ONS

Figure 12.3 Growth of real GDP, 1950–2013 (% change over previous year)

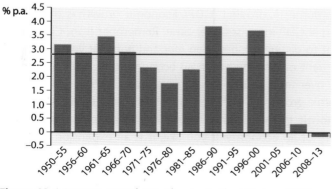

Figure 12.4 Average annual growth rates in the UK since 1950

takes 5-yearly average growth rates over the same period, with the horizontal red line showing the underlying trend rate of growth. This puts the recession of the late 2000s into sharp focus, as it seems out of line with the rest of the period.

Sources of economic growth

At a basic level, production arises from the use of factors of production — capital, labour, entrepreneurship and so on. Capacity output is reached when all factors of production are fully and efficiently utilised. From this perspective, an increase in capacity output can come either from an increase in the quantity of the factors of production, or from an improvement in their efficiency or productivity. **Productivity** is a measure of the efficiency of a factor of production. For example, **labour productivity** measures output per worker, or output per hour worked. The latter is the more helpful measure, as clearly total output is affected by the number of hours worked, which does vary somewhat across countries. **Capital productivity** measures output per unit of capital. **Total factor productivity** refers to the average productivity of all factors, measured as the total output divided by the total amount of inputs used.

An increase in productivity raises aggregate supply and the potential capacity output of an economy, and thus contributes to economic growth.

Capital

Capital is a critical factor in the production process. An increase in capital input is thus one source of economic growth. In order for capital to accumulate and increase the capacity of the economy to produce, **investment** needs to take place.

Notice that in economics 'investment' is used in this specific way. In common parlance the term is sometimes used to refer to investing in shares or putting money into a deposit account at the bank. Do not confuse these different concepts. In economics, 'investment' relates to a firm buying new capital, such as machinery or factory buildings. If you put money into a bank account, that is an act of saving, not investment.

In the national accounts, the closest measurement that economists have to investment is 'gross fixed capital formation'. This covers net additions to the capital stock, but it also includes **depreciation**. Some of the machinery and other capital purchased by firms is bought to replace old, worn-out capital, i.e. to offset depreciation. It does not therefore represent an addition to capital stock. As depreciation cannot be observed easily, the convention in the accounts is to measure gross investment (i.e. including depreciation) and then make an adjustment for depreciation to arrive at **net investment**.

Figure 12.5 shows the time path for gross investment in the UK since 1950, expressed as a percentage of GDP. You can see that the share of investment in GDP has fluctuated a little over the years. It seemed to have settled at around 17% in the 2000s, but it dropped during the recession at the end of the period.

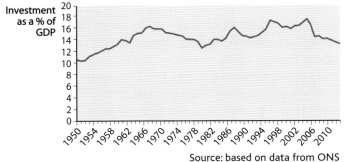

Source: based on data from ONS

Figure 12.5 Gross fixed capital formation in the UK, 1950–2013

Capital stock includes machinery and factory buildings, critical factors in the production process

The choice that any society makes here is between using resources for current consumption and using resources for investment. Investment thus entails sacrificing present consumption in order to have more resources available in the future.

The contribution of capital to growth is reinforced by technological progress, as the productivity of new capital is greater than that of old capital that is being phased out. For example, the speed and power of computers has increased enormously over recent years, which has had a great impact on productivity. Effectively, this means that technology is increasing the contribution that investment can make towards enlarging capacity output in an economy. Innovation can also be important, through the invention of new forms of capital and new ways of using existing capital, both of which can contribute to economic growth.

Labour

Capital has sometimes been seen as the main driver of growth, but labour too has a key contribution to make. There is little point in installing a lot of high-tech equipment unless there is the skilled labour to operate it.

There is relatively little scope for increasing the size of the labour force in a country, except through international migration. (Encouraging population growth is a rather long-term policy.) Nonetheless, the size of the workforce does contribute to the size of capacity output. A number of sub-Saharan African countries experienced this effect in reverse, with the impact of HIV/AIDS. The spread of this epidemic had a devastating impact in a number of countries in the region, seriously affecting capacity output, because the disease affects people of working age disproportionately, diminishing the size of the workforce and the productivity of workers.

The quality of labour input is more amenable to policy action. Education and training can improve the productivity of workers, and can be regarded as a form of investment in human capital.

Chapter 7 discussed how education and healthcare may have associated externalities. In particular, individuals may not perceive the full social benefits associated with education, training and certain kinds of healthcare, and thus may choose to invest less in these forms of human capital than is desirable from the perspective of society as a whole.

Key term

human capital the stock of skills and expertise that contribute to a worker's productivity; can be increased through education and training

Macroeconomics Part 4

142

Another such externality is the impact of human capital formation on economic growth as a justification for viewing education and healthcare as merit goods — which were discussed in Chapter 8.

For many developing countries, the provision of healthcare and improved nutrition can be seen as additional forms of investment in human capital, since such investment can lead to future improvements in productivity.

Exercise 12.1

Which of the following represent genuine economic growth, and which may just mean a move to the *PPC*?

a an increase in the rate of change of potential output

b a fall in the unemployment rate

c improved work practices that increase labour productivity

d an increase in the proportion of the population joining the labour force

e an increase in the utilisation of capital

f a rightward shift in the aggregate supply curve

Summary

- Economic growth is the expansion of an economy's productive capacity.
- This can be envisaged as a movement outwards of the production possibility curve.
- Economic growth can be seen as the underlying trend rate of growth in real GDP.
- Economic growth can stem from an increase in the inputs of factors of production, or from an improvement in their productivity, i.e. the efficiency with which factors of production are utilised.
- Investment contributes to growth by increasing the capital stock of an economy, although some investment is to compensate for depreciation.
- The contribution of capital is reinforced by the effects of technological progress.
- Labour is another critical factor of production that can contribute to economic growth: for instance, education and training can improve labour productivity. This is a form of human capital formation.

GDP and growth

GDP is a way of measuring the total output of an economy over a period of time. Although this measure can provide an indicator of the quantity of resources available to citizens of a country in a given period, as an assessment of the standard of living it has its critics.

GDP does have some things going for it. First, it is relatively straightforward and thus is widely understood. Second, it is a well-established indicator and one that is available for almost every country in the world, so that it can be used to compare income levels across countries. A first point to notice is that if we want to compare across countries, we need to recognise that different countries have differently sized populations, and we need to take this into account.

Calculating GDP per capita

Suppose you want to compare living standards in China and Malaysia. In 2012, real GDP in China was US$4,522 billion, whereas in Malaysia it was US$198.4 billion. However, China's population was 1,351 million, compared to Malaysia's 29 million. It is more meaningful to compare average GDP per person (which is known as **GDP per capita**). For China this was US$4,522,000/1,351 = US$3,347. Notice that because GDP was measured in billions, but population was in millions, it was necessary to convert GDP into millions for this calculation to be correct. For Malaysia, GDP per capita was US$6,841.

GDP per capita the average level of GDP per head of population

It is good to be familiar with generalised facts about regions and countries of the world, but you will *not* be expected to produce lots of facts and figures about individual countries in the exam.

Figure 12.6 provides data on GDP per capita for a range of countries around the world. The extreme differences that exist around the globe are immediately apparent from the data. GDP per capita in Burundi was just $153 in 2012, whereas in the USA the figure was $45,335.

In trying to interpret these data, there are a number of issues that need to be borne in mind, as the comparison is not as straightforward as it looks.

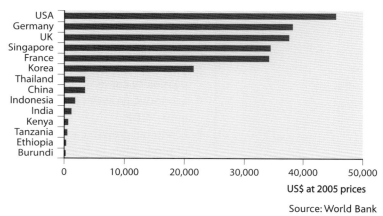

Source: World Bank

Figure 12.6 GDP per capita, 2012, in US$ at constant 2005 prices

Inequality in income distribution

One important point to notice is that looking at the average level of income per person may be misleading if there are wide differences in the way in which income is distributed within countries. In other words, it cannot be assumed that every person living in Burundi receives $153, or that every US citizen receives $45,335. If income is more unequally distributed in some countries, this will affect one's perception of what the term 'average' means. For example, Chile and Croatia had broadly similar GDP per capita levels in 2012, but the income distribution in Croatia was more equitable than in Chile.

The informal sector and the accuracy of data

A further problem with undertaking international comparisons is that it is never absolutely certain that the accuracy with which data are collected is consistent across countries. Definitions of GDP and other variables are now set out in a clear, internationally agreed form, but even when countries are working to the same definitions, some data collection agencies may be more reliable than others.

In many developing countries, substantial economic activity may take place without an exchange of money

One particular area in which this is pertinent relates to the informal sector. In every economy there are some transactions that go unrecorded. In most economies, there are economic activities that take place that cannot be closely monitored because of their informal nature. This is especially prevalent in many developing countries, where substantial amounts of economic activity often take place without an exchange of money. For example, in many countries subsistence agriculture remains an important facet of economic life. If households are producing food simply for their own consumption, there is no reason for a money transaction to take place with regard to its production, and thus such activity will not be recorded as a part of GDP. Equally, much economic activity within the urban areas of less developed countries comes under the category of the 'informal sector'.

Where such activity varies in importance between countries, comparing incomes on the basis of measured GDP may be misleading, as GDP will be a closer indicator of the amount of real economic activity in some countries than in others.

Exchange rate problems

The data presented in Figure 12.6 were expressed in terms of US dollars. This allows economists to compare average incomes using a common unit of measurement. At the same time, however, it may create some problems.

Economists want to compare average income levels so that they can evaluate the standard of living, and compare standards across countries. In other words, it is important to be able to assess people's command over resources in different societies, and to be able to compare the purchasing power of income in different countries.

GDP is initially calculated in terms of local currencies, and subsequently converted into US dollars using official exchange rates. Will this provide information about the relative local purchasing power of incomes? Not necessarily.

One reason for this is that official exchange rates are sometimes affected by government intervention. Indeed, in many of the less developed countries, exchange rates are pegged to an international currency — usually the US dollar. In these circumstances, exchange rates are more likely to reflect the government's policy and actions than the relative purchasing power of incomes in the countries under scrutiny.

Where exchange rates are free to find their own equilibrium level, they are likely to be influenced strongly by the prices of *internationally traded* goods — which are likely to be very different from the prices of the goods that are typically consumed by residents in these countries. Again, it can be argued that the official exchange rates may not be a good reflection of the relative purchasing power of incomes across countries.

The United Nations International Comparison Project has been working on this problem for many years. It now produces an alternative set of international estimates of GDP based on purchasing power parity (PPP) exchange rates, which are designed to reflect the relative purchasing power of incomes in different societies more accurately. Figure 12.7 shows estimates for the same set of countries.

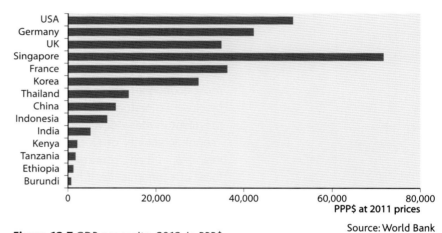

Source: World Bank

Figure 12.7 GDP per capita, 2012, in PPP$

Comparing this with Figure 12.6, you will notice that the gap between the low-income and high-income countries seems less marked when PPP dollars are used as the unit of measurement. In other words, the US dollar estimates exaggerate the gap in living standards between rich and poor countries. This is a general feature of these measurements — that measurements in US dollars tend to understate real incomes for low-income countries and overstate them for high-income countries compared with PPP-dollar data. Put another way, people in the lower-income countries have a stronger command over goods and services than is suggested by US-dollar comparisons of GDP per capita. You can also see that the relative rankings of countries in PPP dollars are different in some cases — for example, compare the UK and Singapore.

Social indicators

A final question that arises is whether GDP can be regarded as a reasonable indicator of a country's standard of living. You have seen that GDP provides an indicator of the total resources available within an economy in a given period, calculated from data about total output, total incomes or total expenditure. This focus on summing the transactions that take place in an economy over a period can be seen as a rather narrow view of what constitutes the 'standard of living'. After all, it may be argued that the quality of people's lives depends on more things than simply the material resources that are available.

For one thing, people need to have knowledge if they are to make good use of the resources that are available. Two societies with similar income levels may nonetheless provide very different quality of life for their inhabitants, depending on the education levels of the population. Furthermore, if people are to benefit from consuming or using the available resources, they need a reasonable lifespan coupled with good health. So, good standards of health are also crucial to a good quality of life.

It is important to remember that different societies tend to set different priorities on the pursuit of growth and the promotion of education and health. This needs to be taken into account when judging relative living standards through a comparison of GDP per capita, as some countries have higher-than-average levels of health and education as compared with other countries with similar levels of GDP per capita.

A reasonable environment in which to live may be seen as another important factor in one's quality of life, and there may be a trade-off between economic growth and environmental standards.

There are some environmental issues that can distort the GDP measure of resources. Suppose there is an environmental disaster — perhaps an oil tanker breaks up close to a beautiful beach. This reduces the overall quality of life by degrading the landscape and preventing enjoyment of the beach. However, it does not have a negative effect on GDP; on the contrary, the money spent on clearing up the damage actually adds to GDP, so that the net effect of an environmental disaster may be to *increase* the measured level of GDP!

Extension material

GDP focuses on the domestic economy, and measures the total amount of output produced in the domestic economy during a period. However, it is also important to recognise that residents of the economy also receive some income from abroad — and some income earned in the domestic economy is sent abroad. Gross national income (GNI) takes into account these income flows between countries, and for some purposes is a more helpful measure — indeed, this is the standard measure used by the World Bank to compare average incomes across countries. For example, suppose we want to compare income levels across different countries in order to monitor the standard of living in a country — in other words, the quality of life that is enjoyed by the country's residents, GNI is to be preferred to GDP in this context, as it more closely reflects the incomes of the residents, including net flows of income between countries. This would be important for some countries such as Pakistan or the Philippines, where there are relatively large inflows of income from abroad from people working abroad and remitting income to their families.

Summary

- GDP is a widely used measure of the total amount of economic activity in an economy over a period of time.
- The trend rate of change of GDP may thus be an indicator of economic growth.
- GDP is a widely understood and widely available measure, but it does have some drawbacks.
- Average GDP per person neglects the important issue of income distribution.
- There may be variation in the effectiveness of data collection agencies in different countries, and variation in the size of the informal sector.
- Converting from a local currency into US dollars may distort the use of GDP as a measure of the purchasing power of local incomes.
- GDP may neglect some important aspects of the quality of life.

Below are some indicators for two countries, A and B. Discuss the extent to which GDP per capita (here measured in PPP$) provides a good indication of relative living standards in the two countries.

	Country A	Country B
GDP per capita (PPP$)	11,989	11,731
Adult literacy rate (%)	92.9	98.0
Life expectancy (in years at birth)	56.1	75.2
Infant mortality rate (per 1,000 live births)	33.3	5.7
% of population living on less than $1 per person per day	31.33	0.74

Discuss what other indicators might be useful in this evaluation.

Economic growth: international experience

The growth performance of different regions around the world has shown contrasting patterns in recent years. As early as the 1950s, a gap had opened up between the early developing countries in North America, Western Europe and Japan and the late developers in sub-Saharan Africa and Latin America.

Between 1960 and 1980 this gap began to widen, except for a small group of countries, mainly in East Asia, that had begun to close it. Figure 12.8 gives some data for countries in different regions. Tanzania and Ethiopia (in sub-Saharan Africa), together with Sri Lanka and India (in South Asia), grew relatively slowly in this period, with only Sri Lanka achieving an average growth rate above 2% per annum. Latin America showed a diverse experience: the examples shown in the figure are Colombia, which grew at about 3% per annum, and Brazil, which achieved growth of above 5% per annum. However, East Asia (represented here by South Korea and Singapore) took off during this period, growing at an average rate of 7% per year and more, achieved partly through exporting to world markets. Japan also grew rapidly at this time, while the UK and the USA grew at a more sedate pace of just above 2% per annum.

Figure 12.9 presents some more recent data, this time by region, for the period 1975–2005 (and for 1990–2005). This reveals some important patterns. The high-income OECD member countries continued to grow at a rather sedate rate of around 2% per annum, and less in the 1990s. Countries in East Asia and the Pacific maintained their impressive high growth of nearly 6% per annum, but again slowed a bit in the 1990s. South Asia showed some improvement, and even accelerated in the 1990s, as indeed did Latin America and the Caribbean. However, sub-Saharan African countries went through a dismal period in which their GDP per capita growth was negative — in other words, GDP per capita was lower in 2005 than it had been in 1975. This is serious indeed.

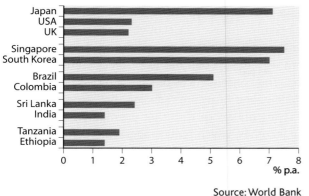

Figure 12.8 Growth of GDP per capita, selected countries, 1960–1980

Source: World Bank

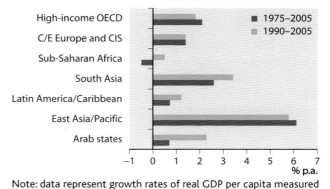

Note: data represent growth rates of real GDP per capita measured in local currency.

Figure 12.9 Growth of GDP per capita

Source: UNDP

The importance of economic growth

Expanding the availability of resources in an economy enables the standard of living of the country to increase. For developing countries this may facilitate the easing of poverty, and may allow investment in human capital that will improve standards of living further in the future. In the industrial economies, populations have come to expect steady improvements in incomes and resources.

Thus for any society, economic growth is likely to be seen as a fundamental objective — perhaps even the most important one, as it could be argued that other policy objectives may be regarded as subsidiary to the growth target. In other words, the control of inflation and the maintenance of full employment are seen as important short-run objectives, because their achievement facilitates long-run economic growth.

Growth versus basic needs

In some less developed countries the perspective may be different, and there has been a long-running debate about whether a society in its early stages of development should devote its resources to achieving the growth objective or to catering for basic needs. By making economic growth the prime target of policy, it may be necessary in the short run to allow inequality of incomes to continue, in order to provide the incentives for entrepreneurs to pursue growth. With such a 'growth-first' approach, it is argued that eventually, as growth takes place, the benefits will trickle down; in other words, growth is necessary in order to tackle poverty and provide for basic needs. However, others have argued that the first priority should be to deal with basic needs, so that people gain in human capital and become better able to contribute to the growth process.

Recession in the late 2000s

For the industrial countries, the importance of economic growth has been brought into sharp focus through the crisis of the late 2000s, which is still affecting many economies. After a period of relative stability during the 2000s, the onset of financial crisis initiated not only a slowdown in the growth of GDP, but a period in which GDP was falling. A **recession** is said to occur when GDP falls for two or more consecutive quarters.

Key term

recession occurs when GDP falls for two or more consecutive quarters

Study tip

Notice that it is *negative* growth that defines a recession: in Figure 12.10 the *growth rate* of GDP fell in 2011, but it did not go negative, so this would not count as a recession.

Figure 12.10 shows how such a recession affected the UK in late 2008, with GDP growth being negative for six consecutive quarters. The UK was not the only economy affected by this, and many advanced countries followed a similar pattern — indeed, countries like Greece were more severely hit in this period. The consequences of such a recession are significant. If output is falling, and firms are reducing their production, it is likely that they are laying off workers, so that unemployment rises. This then leads to falling incomes, which reduce aggregate demand and may lead to further drops in output, prolonging the recession. You can see from Figure 12.10 that the recovery from recession has been sluggish.

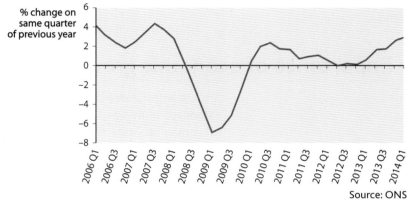

Source: ONS

Figure 12.10 Economic growth in the UK since 2006

The costs of economic growth

Economic growth also brings costs, perhaps most obviously in terms of pollution and degradation of the environment. In designing long-term policy for economic growth, governments need to be aware of the need to maintain a good balance between enabling resources to increase and safeguarding the environment. Pollution reduces the quality of life, so pursuing economic growth without regard to this may be damaging. This means that it is important to consider the long-term effects of economic growth — it may even be important to consider the effects not only for today's generation of citizens, but also for future generations.

This thinking has led to the important notion of **sustainability**, which is of increasing concern in the twenty-first century. The idea has come to the fore with the realisation that the planet does not have unlimited supplies of resources, and that today's generation has a responsibility to approach economic growth in a way that does not endanger the quality of life for future generations. For example, it may be possible to generate income for today's generation by clearing Indonesia's rainforests for timber, but this could have devastating effects in the future — effects that may not be confined to Indonesia.

These costs have been highlighted in recent years by the growing concerns that have been expressed about global climate change and the pressures on non-renewable resources such as oil and natural gas.

Key term

sustainable development
 'development that meets the needs of the present without compromising the ability of future generations to meet their own needs' (Brundtland Commission, 1987)

For example, the rapid growth rates being achieved by large emerging economies such as China and India have raised questions about the sustainability of economic growth in the long run. China in particular has experienced a period of unprecedented growth since 1978, which is shown in Figure 12.11. This shows the average growth between 1978 and 1985 (when reforms began to affect the economy), and for each 5-year period afterwards. No other economy in recent history has been able to achieve an average growth rate of 8.72% per annum over a 34-year period.

These concerns have led to research into the development of renewable energy sources, but progress in promoting sustainability is impeded because of international externality effects. Where there are externality effects that cross international borders, it becomes difficult to ensure regulation or control.

Exercise 12.3

Discuss with your fellow students the various benefits and costs associated with economic growth, and evaluate their relative importance.

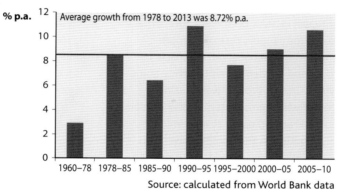

Source: calculated from World Bank data

Figure 12.11 China's average growth in GDP per capita

Summary

- The experience of economic growth has varied substantially in different regions of the world.
- There is a gap in living standards between countries that industrialised early and countries that are now classified as being less developed.
- A few countries, mainly in East Asia, went through a period of rapid growth from the 1960s that has allowed them to close the gap. This was achieved partly through export-led growth, although other factors were also important.
- However, countries in sub-Saharan Africa have stagnated, and remain on very low incomes.
- Economic growth remains important for all countries, at whatever stage of development.
- Recession represents an interruption to the economic growth process, and recovery may be slow.
- There may be costs attached to economic growth, particularly in respect of the environment.

China's economic growth

Since China adopted market reforms in the late 1970s, its economy has enjoyed a period of rapid economic growth that is unprecedented by historical standards. One of the characteristics of this period of rapid growth has been the gradual move towards allowing market forces to operate after a long period of central planning. This would be expected to have benefits for the economy in terms of the efficiency of resource allocation.

Although China's success in achieving such rapid economic progress has been much admired, it has also been much criticised, for a number of reasons.

One source of criticism centres on the environmental damage that results from a rapid rate of economic growth. For example, *The Economist* ran an article in 2007 pointing to several incidents that illustrate some of the ways in which China's growth was causing externalities, some of which cross international borders. One such incident was an explosion at a chemical plant that caused pollution in the Songhua river. This affected the city of Harbin, which had to shut down its water supply, but also had effects on Russia, which is downstream from the spillage.

Such accidents may reflect local problems, but others may be more directly related to economic growth. A key ingredient of the growth process — especially in terms of industrialisation — is an expansion in energy supplies. Factories cannot operate without reliable electricity and other energy sources. Proposals to double

China's production of hydroelectric power have caused concerns about the effects of new dams on river levels in downstream countries in Southeast Asia and in India.

Booming car ownership raises further concerns: one prediction is that the number of cars in China will reach 130 million by 2020 (from just 4 million in 2000). The effect of this on the demand for oil has already been reflected in higher world prices — China is already the world's second biggest oil importer (behind the USA). China is also the world's biggest producer of coal, which accounts for some 80% of China's energy use.

All of this means that China has now overtaken the USA as the largest emitter of carbon dioxide. It seems unlikely that environmental damage on this sort of scale is sustainable from a global perspective.

China is building hydroelectric dams at an unprecedented rate, raising environmental concerns

Follow-up questions

a Explain why a move towards a market-based system would be expected to 'have benefits for the economy in terms of the efficiency of resource allocation'.

b Explain why the new dams would raise concerns.

c Discuss whether China should seek to restrain the growing car ownership that is a by-product of rapid economic growth, which has led to rising real incomes.

SECTION
2

MACROECONOMICS

Part 5
Aggregate demand and
aggregate supply

Aggregate demand

Now that you are familiar with the main macroeconomic variables, it is time to start thinking about how economic analysis can be used to explore the way in which these variables interact. The starting point is to consider the way in which GDP is measured, using the model of the circular flow of income, output and expenditure. The chapter then considers the components of aggregate demand as the first step in building a model of the macroeconomy. The way in which the levels of these components are determined in practice is an important key to the operation of the economy when considered at the aggregate level.

Learning objectives

After studying this chapter, you should:
- be aware of the circular flow of income, expenditure and output
- understand what is meant by aggregate demand
- be able to identify the components of aggregate demand and their determinants
- be aware of the possibility of multiplier effects
- be familiar with the notion of the aggregate demand curve

The circular flow of income, expenditure and output

Chapter 1 introduced the notion of *gross domestic product* (GDP), which was described as the total output of an economy. It is now time to examine this concept more closely, and to see how it may be measured.

Consider a simplified model of an economy. Assume for the moment that there are just two types of economic agent in an economy: households and firms. In other words, ignore the government and assume there is no international trade. (These agents will be brought back into the picture soon.) We also assume that all factors of production are owned and supplied to firms by households.

In this simple world, assume that firms produce goods and hire labour and other factor inputs from households. Also assume that they buy investment goods from other firms, for which purpose they need to borrow in a financial market. Households supply their labour (and other factor inputs) and buy consumer goods. In return for supplying factor inputs, households receive income, part of which they spend on consumer goods and part of which they save in the financial market.

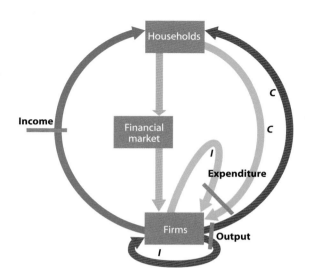

Figure 13.1 The circular flow of income, expenditure and output

If you examine the monetary flows in this economy, you can see how the economy operates. In Figure 13.1 the blue arrow shows the flow of income that goes from firms to households as payment for their factor services (labour, land and capital). The red arrows show what happens to the output produced by firms: part of it goes to households in the form of consumer goods (C); the rest flows back to other firms as investment goods (I). The green arrows show the expenditure flows back to firms, part of which is for consumer goods (C) from households, and part for investment goods (I) from firms. The circle is closed by households' savings, by which part of their income is invested in the financial market; this is then borrowed by firms to finance their purchases of investment goods. These flows are shown by the orange arrows. This model is sometimes known as the circular flow model.

As this is a closed system, these flows must balance. This means that there are three ways in which the total amount of economic activity in this economy can be measured: by the incomes that firms pay out, by the total amount of output that is produced, or by total expenditure. Whichever method is chosen, it should give the same result.

An economy such as the UK's is more complicated than this, so it is also necessary to take into account the economic activities of government and the fact that the UK engages in international trade, so that some of the output produced is sold abroad and some of the expenditure goes on foreign goods and services. However, the principle of measuring total economic activity is the same: GDP can be measured in three ways.

In practice, when the Office for National Statistics (ONS) carries out the measurements, the three answers are never quite the same, as it is impossible to measure with complete accuracy. The published data for GDP are therefore calculated as the average of these three measures, each of which gives information about different aspects of a society's total resources.

What the three measures tell us

The expenditure-side estimate describes how those resources are being used, so that it can be seen what proportion of society's resources is being used for consumption and what for investment etc.

The income-side estimate reports on the way in which households earn their income. In other words, it tells something about the balance between rewards to labour (e.g. wages and salaries), capital (profits), land (rents), enterprise (self-employment) and so on.

The output-side estimate focuses on the economic structure of the economy. One way in which countries differ is in the balance between primary production such as agriculture, secondary activity such as manufacturing, and tertiary activity such as services. Service activity has increased in importance in the UK in recent years, with financial services in particular emerging as a strong part of the UK's comparative advantage.

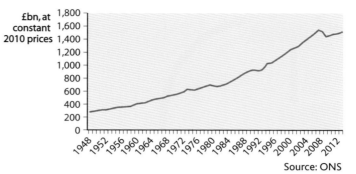

Source: ONS

Figure 13.2 Real GDP, 1948–2013 (£bn)

Figure 13.2 traces real GDP in the UK since 1948. In some ways this is an unhelpful way of presenting the data, as the trend component of the series is so strong. In other words, real GDP has been increasing steadily throughout the period apart from the dip in 2009. There are one or two periods in which there was a movement away from the trend, but these are relatively rare and not easy to analyse. This reflects the nature of economic variables such as GDP, where the fluctuations around trend are small relative to the trend, but can seem substantial when the economy is experiencing them.

It is more revealing to convert these data into annual growth rates, which makes it more straightforward to identify the main periods of fluctuation, particularly periods of negative growth: that is, when the economy contracted. This was the way in which Figure 12.3 was constructed in the discussions about economic growth in the previous chapter.

It should be noted that the measure of GDP has not been without its critics. In particular, economists have questioned whether it provides a reasonable measure of the standard of living enjoyed by the residents of a country, and whether its rate of change is therefore informative about economic growth.

Summary

- The circular flow of income, expenditure and output describes the relationship between these three key variables.
- The model suggests that there are three ways in which the total level of economic activity in an economy during a period of time can be measured: by total income, by total expenditure, and by total output produced.
- In principle, these should give the same answers, but in practice data measurements are not so accurate.
- GDP is a measure of the total economic activity carried out in an economy during a period by residents living on its territory.

The components of aggregate demand

Aggregate demand in the circular flow comprises the combined spending of households (on consumer goods) and firms (on investment goods). It was noted that in the real world it is also necessary to include international trade (exports and imports) and spending by government in this measure. The full version of aggregate expenditure can be written as:

$$AD = C + I + G + X - M$$

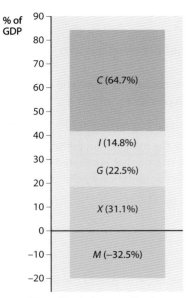

% of GDP

C (64.7%)

I (14.8%)

G (22.5%)

X (31.1%)

M (−32.5%)

Note: C includes spending by non-profit institutions serving households; I includes changes in inventory holdings; the statistical discrepancy is not shown.

Source: ONS

Figure 13.3 The breakdown of real GDP in 2013

Key terms

disposable income the income that households have to devote to consumption and saving, taking into account payments of direct taxes and transfer payments

average propensity to consume the proportion of income that households devote to consumer expenditure

marginal propensity to consume the proportion of additional income devoted to consumer expenditure

marginal propensity to save the proportion of additional income that is saved by households

where *AD* denotes aggregate demand, *C* is consumer expenditure, *I* is investment, *G* is government spending, *X* is exports and *M* is imports.

Figure 13.3 shows the expenditure-side breakdown of real GDP in the UK in 2013. This highlights the relative size of the components of aggregate demand. Consumer expenditure is by far the largest component, amounting to more than 64% of real GDP in 2013. Government current expenditure accounted for more than 20%, but you should realise that this somewhat understates the importance of government in overall spending, as it excludes public spending on investment, which is treated together with private sector investment in the data. Combined public and private sector investment made up almost 15% of total GDP; this includes changes in the inventory holdings of firms. Notice that imports were rather higher than exports, indicating a negative balance of trade in goods and services.

Equilibrium?

In the circular flow model it was noted that total expenditure should be the same as total income and total output if all were measured fully. This seems to suggest that the macroeconomy is always in a sort of equilibrium, in the sense that expenditure and output are always the same. However, this is misleading. Although when you observe the economy, you should find that expenditure and output are the same *after* the event, this does not mean that equilibrium holds in the sense that all economic agents will have found that their plans were fulfilled. In other words, it is not necessarily the case that *planned* expenditure equals *planned* output.

This is the significance of the inclusion of inventory changes as part of investment. If firms find that they have produced more output than is subsequently purchased, their inventory holdings increase. Thus, although after the event expenditure always equals output, this is because any disequilibrium is reflected in unplanned inventory changes.

When in the next chapter you come to consider the conditions under which a macroeconomy will be in equilibrium, you will need to think in terms of the factors that will influence *ex ante* (planned) aggregate demand. The first step is to consider each component in turn.

Consumer expenditure

Consumer expenditure is the largest single component of aggregate demand. What factors could be expected to influence the size of total spending by households? John Maynard Keynes, in his influential book *The General Theory of Employment, Interest and Money*, published in 1936, suggested that the most important determinant is **disposable income**. In other words, as real incomes rise, households will tend to spend more. However, he also pointed out that they would not spend all of an increase in income, but would save some of it. Remember that this was important in the circular flow model. Keynes defined the **average propensity to consume** as the *ratio* of consumer expenditure to income, and the **marginal propensity to consume** as the proportion of an *increase* in disposable income that households would devote to consumer expenditure. The **marginal propensity to save** is the proportion of additional income that is saved by households.

J. M. Keynes's hugely influential book *The General Theory of Employment, Interest and Money* was published in 1936

However, income will not be the only influence on consumer expenditure. Consumer expenditure may also depend partly on the *wealth* of a household. Notice that income and wealth are not the same. Income accrues during a period as a reward for the supply of factor services, such as labour. Wealth, on the other hand, represents the stock of accumulated past savings. If you like, wealth can be thought of in terms of the asset holdings of households. If households experience an increase in the value of their asset holdings, this may influence their spending decisions.

Furthermore, if part of household spending is financed by borrowing, the rate of interest may be significant in influencing the total amount of consumer expenditure. An increase in the rate of interest that raises the cost of borrowing may deter expenditure. At the same time it may encourage saving, as the return on saving is higher when the interest rate is higher. The rate of interest may also have an indirect effect on expenditure through its effect on the value of asset holdings. In addition, households may be influenced in their decisions by their expectations about future inflation. Notice that some of these effects may not be instantaneous: that is, consumer expenditure may adjust to changes in its determinants only after a time lag.

This **consumption function** can be portrayed as a relationship between consumer expenditure and income. This is shown in Figure 13.4, which focuses on the relationship between consumer expenditure and household income, ceteris paribus: in other words, in drawing the relationship between consumer expenditure and income, it is assumed that the other determinants, such as wealth and the interest rate, remain constant. A change in any of these other influences will affect the *position* of the line. Notice that the marginal propensity to consume (*MPC*) is the slope of this line.

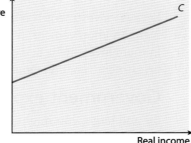

Figure 13.4 The consumption function

In practice, it is not expected that the empirical relationship between consumer expenditure and income will reveal an exact straight line, if only because over a long time period there will be changes in the other influences on consumer expenditure, such as interest rates and expected inflation.

Investment

The rate of interest is also likely to be influential in affecting firms' decisions about investment spending. Again, this is because the interest rate represents the cost of borrowing; so, if firms need to borrow in order to undertake **investment**, they may be discouraged from spending on investment goods when the rate of interest is relatively high.

Investment leads to an increase in the productive capacity of the economy, by increasing the stock of capital available for production. This capital stock comprises plant and machinery, vehicles and other transport equipment, and buildings, including new dwellings, which provide a supply of housing services over a long period.

Although important, the rate of interest is not likely to be the only factor that determines how much investment firms choose to undertake. First, not all investment has to be funded from borrowing — firms may be able to use past profits for this purpose. However, if firms choose to do this, they face an opportunity cost. In other words, profits can be used to buy financial assets that will provide a rate of return dependent on the rate of interest. The rate of interest is thus still important, as it represents the opportunity cost of an investment project.

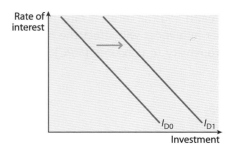

Figure 13.5 Investment and the rate of interest

In considering an investment project, firms will need to form expectations about the future stream of earnings that will flow from the investment. Their expectations about the future state of the economy (and of the demand for their products) will thus be an important influence on current investment. This is one reason why it is argued that inflation is damaging for an economy, as a high rate of inflation increases uncertainty about the future and may dampen firms' expectations about future demand, thereby discouraging investment.

Figure 13.5 shows the relationship between investment and the rate of interest. The investment demand function I_{D0} is downward sloping because investment is relatively low when the rate of interest is relatively high. An improvement in business confidence for the future would result in more investment being undertaken at any given interest rate, so the investment function would move from I_{D0} to I_{D1}.

Government expenditure

By and large, you might expect government expenditure to be decided by different criteria from those influencing private sector expenditures. Indeed, some aspects of government expenditure might be regarded as part of macroeconomic policy, as will be seen in Chapter 15. Some other aspects of government expenditure may vary automatically with variations in the overall level of economic activity over time. For example, unemployment benefit payments are likely to increase during recessionary periods. The effects of this will be examined in Chapter 15.

From the point of view of investigating macroeconomic equilibrium, however, government expenditure can be regarded as mainly *autonomous*: that is, independent of the variables in the model that will be constructed in this chapter.

Trade in goods and services

Finally, there are the factors that may influence the level of exports and imports. One factor that will affect both of these is the exchange rate between sterling and other currencies. This affects the relative prices of UK goods and those produced overseas. Other things being equal, an increase in the sterling exchange rate makes UK exports less competitive and imports into the UK more competitive.

However, the demand for exports and imports will also depend upon the relative prices of goods produced in the UK and the rest of the world. If UK inflation is high relative to elsewhere, again, this will tend to make UK exports less competitive and imports more competitive. These effects will be examined more carefully in Chapter 17, when it will be shown that movements in the exchange rate tend to counteract changes in relative prices between countries.

In addition, the demand for imports into the UK will depend partly upon the level of domestic aggregate income, and the demand for UK exports will depend partly upon the level of incomes in the rest of the world. Thus, a recession in the European Union will affect the demand for UK exports.

Exercise 13.1

Suppose there is an economy in which the values in Table 13.1 apply (all measured in £ million).

Table 13.1 Values for an economy

Consumer expenditure	75
Profits	60
Investment	30
Government expenditure	25
Exports	50
Private saving	50
Imports	55

a Calculate the level of aggregate demand.
b Calculate the trade balance.

The multiplier

Key terms

multiplier the ratio of a change in equilibrium real income to the autonomous change that brought it about; it is defined as 1 divided by the marginal propensity to withdraw

marginal propensity to import the proportion of additional income that is spent on imports of goods and services

marginal propensity to tax the proportion of additional income that is taxed

marginal propensity to withdraw the proportion of additional income that is withdrawn from the circular flow — the sum of the marginal propensities to save, import and tax

In his *General Theory*, Keynes pointed out that there may be **multiplier** effects in response to certain types of expenditure. Suppose that the government increases its expenditure by £1 billion, perhaps by increasing its road-building programme. The effect of this is to generate incomes for households — for example, those of the contractors hired to build the road. Those contractors then spend part of the additional income (and save part of it). By spending part of the extra money earned, an additional income stream is generated for shopkeepers and café owners, who in turn spend part of *their* additional income, and so on. Thus, the original increase in government spending sparks off further income generation and spending, causing the multiplier effect. In effect, equilibrium output may change by more than the original increase in expenditure.

The size of this multiplier effect depends on a number of factors. Most importantly, it depends upon the size of *withdrawals* or *leakages* from the system. In particular, it depends upon how much of the additional income is saved by households, how much is spent on imported goods, and how much is returned to the government in the form of direct taxes. These items constitute withdrawals from the system, in the sense that they detract from the multiplier effect. For example, if households save a high proportion of their additional income, then this clearly reduces the multiplier effect, as the next round of spending will be that much lower. This seems to go against the traditional view that saving is good for the economy.

In the same way that the marginal propensity to consume was defined as the proportion of additional income devoted to consumer expenditure, the **marginal propensity to import** is the proportion of additional income that is spent on imported goods and services, and the **marginal propensity to tax** is the proportion of additional income that is taxed. The sum of the marginal propensities to save, import and tax is the **marginal propensity to withdraw**.

Government spending on road building may increase spending in other areas of the economy due to the multiplier effect

However, there are also *injections* into the system in the form of autonomous government expenditure, investment and exports. One condition of macroeconomic equilibrium is that total withdrawals equal total injections. The fact that injections can have this multiplied effect on equilibrium output and income seems to make the government potentially very powerful, as by increasing its expenditure it can have a multiplied effect on the economy.

It is worth noting that the size of the leakages may depend in part upon the domestic elasticity of supply. If domestic supply is inflexible, and therefore unable to meet an increase in demand, more of the increase in income will spill over into purchasing imports, and this will dilute the multiplier effect.

Quantitative skills 13.3

Calculating the multiplier

A numerical value for the multiplier can be calculated with reference to the withdrawals from the circular flow. Suppose that the marginal propensity to save is 0.25, the marginal propensity to import is 0.1 and the marginal propensity to tax is 0.15. The marginal propensity to withdraw is then 0.25 + 0.1 + 0.15 = 0.5. The multiplier formula is 1 divided by the marginal propensity to withdraw $\left(\dfrac{1}{MPW}\right)$. If the *MPW* is 0.5, then the value of the multiplier is 2, so for every £100 million injection into the circular flow, there will be a £200 million increase in equilibrium output.

Extension material

The accelerator

The idea of the multiplier is based on the induced effects of expenditure that spread the initial effects of an increase in spending. A similar notion is that of the *accelerator*. The notion of the accelerator arises from one of the driving forces behind firms' investment. Although some investment is needed to replace old equipment (known as depreciation), most investment is needed when firms wish to expand capacity. If there is an increase in demand for a firm's product (or if a firm *expects* there to be an increase in demand), it may need to expand capacity in order to meet the increased demand. This suggests that one of the determinants of the level of investment is a *change* in expected demand. Notice that it is the change in demand that is important, rather than the level, and it is this that leads to the notion of the accelerator.

Suppose that the economy is in recession and begins to recover. As the recovery begins, demand begins to increase, and firms have to undertake investment in order to expand capacity. However, as the economy approaches full capacity, the growth rate slows down — and hence investment falls, as it reacts to the change in output.

The multiplier and accelerator interact with each other. If there is an increase in output following an increase in aggregate demand, the accelerator induces an increase in investment. The increase in investment then has a multiplier effect that induces an additional increase in demand. In this way, the multiplier and accelerator reinforce each other. The downside to this is that the same thing happens when output slows as this leads to a fall in investment, which has negative multiplier effects. This interaction between the multiplier and the accelerator can result in cyclical fluctuations in the level of output.

The aggregate demand curve

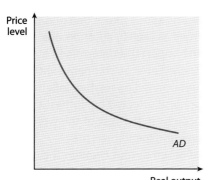

Figure 13.6 An aggregate demand curve

The key relationship to carry forward is the **aggregate demand (*AD*) curve**, which shows the relationship between aggregate demand and the overall price level. Formally, this curve shows the total amount of goods and services demanded in an economy at any given overall level of prices.

It is important to realise that this is a very different sort of demand curve from the microeconomic demand curves that were introduced in Chapter 3, where the focus was on an individual product and its relationship with its own price. Here the relationship is between the *total* demand for goods and services and the overall price level. Thus, aggregate demand is made up of all the components discussed above, and price is an average of all prices of goods and services in the economy.

Figure 13.6 shows an aggregate demand curve. The key question is why it slopes downwards. To answer this, it is necessary to determine the likely influence of the price level on the various components of aggregate demand that have been discussed in this chapter, as prices have not been mentioned explicitly (except for how expectations about inflation might influence consumer spending). First, however, the discussion needs to be cast in terms of the price *level*.

When the overall level of prices is relatively low, the purchasing power of income is relatively high. In other words, low overall prices can be thought of as indicating relatively high real income. Furthermore, when prices are low, this raises the real value of households' wealth. For example, suppose a household holds a financial asset such as a bond with a fixed money value of £100. The relative (real) value of that asset is higher when the overall price level is relatively low. From the above discussion, this suggests that, ceteris paribus, a low overall price level means relatively high consumption.

A second argument relates to interest rates. When prices are relatively low, interest rates also tend to be relatively low, which, it was argued, would encourage both investment and consumption expenditure, as interest rates can be seen as representing the cost of borrowing.

A third argument concerns exports and imports. It has been argued that, ceteris paribus, when UK prices are relatively low compared with the rest of the world, this will increase the competitiveness of UK goods, leading to an increase in foreign demand for UK exports, and a fall in the demand for imports into the UK as people switch to buying UK goods and services.

All of these arguments support the idea that the aggregate demand curve should be downward sloping. In other words, when the overall price level is relatively low, aggregate demand will be relatively high, and when prices are relatively high, aggregate demand will be relatively low.

Other factors discussed above will affect the *position* of the *AD* curve. This point will be explored after the introduction of the other side of the coin — the aggregate supply curve.

Exercise 13.3

State whether each of the following statements about aggregate demand and/or the aggregate demand curve is true or false.

a The aggregate demand curve shows the relationship between the level of aggregate demand and the overall price level in an economy.

b The aggregate demand curve shows planned expenditure in an economy at any given possible overall price level.

c As the aggregate price level falls, the demand for goods and services in the economy rises and more of each good or service will be demanded.

d Government expenditure is regarded as autonomous, and affects the shape of the aggregate demand curve.

e The value of the multiplier depends upon the level of government spending.

f An increase in government spending may induce a multiplier effect.

g The way in which consumption and investment respond to changes in the interest rate affects the shape of the aggregate demand curve.

h Investment expenditure by firms is the largest component of aggregate demand in an economy.

Summary

- Aggregate demand is the total demand in an economy, made up of consumer expenditure, investment, government spending and net exports.
- Consumer expenditure is the largest of these components and is determined by income and other influences, such as interest rates, wealth and expectations about the future.
- Investment leads to increases in the capital stock and is influenced by interest rates, past profits and expectations about future demand.
- Government expenditure may be regarded as largely autonomous.
- Trade in goods and services (exports and imports) is determined by the competitiveness of domestic goods and services compared with the rest of the world, which in turn is determined by relative inflation rates and the exchange rate. Imports are also affected by domestic income, and exports are affected by incomes in the rest of the world.
- Autonomous spending, such as government expenditure, may give rise to a magnified impact on equilibrium output through the multiplier effect.
- The aggregate demand curve shows the relationship between aggregate demand and the overall price level.

Aggregate supply and macroeconomic equilibrium

Having seen what is meant by aggregate demand, it is now time to investigate aggregate supply and the factors that will influence it. This chapter explores the notion of macroeconomic equilibrium. As in microeconomics, this relates to the process by which balance can be achieved between the opposing forces of demand and supply. However, there are some important differences in these concepts when applied at the macroeconomic level.

> ## Learning objectives
>
> After studying this chapter, you should:
> - understand what is meant by aggregate supply
> - be able to identify the factors that influence aggregate supply
> - be familiar with the notion of the aggregate supply curve
> - understand the nature of equilibrium in the macroeconomy
> - be able to undertake comparative static analysis of external shocks affecting aggregate demand and aggregate supply

The aggregate supply curve

The previous chapter discussed the notion of aggregate demand and introduced the aggregate demand curve. In order to analyse the overall macroeconomic equilibrium, it is necessary to derive a second relationship: that between aggregate supply and the price level. It is important to remember that the level of aggregate supply covers the output of all sorts of goods and services that are produced within an economy during a period of time. However, it is not simply a question of adding up all the individual supply curves from individual markets. Within an individual market, an increase in price may induce higher supply of a good because firms will switch from other markets in search of higher profits. What you now need to be looking for is a relationship between the *overall* price level and the total amount supplied, which is a different kettle of fish.

The total quantity of output supplied in an economy over a period of time depends upon the quantities of inputs of factors of production employed: that is, the total amounts of labour, capital and other factors used. The ability of firms to vary output in the short run will be

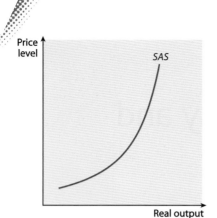

Figure 14.1 Aggregate supply in the short run

influenced by the degree of flexibility the firms have in varying inputs. This suggests that it is necessary to distinguish between short-run and long-run aggregate supply.

In the short run, firms may have relatively little flexibility to vary their inputs. Money wages are likely to be fixed, and if firms wish to vary output, they may need to do so by varying the intensity of utilisation of existing inputs. For example, if a firm wishes to expand output, the only way of doing so in the short run may be by paying its existing workers overtime, and it will be prepared to do this only in response to higher prices. This suggests that in the short run, aggregate supply may be upward sloping, as shown in Figure 14.1, where *SAS* represents **short-run aggregate supply**.

Firms will not want to operate in this way in the long run. It is not good practice to be permanently paying workers overtime. In the long run, therefore, firms will adjust their working practices and hire additional workers to avoid this situation.

> **Key term**
>
> **short-run aggregate supply curve** a curve showing how much output firms would be prepared to supply in the short run at any given overall price level

The position of the aggregate supply curve

What factors influence the position of aggregate supply? Given that aggregate supply arises from the use of inputs of factors of production, one important influence is the availability and effectiveness of factor inputs. Factors that influence the costs faced by firms will also be important.

The quantity of inputs

As far as labour input is concerned, an increase in the size of the workforce will affect the position of aggregate supply. In practice, the size of the labour force tends to change relatively slowly unless substantial international migration is taking place: for example, the expansion of membership of the EU in May 2004 led to significant migration into the UK.

An increase in the quantity of capital will also have this effect, by increasing the capacity of the economy to produce. However, such an increase requires firms to have undertaken investment activity. In other words, the balance of spending between consumption and investment may affect the position of the aggregate supply curve in future periods.

The effective use of inputs

The effectiveness with which inputs are utilised is another important influence on the position of the aggregate supply curve. For example, an increase in the skills that workers have will increase the amount of aggregate output that can be produced and lead to a shift in the aggregate supply curve. This is shown in Figure 14.2, where aggregate supply was originally at SAS_0. An increase in the skills of the workforce means that firms are prepared to supply more output at any given overall price level, so the aggregate supply curve shifts to SAS_1.

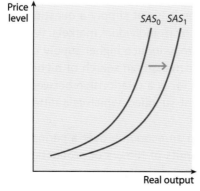

Figure 14.2 A shift in aggregate supply

The ability to attract highly skilled migrant workers has an effect on the productive capacity of the economy

An increase in the efficiency of capital, perhaps arising from improvements in technology, would have a similar effect, enabling greater aggregate supply at any given overall price level, and raising the productive capacity of the economy. Notice that these factors that determine the position of the aggregate supply curve are likely to be more significant in the long run.

The costs faced by firms

Underlying the aggregate supply curve are the decisions taken by firms about production levels at any given price. A change in the costs faced by firms may induce them to choose to supply more (or less) output. There are several factors that could influence costs in this way. It might be that there is a change in the cost of raw materials. If a key raw material becomes more limited in supply, perhaps because reserves are exhausted, then prices will tend to rise, thus raising firms' costs of production. They may then choose to supply less output at any given price — and the aggregate supply curve would shift to the left. A change in the exchange rate could have similar effects, by affecting the domestic price of imported inputs. This could be favourable, of course. It may be that the exchange rate moves to reduce the domestic price of imports. Firms may then be prepared to supply more output at any given price, so the aggregate supply curve would shift to the right.

It may be that changes in the domestic production environment could affect the costs faced by firms — either for better or for worse. An increase in regulation that forced firms to spend more on health and safety measures would raise costs, as would an increase in congestion on the roads that raised transport costs. These effects would tend to result in a leftward shift of the aggregate supply curve. On the other hand, improvements to infrastructure in the domestic economy, such as improvements to the transport system, would have the opposite effect of reducing the costs faced by firms, which could then lead to a rightward shift of the aggregate supply curve.

Macroeconomic equilibrium

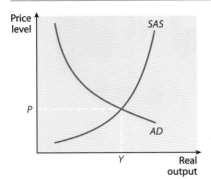

Figure 14.3 Macroeconomic equilibrium

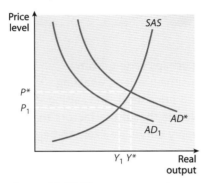

Figure 14.4 Will macroeconomic equilibrium be at full employment?

Bringing aggregate demand and aggregate supply together, the overall equilibrium position for the macroeconomy can be identified. In Figure 14.3, with aggregate supply given by *SAS* and aggregate demand by *AD*, equilibrium is reached at the real output level *Y*, with the price level at *P*.

This is an equilibrium, in the sense that if nothing changes then firms and households will have no reason to alter their behaviour in the next period. At the price *P*, aggregate supply is matched by aggregate demand.

Can it be guaranteed that the macroeconomic equilibrium will occur at the full employment level of output? For example, suppose that in Figure 14.4 the output level *Y** corresponds to the full employment level of output — that is, the level of output that represents productive capacity when all factors of production are fully employed. It may be possible to produce more than this in the short run, but only on a temporary basis, perhaps by the use of overtime. If aggregate demand is at *AD**, the macroeconomic equilibrium is at this full employment output *Y**. However, if the aggregate demand curve is located at *AD*$_1$ the equilibrium will occur at *Y*$_1$, which is below the full employment level, so there is surplus capacity in the economy.

Exercise 14.1

For each of the following, state whether the aggregate supply curve would shift to the left or to the right:
a the discovery of a new source of a raw material, reducing its price
b an increase in the rate of migration from a country
c an increase in the exchange rate
d improvements to the transportation system in a country
e a technological advance that improves efficiency
f an increase in investment by firms

Summary
- The aggregate supply (*SAS*) curve shows the relationship between aggregate supply and the overall price level.
- Macroeconomic equilibrium is reached at the intersection of *AD* and *AS*.

Changes to macroeconomic equilibrium

Having identified macroeconomic equilibrium, it is possible to undertake some analysis of how this will change in response to changes in the macroeconomic environment. In other words, comparative static analysis can be used.

An increase in aggregate demand

The position of the aggregate demand curve depends on the components of aggregate demand: consumption, investment, government spending and net exports. Factors that affect these components will affect the position of aggregate demand.

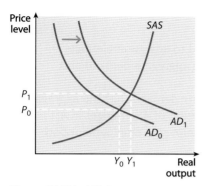

Figure 14.5 A shift in aggregate demand

Consider Figure 14.5. Suppose that the economy begins in equilibrium with aggregate demand at AD_0. The equilibrium output level is Y_0, and the price level is at P_0. An increase in government expenditure will affect the position of the aggregate demand curve, shifting it to AD_1. The economy will move to a new equilibrium position, with a higher output level Y_1 and a higher price level P_1.

This seems to suggest that the government can always reach full employment, simply by increasing its expenditure. However, you should be a little cautious in reaching such a conclusion, as the effect on equilibrium output and the price level will depend upon how close the economy is to the full employment level. Notice that the aggregate supply curve becomes steeper as output and the price level increase. In other words, the closer the economy is to the full employment level, the smaller is the elasticity of supply, so an increase in aggregate demand close to full employment will have more of an effect on the price level (and hence potentially on inflation) than on the level of real output.

The effect of a supply shock

The AD/AS model can also be used to analyse the effects of an external shock that affects aggregate supply. For example, suppose there is an increase in oil prices arising from a disruption to supplies in the Middle East. This raises firms' costs, and leads to a reduction in aggregate supply. Comparative static analysis can again be employed to examine the likely effects on equilibrium.

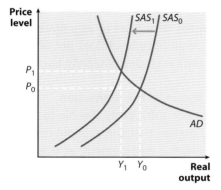

Figure 14.6 A supply shock

Figure 14.6 analyses the situation. The economy begins in equilibrium with output at Y_0 and the overall level of prices at P_0. The increase in oil prices causes a movement of the aggregate supply curve from SAS_0 to SAS_1, with aggregate demand unchanged at AD. After the economy returns to equilibrium, the new output level has fallen to Y_1 and the overall price level has increased to P_1.

At the time of the first oil price crisis back in 1973–74, the UK government of the day tried to maintain the previous level of real output by stimulating aggregate demand. This had the effect of pushing up the price level, but did not have any noticeable effect on real output. Such a result is not unexpected, given the steepness of the aggregate supply curve. Indeed, in Figure 14.6 the previous output level Y_0 cannot be reached with aggregate supply in its new position. You can see the effects of the oil shock on the UK economy by looking back at Figures 10.2 and 11.3.

Shifts of and movements along *AD* and *AS*

It is important to be aware of the distinction between shifts *of* the *AD* and *AS* curves, and movements *along* them. Typically, if a shock affects the position of one of the curves, it will lead to a movement *along* the other. For example, if the *AS* curve shifts as a result of a supply shock, the response is a movement *along* the *AD* curve, and vice versa. Thus, in trying to analyse the effects of a shock, the first step is to think about whether the shock affects *AD* or *AS*, and the second is to analyse whether the shock is positive or negative: that is, which way the relevant curve will shift. The move towards a new equilibrium can then be investigated.

Summary

- Comparative static analysis can be used to analyse the effects of changes in the factors that influence aggregate demand and aggregate supply.
- Changes in the components of aggregate demand shift the aggregate demand curve. Within the vertical segment of *AS*, changes in *AD* affect only the overall price level, but below full employment both price and real output will be affected.
- Changes in the factors affecting aggregate supply alter the long-run potential productive capacity of the economy.

Aggregate supply in the long run

Key terms

Monetarist School a group of economists who believed that the macroeconomy always adjusts rapidly to the full employment level of output

natural rate of output the long-run equilibrium level of output to which monetarists believe the macroeconomy will always tend; corresponds to full employment

Keynesian School a group of economists who believed that the macroeconomy could settle at an equilibrium that was below full employment

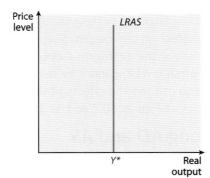

Figure 14.7 Aggregate supply in the long run (the 'monetarist' view)

The discussion so far has focused on short-run aggregate supply. However, it is also important to consider how aggregate supply can be seen in the longer term. An important debate developed during the 1970s over the shape of the aggregate supply curve, which has implications for the conduct and effectiveness of policy options. An influential school of macroeconomists, known as the **Monetarist School**, argued that the economy would always converge on an equilibrium level of output that they referred to as the **natural rate of output**. This corresponds to a situation in which the economy is at full employment. If this were the case, then the long-run relationship between aggregate supply and the price level would be vertical, shown as *LRAS* in Figure 14.7. Here Y^* is the natural rate of output: that is, the full employment level of aggregate output. In other words, a change in the overall price level does not affect aggregate output, because the economy always readjusts rapidly back to full employment.

An opposing school of thought (often known as the **Keynesian School**) held that the macroeconomy was not sufficiently flexible to enable continuous full employment. They argued that the economy could settle at an equilibrium position below full employment, at least in the medium term. In particular, inflexibilities in labour markets would prevent adjustment. For example, if firms had pessimistic expectations about aggregate demand, and thus reduced their supply of output, this would lead to lower incomes because of the workers being laid off. This would then mean that aggregate demand was indeed deficient, so firms' pessimism was self-fulfilling.

These sorts of argument led to a belief that there would be a range of output over which aggregate supply would be upward sloping. Figure 14.8 illustrates such an aggregate supply curve, in which Y^* represents full employment; however, when the economy is operating below this level of output, aggregate supply is somewhat sensitive to the price level, becoming steeper as full employment is approached.

The policy implications of the monetarist *LRAS* curve are strong. If the economy always converges rapidly on the full employment level of output, no manipulation of aggregate demand can have any effect except on the price level. This is readily seen in Figure 14.9 where, regardless of the position of the aggregate demand curve, the level of real output remains at Y^*. If aggregate demand is low at AD_0, then the price level is also relatively low, at P_0. An increase in aggregate demand to AD_1 raises the price level to P_1 but leaves real output at Y^*.

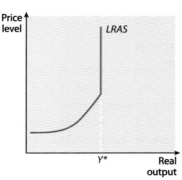

Figure 14.8 Aggregate supply in the long run (the 'Keynesian' view)

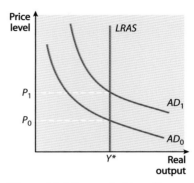

Figure 14.9 Demand-side policy with a vertical AS curve

Extension material

The Keynesian and Monetarist Schools of thought were dominant at different times during the period after the Second World War, both in the development of macroeconomic theory and in the influence they had on economic policy. Keynes was influential in the immediate period, and you will see how his thought affected the way in which fiscal policy was used in particular. The Monetarist economists then became more influential in the 1970s when inflation began to accelerate in many of the advanced economies, and this shaped the policies adopted by Margaret Thatcher in the UK and Ronald Reagan in the USA. In more recent years, the divergences between the views have diminished, with a greater sense of agreement on some issues beginning to emerge — at least until the financial crisis of the late 2000s, which raised new controversies.

Exercise 14.2

For each of the following, decide whether the change affects aggregate demand or aggregate supply, and sketch a diagram to illustrate the effects on equilibrium real output and overall price level. Undertake this exercise first for a starting position in the steep part of the AS curve, and then for an initial position further to the left, where $LRAS$ is more elastic:

a an advancement in technology that improves the efficiency of capital
b a financial crisis in Asia that reduces the demand for UK exports
c an improvement in firms' expectations about future demand, such that investment expenditure increases
d the introduction of new health and safety legislation that raises firms' costs

For each of these changes, indicate whether the result is a shift of or a movement along the AD and AS curves.

Changes in aggregate demand and aggregate supply can help to analyse macroeconomic performance as discussed earlier in terms of inflation, unemployment and economic growth.

Inflation

The *AD/AS* model explains how the equilibrium overall price level for an economy is reached. It also explains how an increase in aggregate demand when the economy is at full employment will result in a higher equilibrium price level, but with no change in the level of real output. If aggregate demand continues to increase, then the price level will continue to rise, and the result is inflation.

Employment and unemployment

When the macroeconomy is in equilibrium at a given level of real output, there is an implied level of employment — and hence a level of unemployment. The position of the *AD/AS* equilibrium thus determines whether the economy is at full employment. With a monetarist vertical *LRAS* curve, the economy always returns rapidly to full employment. However, with a Keynesian interpretation of the *AD/AS* model it is possible for the macroeconomy to settle in equilibrium below the full employment level. In this situation, a shift in aggregate demand is needed to take the economy back towards full employment.

Economic growth

In Chapter 12, economic growth was discussed in terms of an outward movement in the production possibility curve. The *AD/AS* model now offers an alternative interpretation. Long-run economic growth can now be seen as a shift to the right of the long-run aggregate supply curve. This may be caused by an increase in the quantity of factors of production available in the economy, or an improvement in the efficiency with which they are utilised. Short-run economic growth in the *AD/AS* model may be a short-run response to an increase in aggregate demand, which may not be sustainable if it takes the economy temporarily beyond the full employment level. Alternatively, it may be a situation in which the macroeconomy is returning to equilibrium having been positioned below full employment.

Summary
- In using the *AD/AS* model to analyse policy options, it is useful to distinguish between monetarist and Keynesian views about the shape of the aggregate supply curve.
- Monetarist economists have argued that the economy always converges rapidly on equilibrium at the natural rate of output, implying that policies affecting aggregate demand have an impact only on prices, leaving real output unaffected. The aggregate supply curve in this world is vertical.
- The Keynesian view is that the economy may settle at an equilibrium that is below full employment, and that there is a range over which the aggregate supply curve slopes upwards.

The importance of expectations

In mid-2008, the UK economy was seen to be in a state of crisis. Economic growth had slowed (although it was still positive, so technically the economy had not yet entered into recession). Inflation had been affected by a number of world events. China's economy was continuing to expand at an unprecedented rate, and was having an impact on world prices by its strong demand for oil, foodstuffs and other commodities. The growth in demand for biofuels was fuelling a rise in the prices of some key food items, including rice and wheat. This was partly because land previously used to grow food was being turned over to grow crops to be made into biofuels. These effects were beginning to take their toll on the UK economy. Surveys of business confidence showed that firms were expecting a recession, and house prices were falling.

Demand for biofuels affected the price of crops such as rice and wheat

Follow-up question

Using a diagram, explain how the events described above would be expected to affect aggregate demand and/or aggregate supply.

MACROECONOMICS

Part 6
The application of policy instruments

Chapter 15

Macroeconomic policy instruments

Previous chapters have shown that there may be a range of macroeconomic policy objectives, such as economic growth, full employment and the control of inflation. Other objectives may also be important, such as reaching equilibrium on the current account of the balance of payments, and concerns about the environment or the distribution of income. Attention now turns to the sorts of policy that might be implemented to try to meet these targets. Policies at the macroeconomic level are designed to affect either aggregate demand or aggregate supply, and each will be examined in turn.

> **Learning objectives**
>
> After studying this chapter, you should:
> - understand and be able to evaluate policies that affect aggregate demand, including fiscal, monetary and exchange rate policies
> - understand and be able to evaluate policies that affect aggregate supply
> - be able to appraise the relative merits of policies applied to the demand and supply sides of the macroeconomy
> - be familiar with how macroeconomic policy has been conducted in the UK in recent years

Macroeconomic policy objectives

Chapters 10–12 explained that there are a range of objectives that might be seen as desirable for the macroeconomy. These can be interpreted in terms of Figure 15.1, which shows an economy in macroeconomic equilibrium.

Price stability

The first objective discussed related to the control of inflation, where it was pointed out that prices can increase because of shifts in either aggregate demand or aggregate supply. However, it was also pointed out that *persistent* inflation would arise only in a situation in which money stock was growing more rapidly than real output. This seems to suggest that one policy response to persistent inflation would be to control the growth of the money stock.

An increase in money stock affects aggregate demand, shifting the aggregate demand curve to the right and causing prices to rise in an attempt to regain macroeconomic equilibrium. Thus, attempts to control inflation can be interpreted as attempts to create stability in the overall equilibrium price level.

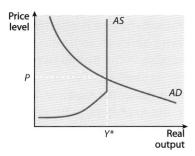

Figure 15.1 Macroeconomic policy objectives

Full employment

A second macroeconomic policy objective is full employment, which occurs at $Y*$ in Figure 15.1. If the aggregate demand curve is positioned well to the left in Figure 15.1, macroeconomic equilibrium occurs at less than the full employment level of real output. This suggests that, to restore full employment, policy should be aimed at altering the position of the aggregate demand curve in order to bring the economy back to $Y*$.

The balance of payments

Policy-makers need to be aware of the dangers of a prolonged and substantial deficit on the balance of payments current account, which can have long-run effects on the ownership pattern of UK assets, as will be explained in Chapter 17. If these assets are sold to foreigners, their sale will have a long-run effect on the aggregate supply curve. However, the deficit is caused by an imbalance between the components of aggregate demand, so in a sense the current account objective is related to both aggregate supply and aggregate demand. In effect, the need to achieve current account balance acts as a constraint on attempts to meet other policy objectives, so the trade-offs between objectives are of the greatest importance in this case.

Economic growth

The achievement of economic growth is a long-term objective, the aim of which is to increase the economy's productive capacity. With respect to Figure 15.1, this can be interpreted in terms of policies affecting the position of the long-run aggregate supply curve. Economic growth occurs when the aggregate supply curve moves to the right. Thus, in order to influence the economic growth rate of a country, economists need to look for policies that can affect aggregate supply.

Demand-side policies

Policies that aim to influence an economy's aggregate demand are designed either to stabilise the level of output and employment or to stabilise the price level. The prime focus is thus on the short-run position of the macroeconomy. The two major categories of policy are fiscal policy and monetary policy.

Fiscal policy

The term **fiscal policy** covers a range of policy measures that affect government expenditures and revenues. For example, an expansionary fiscal policy would be seen as an increase in government spending (or reduction in taxes) that shifts the aggregate demand curve to the right.

In Figure 15.2 macroeconomic equilibrium is initially at the intersection of aggregate supply (AS) and the initial aggregate demand curve (AD_0), so that real output is at Y_0, which is below the full employment level of output at $Y*$. As government expenditure is one of the components of aggregate demand, an increase in such expenditure shifts the aggregate demand curve from AD_0 to AD_1. In response, the economy moves to a new equilibrium, in which the overall price level has risen to P_1 but real output has moved to Y_1, which is closer to the full employment level $Y*$.

> **Key term**
>
> **fiscal policy** decisions made by the government on its expenditure, taxation and borrowing

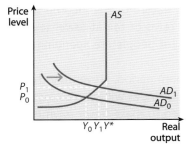

Figure 15.2 The use of fiscal policy

In this scenario, government expenditure is treated as an injection into the circular flow, and it will be reinforced by a multiplier effect. In the present context, an increase in government expenditure is effective in raising the level of real output in the economy, although some of the increase is dissipated in the form of an increase in the overall level of prices. Notice that such a move can be seen as short-run (actual) economic growth, although the full employment (potential capacity) level of real output, Y^*, has not been affected. It is also important to be aware that, if the multiplier is relatively low, the reinforcement of fiscal policy through this route will also be relatively weak.

This kind of policy is effective only if the aggregate demand curve intersects the aggregate supply curve in the upward-sloping segment of *AS*. If the economy is already at the full employment level of output, an increase in aggregate demand merely results in a higher overall level of prices. The effective use of such policy thus requires policy-makers to have good information about the current state of the economy; in particular, they need to know whether the economy is at or below full employment. Otherwise, the results could be damaging for the price stability target. In other words, there is a danger that an expansionary fiscal policy will lead to inflation, but not affect output very much, if the *AS* curve is relatively steep.

The effect on the balance of payments must also be borne in mind. Part of an increase in aggregate demand is likely to be spent on imports, but there is no immediate reason for exports to change, so in the short run there is likely to be an increase in the current account deficit on the balance of payments.

Although the focus of the discussion so far has been on government expenditure, fiscal policy also refers to taxation. In fact, the key issue in considering fiscal policy is the *balance* between government expenditure and government revenue, as it is this balance that affects the position of aggregate demand directly.

An increase in the **government budget deficit** (or a decrease in the **government budget surplus**) moves the aggregate demand curve to the right. The budget deficit may arise either from an increase in expenditure or from a decrease in taxation, although the two have some differential effects.

To a certain extent, the government budget deficit changes automatically, without active intervention from the government. If the economy goes into a period of recession, unemployment benefit payments will rise, thereby increasing government expenditure. At the same time, tax revenues will decrease, partly because people who lose their jobs no longer pay income tax. In addition, people whose income is reduced — perhaps because they no longer work overtime — also pay less tax. This is reinforced by the progressive nature of the income tax system, which means that people pay lower rates of tax at lower levels of income. Furthermore, VAT receipts will fall if people are spending less on goods and services.

The opposite effects will be evident in a boom period, preventing the economy from overheating. For example, tax revenues will tend to increase during the boom, and the government will need to make fewer payments of social security benefits. By such **automatic stabilisers**, government expenditure automatically rises during a recession and falls during a boom.

In the past there was a tendency for governments to use fiscal policy in a *discretionary* way in order to influence the path of the economy. A government might use its discretion to increase government expenditure to prevent a recession, for example. Indeed, there have been accusations that governments have sometimes, in some countries, used fiscal policy to create a 'feel-good' factor in the run-up to a general election, by allowing the economy to boom as the election approaches, only to impose a clampdown afterwards.

Such intervention has been shown to be damaging to the long-run path of the economy because of its effect on inflation. Furthermore, there are other problems with using fiscal policy in this way. Apart from anything else, it takes time to collect data about the performance of the economy, so its *current* state is never known for certain. Because the economy responds quite sluggishly to policy change, it is often the case that the policy comes into effect just when the economy is already turning around of its own accord. This is potentially destabilising, and can do more harm than good.

Fiscal policy in the UK

If the government spends more than it raises in revenue, the resulting deficit has to be financed in some way. The government deficit is the difference between public sector spending and revenues, and is known as the *public sector net cash requirement* (PSNCR), which until 1999 was known as the *public sector borrowing requirement* (PSBR). Part of the PSNCR is covered by borrowing, and the government closely monitors its *net borrowing*. Over time, such borrowing leads to *net debt*, which is the accumulation of past borrowing. Figure 15.3 shows public sector net debt as a percentage of GDP. The Labour government aimed to keep this below 40%. As you can see in the figure, this was achieved until the financial crisis hit, when the bail-out of banks to avert financial meltdown led to a dramatic rise in public sector debt.

The Labour government had established the 40% rule as part of a strategy to maintain what was seen as an appropriate balance in fiscal policy. There was a concern for the long-run effects of policy on spending and borrowing, recognising that sustainable economic growth must take into account the needs of future generations. The government therefore took the view that its current spending should be met out of current revenues, and that only investment for the future should be met through borrowing. There was also a commitment to avoid using discretionary fiscal policy. This clear statement was intended to increase the credibility of government policy by indicating the government's refusal to take action that could destabilise the macroeconomy.

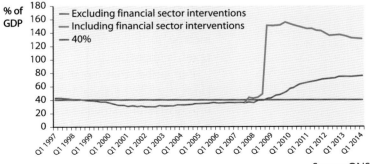

Source: ONS

Figure 15.3 Public sector net debt (% of GDP)

The turmoil of the late 2000s required some rethinking. The Coalition government responded to the high level of public sector net debt by using fiscal policy, in the form of cuts to public expenditure, in an attempt to reduce the debt.

Balance between the public and private sectors

Even if the size of the budget deficit limits the government's actions in terms of fiscal policy, there are still decisions to be made about the overall balance of activity in the economy. A neutral government budget can be attained either with high expenditure and high revenues, or with relatively small expenditure and revenues. Such decisions affect the overall size of the public sector relative to the private sector. Over the years, different governments in the UK have taken different decisions on this issue — and different countries throughout the world have certainly adopted different approaches.

In part, such issues are determined through the ballot box. In the run-up to an election, each political party presents its overall plans for taxation and spending, and typically they adopt different positions as to the overall balance. It is then up to those voting to give a mandate to whichever party offers a package that most closely resembles their preferences.

Extension material

If the government runs a budget deficit, this can affect the balance between the public and private sectors through the operation of interest rates. When the government runs a budget deficit, and finances it by borrowing, it puts upward pressure on the rate of interest. This in turn means that private firms also face an increase in the cost of borrowing, and may thus reduce their investment expenditure. This effect is known as *crowding-out*, as the private sector is being crowded out of financial markets through the effects of government borrowing.

If the reverse happens, for example if the government runs a budget surplus and thus needs to borrow less, then the opposite effect can happen, and there could be *crowding-in*, with firms being encouraged by low interest rates to undertake more investment.

Direct and indirect taxes

Fiscal policy, and taxation in particular, has not only been used to establish a balance between the public and private sectors of an economy. In addition, taxation remains an important weapon against some forms of market failure, and it also influences the distribution of income. In this context, the choice between using direct and indirect taxes is important.

Remember that direct taxes are taxes levied on income of various kinds, such as personal income tax. Such taxes are designed to be progressive and so can be effective in redistributing income: for example, a higher income tax rate can be charged to those earning high incomes. In contrast, indirect taxes — taxes on expenditure, such as VAT and excise duties — tend to be regressive. As poorer households tend to spend a higher proportion of their income on items that are subject to excise duties, a greater share of their income is taken up by indirect taxes. Even VAT can be regressive if higher-income households save a greater proportion of their incomes.

Indirect taxes can be targeted at specific instances of market failure; hence the high excise duties on such goods as tobacco (seen as a demerit good) and petrol (seen as damaging to the environment because of the externality of greenhouse gas emissions).

What is a 'good' tax?

Adam Smith set out four maxims that he believed should form the underpinning of any good tax. These later became known as the 'Canons of Taxation'. They were as follows:

- *Equity*: 'The subjects of every state ought to contribute towards the support of the government, as nearly as possible, in proportion to their respective abilities; that is, in proportion to the revenue which they respectively enjoy under the protection of the state.'
- *Certainty*: 'The tax which each individual is bound to pay ought to be certain, and not arbitrary.'
- *Convenience*: 'Every tax ought to be levied at the time, or in the manner, in which it is likely to be convenient for the contributor to pay it.'
- *Economy*: 'Every tax ought to be contrived as both to take out and to keep out of the pockets of people as little as possible over and above what it brings into the public treasury of the state.'

These desirable characteristics of a tax would still command widespread support today, although the focus would normally be on the incidence of a tax and on whether the tax is implemented in a way that is efficient. In this context, efficiency would be seen not only in terms of the cost of collection, but also in relation to the impact that it may have on resource allocation. In a modern economy, it may also be important to see that levels of taxation reflect changing prices in an inflationary environment. Where countries have close trade links with other countries (and especially when they are part of regional trade agreements), it is also important to ensure that tax rates are compatible with those of their trading partners.

It has been argued by some commentators that a **flat-rate tax system** would be beneficial. Under such a system, all taxpayers would pay the same rate of tax, regardless of their income. This would meet the 'certainty' maxim, and would be efficient to implement. It might also provide better incentives to work for those on relatively high incomes. Under a progressive tax system, high income-earners find that a high proportion of additional income is taxed away, so they face weak incentives to continue to provide effort. Furthermore, a tax system with multiple rates at different income levels is complex and expensive to implement. Estonia introduced such a system in 1994, followed by other countries in the Baltic and eastern Europe, including Russia and Ukraine.

The main argument against such a system concerns equity (another of Adam Smith's Canons). Perhaps the most important advantage of a progressive tax system is that it enables redistribution of income between rich and poor groups within society.

Key terms

Canons of Taxation four maxims devised by Adam Smith, setting out the characteristics of a good tax

flat-rate tax system a system of income tax in which each taxpayer pays the same rate of tax on income

Adam Smith first proposed his Canons of Taxation in 1776

Summary

- Fiscal policy is concerned with the decisions made by government about its expenditure, taxation and borrowing.
- As government expenditure is an autonomous component of aggregate demand, an increase in expenditure will shift the *AD* curve to the right.
- If the *AD* curve intersects the *AS* curve in the vertical segment of *AS*, the effect of the increase in aggregate demand is felt only in prices.
- However, if the initial equilibrium is below the full employment level, the shift in *AD* will lead to an increase in both equilibrium real output and the overall price level.
- In fact, it is net spending that is important, so government decisions on taxation are also significant.
- The government budget deficit (surplus) is the difference between government expenditure and revenue.
- The budget deficit varies automatically through the business cycle because of the action of the automatic stabilisers.
- If the government runs a budget deficit, it may need to undertake net borrowing, which over time affects the net debt position.
- Adam Smith set out the desirable features of a good tax in his Canons of Taxation.

Monetary policy

Key term

monetary policy the decisions made by government regarding monetary variables such as the money supply and the interest rate

Monetary policy is the approach currently favoured by the UK government to stabilise the macroeconomy. It entails the use of monetary variables such as the money supply and interest rates to influence aggregate demand.

The prime instrument of monetary policy in recent years has been the interest rate. Through the interest rate, monetary policy affects aggregate demand. At higher interest rates, firms undertake less investment expenditure and households undertake less consumption expenditure. This is partly because when the interest rate is relatively high, the cost of borrowing becomes high and people are discouraged from borrowing for investment or consumption purposes. There are reinforcing effects that operate through the exchange rate if UK interest rates are high relative to elsewhere in the world. If the exchange rate rises because of high interest rates, this will reduce the competitiveness of UK goods.

Suppose the government believes that the economy is close to full employment and is in danger of overheating. Overheating could push prices up without any resulting benefit in terms of higher real output. An increase in the interest rate will lead to a fall in aggregate demand, thereby relieving the pressure on prices. This is illustrated in Figure 15.4, where the initial position has aggregate demand relatively high at AD_0, real output at the full employment level Y_0 and the overall price level at P_0. The increase in interest rates shifts aggregate demand to the left, to AD_1. Real output falls slightly to Y_1 and the equilibrium price level falls to P_1.

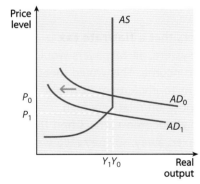

Figure 15.4 The use of monetary policy

Monetary policy in the UK

One of the first steps taken by Tony Blair's government after it was first elected in 1997 was to devolve the responsibility for monetary policy to the Bank of England, which was given the task of achieving

Monetary Policy Committee
body within the Bank of England
responsible for the conduct of
monetary policy

inflation targeting an approach
to macroeconomic policy
whereby the central bank is
charged with meeting a target
for inflation

bank rate the interest rate that
is set by the Monetary Policy
Committee of the Bank of
England in order to influence
inflation

the government's stated inflation target, initially set at 2.5% for RPIX
inflation. As noted in Chapter 10, the target was amended in 2004, when
it became 2% per annum as measured by the CPI.

According to this arrangement, the **Monetary Policy Committee**
(MPC) of the Bank of England sets interest rates in order to achieve the
target rate of inflation. If inflation moves beyond 1 percentage point
above or below the target, the Bank has to write an open letter to the
chancellor of the exchequer to explain why the target has not been met.
Such a letter became necessary for the first time in March 2007, when
CPI inflation touched 3.1%. This was to become the norm in 2010/11.

The idea underpinning **inflation targeting** is that it raises the
credibility of macroeconomic policy. If economic agents realise that the
central bank is committed to meeting the target for inflation, and that
it does this independently of the government, then this will stabilise
expectations. In particular, if firms believe that the target will be met,
this improves expectations about the future stability of the economy and
should encourage investment.

Operationally, the MPC sets the interest rate which it pays on
commercial bank reserves. This is known as the **bank rate**. The commercial
banks tend to use this rate as their own base rate, from which they
calculate the rates of interest that they charge to their borrowers. Thus, if
the MPC changes the bank rate, the commercial banks soon adjust the
rates they charge to borrowers. These will vary according to the riskiness
of the loans; thus credit cards are charged at a higher rate than mortgages,
but all the rates are geared to the base rate set by the commercial banks,
and hence indirectly to the bank rate set by the Bank of England.

Although inflation remained within the 1% band from 1997 right through
until March 2007, the following period showed a much more unstable
pattern. Figure 15.5 shows the bank rate and the inflation rate since 2004.

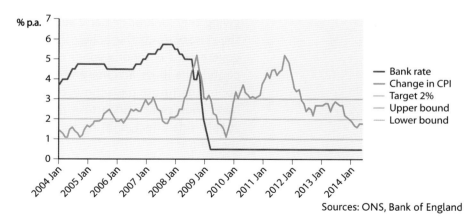

Sources: ONS, Bank of England

Figure 15.5 UK bank rate and the inflation target, 2004–14

Monetary policy until 2007

In the first part of this period, inflation seemed under control. The
association between the bank rate and movements in the inflation rate
is not close. This is because the relationship between them is partly
obscured by other influences. It also reflects the fact that the MPC took
into account a wide range of factors when deciding whether to move the
bank rate or to leave it as it was in the previous month.

A Monetary Policy Committee briefing led by Mark Carney, Governor of the Bank of England

At a typical meeting, the MPC discusses financial market developments, the international economy, money, credit, demand and output, and costs and prices. In other words, the inflation target is considered within the broad context of developments in various aspects of the economy. All these factors would be discussed in some detail before taking a decision on the bank rate. In the interests of transparency, the minutes of the regular MPC meetings are published on the internet — you can see them at www.bankofengland.co.uk/mpc. This means that you can readily check recent developments in the economy.

The underlying idea is that by influencing the level of aggregate demand, the MPC could affect the rate of inflation so as to keep it within the target range, although the effects of a change in the bank rate are not likely to take immediate effect. One reason for giving the Bank of England such independence was that it increases the credibility of the policy. If firms and households realise that the government is serious about controlling inflation, they will have more confidence in its actions, and will be better able to form expectations about the future path the economy will take. In particular, firms will be encouraged to undertake more investment, and this will have a supply-side effect, shifting the aggregate supply curve to the right in the long run.

When inflation began drifting towards 3% in early 2007, you can see that the bank rate was increased in an attempt to bring inflation down. You can also see that this did indeed happen during 2007, with inflation coming back down to around 2%.

Monetary policy from 2008

Inflation accelerated during 2008, but the MPC was aware that this was likely to be a temporary surge. The financial crisis began to bite, and with many commercial banks finding themselves in trouble, the MPC was aware that credit in the economy was tight. Instead of raising the bank rate in order to curb inflation, the MPC reduced the bank rate, and by early 2009 the bank rate had reached 0.5%, which was effectively as low as it could go.

Key term

quantitative easing a process by which the central bank purchases assets such as government and corporate bonds in order to release additional money into the financial system

With the economy heading into recession, reducing the bank rate in order to boost aggregate demand was no longer an option, and the Bank of England instead turned to a policy that became known as **quantitative easing**. This was a process by which the Bank of England purchased assets (mainly government securities) from the banks, thus affecting the banks' liquidity positions. The aim of this was to encourage lending by the banks, which had dried up during the credit crunch, thus making it difficult for firms to borrow. Quantitative easing was effectively a way in which the Bank of England could increase money supply in order to boost aggregate demand and help to counter the recession.

The bank rate remained at 0.5%, even during 2011 when inflation again accelerated beyond its target. You can see this clearly in Figure 15.5.

Exercise 15.3

Visit the Bank of England website and check whether the MPC chose to change the interest rate at its most recent meeting. Take a look at the minutes of the meeting to see the factors that were considered in taking this decision.

Summary

- Monetary policy is concerned with the decisions made by government on monetary variables such as money supply and the interest rate.
- A change in the interest rate influences the level of aggregate demand through the investment expenditure of firms, the consumption behaviour of households and (indirectly) net exports.
- Since 1997, the Bank of England has been given independent responsibility to set interest rates in order to meet the government's inflation target.
- The Monetary Policy Committee (MPC) of the Bank sets the bank rate, which is then used as a base rate by the commercial banks and other financial institutions.
- Giving independence to the Bank of England in this way increases the credibility of monetary policy.
- If this encourages investment, there may be a long-run impact on aggregate supply.
- In 2009, the depth of the recession induced the Bank of England to introduce quantitative easing, a process by which money supply was increased.

Policies affecting aggregate supply

Key term

supply-side policies range of measures intended to have a direct impact on aggregate supply — and specifically the potential capacity output of the economy

Demand-side policies have been aimed primarily at stabilising the macroeconomy in the relatively short run, but with the intention of affecting aggregate supply in the long run, by influencing firms' and households' confidence in the future path of the economy. However, there are also a number of policies that can be used to influence the aggregate supply curve directly.

Chapter 14 indicated that the position of the aggregate supply curve depends primarily on the quantity of factor inputs available in the economy, and on the efficiency of those factors. **Supply-side policies** thus focus on affecting these determinants of aggregate supply in order to shift the *AS* curve to the right.

Investment is one key to this in the long run, and this chapter has already shown how demand-side policies that stabilise the macroeconomy in the short run may also have long-run effects on aggregate supply by encouraging investment.

Education and training

Investment is also needed in human capital, and one form that this can take is education and training. An important supply-side policy therefore takes the form of encouraging workers (and potential workers) to undertake education and training to improve their productivity.

This takes place partly through education in schools and colleges in preparation for work. It is important, therefore, that the curriculum is designed to provide key skills that will be useful in the workplace. However, this does not mean that all education has to be geared directly to providing skills; problem-solving and analytical skills, for example, can be developed through the study of a wide range of disciplines.

Adult education is also important. When the structure of the economy is changing, retraining must be made available to enable workers to move easily between sectors and occupations. This is crucial if structural unemployment is not to become a major problem. For any society — whether industrialised or less developed and needing to reduce its dependence on agriculture — education and skills are necessary to enable workers to switch into new activities in response to structural changes in the economy.

Figure 15.6 shows how such a policy can affect the aggregate supply curve, moving it from AS_0 to AS_1. This move enables an increase in the potential output capacity of the economy, and it need not be inflationary. Indeed, in the figure the overall price level falls from P_0 to P_1 following the shift in aggregate supply, with real output increasing from Y^* to Y^{**}.

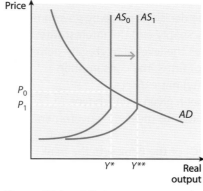

Figure 15.6 A shift in aggregate supply

Flexibility of markets

The rationale for including retraining as a supply-side policy rests partly on the argument that this provides for greater flexibility in labour markets, enabling workers to switch between economic activities to improve the overall workings of the economy.

There are other ways of improving market flexibility. One is to limit the power of the trade unions, whose actions can sometimes lead to inflexibility in the labour market, either through resistance to new working practices that could improve productivity or by pushing up wages so that the level of employment is reduced.

Indeed, maintaining the flexibility of markets is one way in which the macroeconomic stability promoted by disciplined fiscal and monetary policy can improve aggregate supply. Macroeconomic stability enables price signals to work more effectively, as producers are better able to observe changes in relative prices. This can promote allocative efficiency.

Promotion of competition

If firms gain dominance in a market, the pursuit of profits may lead them to use their market position to restrict output and raise prices. Such market dominance arises because of a lack of competition. In addition, it is possible that in some markets the lack of competition will produce complacency, depriving firms of the incentive to operate at maximum efficiency. This was especially true in the UK for the formerly nationalised industries such as electricity and gas supply, which were widely believed to have operated with widespread productive inefficiency.

Policies that promote competition may thus lead to improvements in both allocative and productive efficiency. This was one of the motivations behind the privatisation drive that began in the 1980s under Margaret Thatcher. However, it should be noted that there is not wholesale agreement on whether privatisation has invariably led to improvements in efficiency, in industries such as the railways and water supply.

Unemployment benefits

An important influence on labour supply, particularly for low-income workers, is the level of unemployment benefit. If unemployment benefit is provided at too high a level, it may inhibit labour force participation, in that some workers may opt to live on unemployment benefit rather than take up low-skilled (and low-paid) employment. In such a situation, a reduction in unemployment benefit may induce an increase in labour supply, which again will shift the aggregate supply curve to the right.

However, such a policy needs to be balanced against the need to provide protection for those who are unable to find employment. It is also important that unemployment benefit is not reduced to such a level that workers are unwilling to leave their jobs to search for better ones, as this may inhibit the flexibility of the labour market.

Incentive effects

Similarly, there are dangers in making the taxation system too progressive. Most people accept that income tax should be progressive — that is, that those on relatively high incomes should pay a higher rate of tax than those on low incomes — as a way of redistributing income within society and preventing inequality from becoming extreme. However, there may come a point at which marginal tax rates are so high that a large proportion of additional income is taxed away, reducing incentives for individuals to supply additional effort or labour. This could also have an effect on aggregate supply. Again, however, it is important to balance these incentive effects against the distortion caused by having too much inequality in society.

Low-skilled workers may be better off on unemployment benefits

---

Exercise 15.4

For each of the following policies, identify whether it is an example of fiscal, monetary or supply-side policy. Discuss how each policy affects either aggregate demand or aggregate supply (or both), and examine its effects on equilibrium real output and the overall price level:

a an increase in government expenditure
b a decrease in the rate of unemployment benefit
c a fall in the rate of interest
d legislation limiting the power of trade unions
e encouragement for more students to attend university
f provision of retraining in the form of adult education
g a reduction in the highest rate of income tax
h measures to break up a concentrated market
i an increase in the bank rate

With the range of policy instruments available to the authorities, it is important to investigate whether they will be mutually compatible, or whether conflict could arise between them.

It was seen earlier that fiscal policy may have implications for the interest rate. If the government increases its expenditure, perhaps with the intention of improving infrastructure or subsidising education and training, one side-effect could be to require higher borrowing and push up interest rates. This could in turn lead to an inflow of hot money, affecting the exchange rate and the competitiveness of domestic goods in international markets. This suggests that there may be circumstances in which fiscal and monetary policy come into conflict, given that interest rates are a key part of the transmission of monetary policy. Consequently, a way must be found of coordinating fiscal and monetary policy. This is naturally difficult to do, given the way that the Bank of England is intended to act independently of the government in conducting monetary policy in order to meet the inflation target.

In creating a stable macroeconomic environment, the ultimate aim of monetary policy is not simply to keep inflation low, but to improve the confidence of decision-makers. This will encourage firms to invest in order to generate an increase in productive capacity — which will stimulate economic growth and create an opportunity to improve living standards. In other words, the hope is to stimulate investment and thus enable an increase in the productive capacity of the economy by shifting the *AS* curve. The problem is that high interest rates may be needed at times in order to achieve the inflation target — and high interest rates will tend to discourage investment.

Conflict may also arise because of trade-offs that exist between other policy objectives. Too rapid a rate of economic growth may put upwards pressure on prices, thus leading to inflation. Inflation may cause problems with international competitiveness, and thus have an impact on the balance of payments. However, reducing demand in order to control inflation may lead to unemployment. Rapid economic growth may also increase inequity within a society, if the benefits are enjoyed by a minority of people — and growth may also cause damage to the environment.

Designing the policy mix

The existence of these trade-offs makes it important to be able to design a policy mix that can resolve the conflicts, or at least reduce their consequences.

In the context of the aggregate demand/aggregate supply model, it is clear that demand- and supply-side policies are aimed at achieving rather different objectives.

Study tip

The potential conflict between policy objectives is an important topic, so spend some time thinking about where such conflict may arise, and why.

The primary rationale for monetary and fiscal policies is to stabilise the macroeconomy. In this, fiscal policy has come to take on a subsidiary role, supporting monetary policy. This was not always the case, and there have been periods in which fiscal policy has been used much more actively to try to stimulate the economy. There are still some countries in which such policies are very much the vogue: for example, it has been suggested that much of Latin America's problem with high inflation has stemmed from fiscal indiscipline, although not all Latin American economists accept this argument. The fact that fiscal policy has not always been well implemented does not mean that such policies cannot be valuable tools — but it does warn against misuse.

In the UK, the use of monetary policy with the support of fiscal policy seemed to be working reasonably effectively until the onset of the financial crisis in late 2008. Furthermore, it seemed to be operating in such a way as to complement the supply-side policies. When a stable macroeconomic environment is created, microeconomic markets are able to operate effectively and investment is encouraged, thereby leading to a boost in aggregate supply. Supply-side policies aim to influence aggregate supply directly, either raising the supply of factor inputs or improving productivity and efficiency. However, the UK operates within the global economy, and the financial crisis brought with it a period of recession from which the economy was slow to recover. The global context is explored in the next part of the book.

Policy design is a balancing act

The design and conduct of economic policy may therefore be seen as an elaborate balancing act. Differing policy objectives need to be prioritised, as in many cases there may be conflict between them. Choices have to be made about the balance to be achieved between fiscal, monetary and supply-side policies.

The consensus view in the early part of the twenty-first century was that fiscal policy should be used to achieve the desired balance between the public and private sectors. Monetary policy should be devoted to meeting the government's inflation target in order to create a stable macroeconomic environment; this would then encourage growth and enable improvements in the standard of living. Problems arose when fiscal policy was forced into action in order to protect the financial system, resulting in an escalation of public debt.

In the long run, supply-side policies are perhaps the most important, as these contribute to raising efficiency and increasing the productive capacity of the economy. The keynote in policy design lies in enabling markets to operate as effectively as possible.

Summary

- Policies to shift the aggregate supply curve may be used to encourage economic growth.
- Education and training can be viewed as a form of investment in human capital, which is designed to improve the productivity of workers.
- Measures to improve the flexibility of labour and product markets may lead to an overall improvement in productivity and thus may affect aggregate supply.
- Promoting competition can also improve the effectiveness of markets in the economy.
- Incentive effects are an important influence on aggregate supply. For example, if unemployment benefits are set too high, this may discourage labour force participation. An over-progressive income taxation structure can also have damaging incentive effects.
- Demand-side and supply-side policies have different objectives. Demand-side policies such as fiscal and monetary policy are aimed primarily at stabilising the economy. Supply-side policies are geared more towards promoting economic growth.
- However, effective stabilisation of the economy may also have long-term effects on aggregate supply. There are situations in which different policies have conflicting impacts on the economy.
- The financial crisis and the recession that it triggered have led to some rethinking of the relationship between monetary and fiscal policy, with fiscal policy being invoked to protect the financial system.

Case study 15.1

Policy dilemmas

Imagine you are the economic dictator of a country called Nowhere. The economy has been experiencing a period of prosperity, with low inflation and unemployment and steady economic growth. However, you are aware that you soon face re-election, and there are some problems on the horizon. Imports of consumer goods from China are growing rapidly, and unemployment has begun to creep up as some firms go out of business. Global commodity prices are rising, putting additional pressures on the prices of some key strategic imports. There is a growing environmental lobby putting pressure on you to reduce the environmental impact of economic growth and tackle carbon dioxide emissions. Inflation is towards the top end of the acceptable range. A house price bubble is threatening to burst.

Follow-up question
Discuss to which objective you should give top priority.

Case study 15.2

Macroeconomic policy instruments

Governments in a modern economy have three main types of policy instrument for affecting the macroeconomy — monetary policy, fiscal policy and supply-side policy. Monetary policy is dedicated to ensuring the stability of the economy by influencing aggregate demand. Fiscal policy is used to maintain balance in the economy between public and private sectors and between present and future generations of citizens. Supply-side policies are dedicated to affecting the productive capacity of the economy, operating primarily through microeconomic incentives.

Follow-up question
Explain these distinctions between the types of policy instrument. Which type do you consider to be of most importance?

SECTION
2

MACROECONOMICS

Part 7
The global context

International trade

The world economy is becoming increasingly integrated, and it is no longer possible to think of any single economy in isolation. The UK economy is no exception. It relies on international trade, engaging in exporting and importing activity, and many UK firms are increasingly active in global markets. This situation has created opportunities for UK firms to expand and become global players, and for UK consumers to have access to a wider range of goods and services. However, there is also a downside: global shocks, whether caused by increases in oil prices, financial crises or the emergence of China as a world economic force, can reverberate throughout economies in all parts of the world. It is also apparent that, although economic analysis suggests that there are potential gains to be reaped from international trade, it is still the case that many countries interfere with freedom of trade and try to protect their domestic markets. These are some of the issues that will be explored in this chapter.

Learning objectives

After studying this chapter, you should:
- appreciate the importance of trade and exchange between nations
- realise how countries may be able to gain from engaging in international trade
- be aware of the risks that come from overspecialisation
- understand what is meant by globalisation, and be aware of the factors that have given rise to this phenomenon
- be familiar with the arguments for trade liberalisation as opposed to protectionism

Gains from international trade

Key term

absolute advantage a country's ability to produce a good using less resources than another country

Chapter 1 highlighted the importance of specialisation, by which, it was argued, workers could become more productive. This same principle can be applied in the context of international trade. Suppose there are two countries — call them Anywhere and Somewhere. Each country can produce combinations of agricultural goods and manufactured goods.

There are differences between countries in the efficiency with which they use their factors of production. For example, it may be that Anywhere can produce manufactured goods using less resources than Somewhere. Anywhere would then be said to have an **absolute advantage** in the production of manufactured goods as compared with Somewhere. It could be the case that Anywhere has an absolute advantage in the production of

comparative advantage a
country's ability to produce a
good *relatively* more efficiently
(i.e. at lower opportunity cost)
than another country

trading possibilities curve
shows the consumption
possibilities under conditions of
free trade

law of comparative advantage
a theory arguing that there
may be gains from trade arising
when countries specialise in
the production of goods or
services in which they have a
comparative advantage

both manufactured and agricultural goods as compared with Somewhere. However, this does not mean that trade could not be beneficial. This turns on the *relative* efficiency with which the two countries produce the two types of goods. If Somewhere is relatively more efficient at producing agricultural goods than manufactured goods, then it has a **comparative advantage** in producing agricultural goods, by producing them at lower opportunity cost.

Consider the example of Anywhere and Somewhere from the previous paragraph. Assume (for simplicity) that the two countries are of similar size in output terms, although Somewhere uses more resources in production than Anywhere because of the absolute advantage held by Anywhere. Their respective *PPC*s are shown in Figure 16.1.

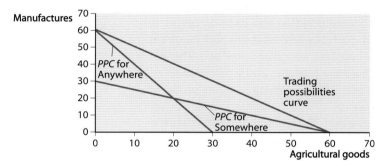

Figure 16.1 Trading possibilities for Anywhere and Somewhere

The pattern of comparative advantage held by the two countries is reflected in the different slopes of the countries' *PPC*s. In the absence of trade, each country is constrained to consume along its *PPC*. For example, if Somewhere wants to consume 20 units of manufactures, it can consume a maximum of 20 units of agricultural goods.

However, suppose that each country were to specialise in producing the product in which it has a comparative advantage. Anywhere could produce 60 units of manufactures and Somewhere could produce 60 units of agricultural goods. If each country were to specialise completely in this way, and if trade were to take place on a one-to-one basis (i.e. if one unit of manufactures is exchanged for one unit of agricultural goods), then it can be seen that this would expand the consumption possibilities for both countries. The **trading possibilities curve** in Figure 16.1 shows the potential consumption points for each country in this situation.

For example, if Somewhere still wishes to consume 20 units of manufactures, it could now produce 60 units of agricultural goods, and exchange 20 units of them for 20 units of manufactures. It would then have its 20 units of manufactures, but have more agricultural goods than without trade. In this particular exchange, Anywhere would now have 40 units of manufactures and 20 units of agricultural goods, and would also be better off than without trade.

The **law of comparative advantage** states that overall output can be increased if countries specialise in producing the goods in which they have a comparative advantage.

193

Calculating opportunity cost ratios

The key to comparative advantage is the difference in the opportunity costs faced by each country in the production of these goods. This can be calculated. First, notice that if Anywhere chooses to increase output of agricultural goods by 10 units, it must sacrifice 20 units of manufactures, so the opportunity cost ratio is 2:1, meaning that for every unit of extra agricultural goods it must sacrifice 2 units of manufactures. However, for Somewhere 10 units of manufactures are sacrificed if 10 more units of agricultural goods are to be produced, so the opportunity cost ratio is 1:1. Similarly, the opportunity cost ratios for manufactured goods are 0.5 for Anywhere and 1 for Somewhere.

Exercise 16.1

Figure 16.2 shows production possibility curves for two countries, each of which produces both coats and scooters. The countries are called 'Here' and 'There'.

a Suppose that Here produces 200 scooters and There produces 100: how many coats are produced in each country?

b Now suppose that 300 scooters and 200 coats are produced by Here, and that There produces only coats. What has happened to total production of coats and scooters?

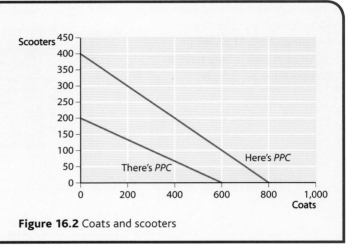

Figure 16.2 Coats and scooters

In the above examples and exercises, specialisation and trade are seen to lead to higher overall production of goods. Although the examples have related to goods, you should be equally aware that services too may be a source of specialisation and trade. This is potentially important for an economy such as the UK's, where there is a comparative advantage in the provision of financial services.

Extension material

Two Swedish economists, Eli Heckscher and Bertil Ohlin, argued that a country's comparative advantage would depend crucially on its relative endowments of factors of production. They argued that the optimal techniques for producing different commodities varied. Some commodities are most efficiently produced using labour-intensive techniques, whereas others could be more efficiently produced using relatively capital-intensive methods. This then suggests that if a country has abundant labour but scarce capital, then its natural comparative advantage would lie in the production of goods that require little capital but lots of labour. In contrast, a country with access to capital but facing a labour shortage would tend to have a comparative advantage in capital-intensive goods or services.

This suggests that countries whose comparative advantage lies in the production of labour- or land-intensive goods, but who wish to develop into a more industrial society are likely to face significant challenges in seeking to alter the pattern of their comparative advantage. This important issue will be explored in the later part of the A Level course.

terms of trade the relative prices at which exchange takes place; the ratio of export prices to import prices

Who gains from international trade?

A key factor that determines which of the countries will gain from trade — and whether trade will take place at all — is the relative prices at which trade takes place, known as the **terms of trade**. In practice, the relative prices are set in world markets, although it is possible that for some commodities there are countries large enough to influence prices.

The terms of trade will depend partly upon the relative demand and supply conditions in the two countries — and also upon whether markets are in fact competitive, or whether one of the trading partners has some form of market power that can be used to influence the terms of trade between the two countries. In other words, the relative prices at which goods are exchanged will influence the way in which the gains from trade are distributed between the trading partners.

In particular, specialisation may bring dangers and risks, as well as benefits. One obvious way in which this may be relevant is that, by specialising, a country allows some sectors to run down. For example, suppose a country came to rely on imported food and allowed its agricultural sector to waste away. If the country then became involved in a war, or for some other reason was unable to import its food, there would clearly be serious consequences if it could no longer grow its own foodstuffs. For this reason, many countries have in place measures designed to protect their agricultural sectors — or other sectors that are seen to be strategic in nature. This is a contentious area, and there has been considerable criticism of the European Common Agricultural Policy — especially from the vantage point of developing countries, which argue that they are disadvantaged by the overprotection of European agriculture.

Overreliance on some commodities may also be risky. For example, the development of artificial substitutes for rubber had an enormous impact on the demand for natural rubber; this was reflected in falls in its price, which caused difficulties for countries that had specialised in producing rubber.

Trade between nations

Over 5 billion bananas are imported into the UK every year

Countries all around the world engage in international trade. This is partly for obvious reasons: for example, the UK is not a sensible place to grow bananas on a commercial scale, but people living in the UK like to eat bananas. International trade enables individuals to consume goods that cannot be easily produced domestically. It makes sense for bananas to be produced in countries where the relative opportunity cost is low.

The extent to which countries engage in international trade varies enormously, as can be seen in Figure 16.3, which shows total trade (exports plus imports) as a percentage of GDP. In some cases, the extent of dependence on trade reflects the availability of natural resources in a country, but it may also reflect political attitudes towards trade.

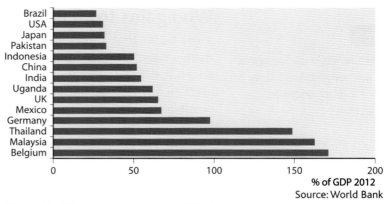

Figure 16.3 Trade as a percentage of GDP

The USA has a large and diverse economy, with a wealth of natural resources, and does not depend so heavily on trade. Brazil, India and Pakistan have a similarly low level of dependence, but this partly reflects a conscious policy over many years to limit the extent to which their economies have to rely on external trade. At the other extreme, countries such as Malaysia and Thailand have followed policies that promote exports, believing that this will allow more rapid economic growth. China was closed to international trade for a long period but is now increasingly relying on exporting in order to stimulate economic growth. The share of trade in GDP for China is expanding rapidly.

You may be curious as to how it is possible for a country to display a ratio of trade to GDP that is greater than 100%. The reason is that exports include re-exports, i.e. goods that are imported, perhaps as components for other goods, and then exported again. In other words, there is some double-counting going on here.

The pattern of global trade

Moves towards closer integration between countries have strongly affected the pattern of world trade. For example, the moves towards European integration have made Europe a major player in world trade. Something of this can be seen in Figure 16.4(a), which shows the destination of world exports in 2012 (i.e. the percentage of the world's exports *imported* by each region). You can see that almost 40% of the world's exports head for Europe and 17% to North America. Asia has also become an important part of the world trade scene, with China expanding its trading at an unprecedented rate in recent years.

Figure 16.4(b) shows the origin of world imports (i.e. the percentage of the world's imports *exported* by each region). Given the size of its population, Africa contributes very little to world trade.

Exercise 16.2

Next time you go shopping, make a list of the goods that you see on offer that have been imported from elsewhere in the world. See if you can detect any patterns in the sorts of goods that come from different parts of the world.

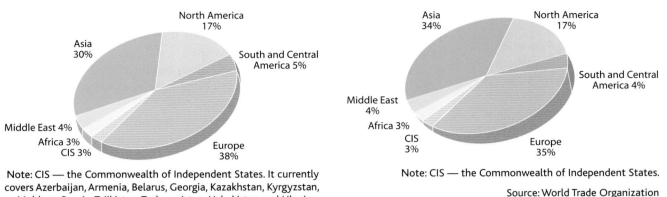

North America
17%

Asia
30%

South and Central
America 5%

Middle East 4%

Africa 3%

CIS 3%

Europe
38%

Note: CIS — the Commonwealth of Independent States. It currently covers Azerbaijan, Armenia, Belarus, Georgia, Kazakhstan, Kyrgyzstan, Moldova, Russia, Tajikistan, Turkmenistan, Uzbekistan and Ukraine.

Source: World Trade Organization

Figure 16.4(a) Destination of world exports, 2012

Asia
34%

North America
17%

South and Central
America 4%

Middle East
4%

Africa 3%

CIS
3%

Europe
35%

Note: CIS — the Commonwealth of Independent States.

Source: World Trade Organization

Figure 16.4(b) Origin of world imports, 2012

Globalisation

The term 'globalisation' has been much used in recent years, especially by the protest groups that have demonstrated against it. It is therefore important to be clear about what the term means before seeking to evaluate the strengths and weaknesses of the phenomenon.

Ann Krueger, the first deputy managing director of the IMF, defined globalisation as 'a phenomenon by which economic agents in any given part of the world are much more affected by events elsewhere in the world'. Joseph Stiglitz, the Nobel laureate and former chief economist at the World Bank, defined it as follows:

> Fundamentally, [globalization] is the closer integration of countries and peoples of the world which has been brought about by the enormous reduction of costs of transportation and communication, and the breaking down of artificial barriers to the flows of goods, services, capital, knowledge, and (to a lesser extent) people across borders.

J. Stiglitz, *Globalization and its Discontents* (Penguin, 2004)

On this basis, globalisation is crucially about the closer integration of the world's economies. Critics have focused partly on the environmental effects of rapid global economic growth, and partly on the opportunities that powerful nations and large corporations have for exploiting the weak.

The quotation from the book by Joseph Stiglitz not only defines what is meant by globalisation, but also offers some reasons for its occurrence.

Transportation costs

One of the contributory factors to the spread of globalisation has undoubtedly been the rapid advances in the technology of transportation and communications.

Improvements in transportation have enabled firms to fragment their production process to take advantage of varying cost conditions in different parts of the world. For example, it is now possible to site labour-intensive parts of a production process in areas of the world where labour is relatively plentiful, and thus relatively cheap. This is one way in which **multinational corporations (MNCs)** arise, in some cases operating across a wide range of countries.

Furthermore, communications technology has developed rapidly with the growth of the worldwide web and e-commerce, enabling firms to compete more easily in global markets.

These technological changes have augmented existing economies of scale and scope, enabling firms to grow. If the size of firms were measured by their gross turnover, many of them would be found to be larger in size than a lot of the countries in which they operate (when size is measured by GDP): for instance, on this basis General Motors is bigger than Hong Kong or Norway.

Reduction of trade barriers

A second factor that has contributed to globalisation has been the successive reductions in trade barriers during the period since the Second World War, first under the auspices of the **General Agreement on Tariffs and Trade (GATT)**, and later under the **World Trade Organization (WTO)**, which replaced it.

In addition to these trade-liberalising measures, there has been a trend towards the establishment of free trade areas and customs unions in various parts of the world, with the European Union being just one example.

By facilitating the process of international trade, such developments have encouraged firms to become more active in trade, and thus have added to the impetus towards globalisation.

Deregulation of financial markets

Hand in hand with these developments, there have been moves towards removing restrictions on the movement of financial capital between countries. Many countries have removed capital controls, thereby making it much easier for firms to operate globally. This has been reinforced by developments in technology that enable financial transactions to be undertaken more quickly and efficiently.

The pattern of world trade

In order to provide the context for a discussion of the place of the UK economy in the global economy, it is helpful to examine the pattern of world trade.

Table 16.1 presents some data on this pattern. It shows the size of trade flows between regions. The rows of the table show the exports from each of the regions to each other region, while the columns show the pattern of imports from each region. The numbers on the 'diagonal' of the table (in bold type) show the trade flows *within* regions. One remarkable feature of the table is the high involvement of Europe in world trade, accounting for 35.7% of imports and 34.2% of the exports. Of course, this includes substantial flows within Europe. In contrast, Africa shows very little involvement in world trade, in spite of the fact that, in population terms, it is far larger.

Many East Asian countries have adopted very open policies towards trade

Indeed, trade flows between the developed countries — and with the more advanced developing countries — have tended to dominate world trade, with the flows between developing countries being relatively minor. This is not surprising, given that by definition the richer countries have greater purchasing power. However, the degree of openness to trade of economies around the world also varies as a result of conscious policy decisions. Some countries, especially in East Asia, have adopted very open policies towards trade, promoting exports in order to achieve export-led growth. In contrast, countries such as India and a number of Latin American countries have been much more reluctant to become dependent on international trade, and have adopted a more closed attitude towards trade.

The global pattern of trade has changed over time. The expansion of the European Union and the Single European Market has altered the pattern of trade, with member countries more likely to trade with each other because of the falling transactions costs when markets are deregulated. The rapid growth of China and India as active trading nations has also had an impact on the direction of trade flows.

Table 16.1 Intra- and interregional merchandise trade, 2011 (US$bn)

	Destination								
Origin	North America	South and Central America	European Union	Other Europe	CIS	Africa	Middle East	Asia	World
North America	**1,103**	201	328	54	15	37	63	476	2,278
S & C America	181	**200**	120	17	8	21	18	169	736
European Union	433	109	**3,906**	388	211	183	159	575	5,965
Other Europe	47	9	352	**22**	23	16	35	63	567
CIS	43	11	356	53	**154**	12	24	117	770
Africa	102	19	182	23	2	**77**	21	146	572
Middle East	107	10	133	25	6	38	**110**	660	1,089
Asia	906	189	847	75	110	152	242	**2,926**	5,447
World	2,923	749	6,223	658	530	538	672	5,133	**17,425**

The pattern of UK trade

Figures 16.5(a) and (b) show the destination of UK exports of goods and services to major regional groupings in the world. The most striking feature of this graph is the extent to which the UK relies on Europe and the USA for almost three-quarters of its exports. Figures 16.6(a) and (b) reveal a similar pattern for the UK's imports of goods and services.

The proportion of UK trade (both exports and imports) that is with Europe has undergone substantial change over the past 50 years. By 2000, more than 60% of UK exports of goods went to the countries that now make up the EU. This has fallen back a little, to about 50% in 2012, but this still represents a significant reliance on Europe for international trade.

A substantial share of exports of goods from the UK consists of manufactured goods, especially road vehicles together with machinery and equipment of various types, and pharmaceuticals — and oil, of course. Many of these commodities are also imported in large volumes. In part, this reflects the way in which commodity groups are defined. For example, there are many different types of road vehicle or pharmaceutical product, and specialisation may mean that firms in particular countries focus on particular types of vehicle or drug. By specialising in this way, they may be able to tap economies of scale that would otherwise not be available within the domestic market. Exports of services are also a large share of UK exports, particularly financial services and insurance.

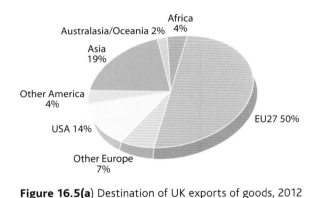

Figure 16.5(a) Destination of UK exports of goods, 2012

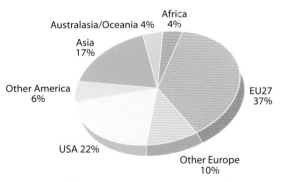

Figure 16.5(b) Destination of UK exports of services, 2012

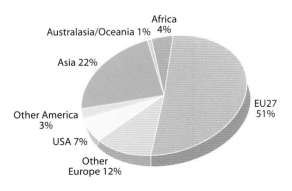

Figure 16.6(a) Source of UK imports of goods, 2012

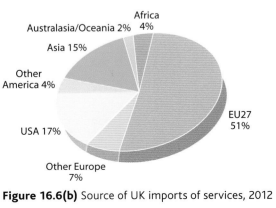

Figure 16.6(b) Source of UK imports of services, 2012

Source for all figures: Pink Book

The benefits from specialisation revisited

It has been argued that countries can gain from engaging in international trade by specialising in the production of goods and services in which they have a lower opportunity cost of production. This helps to explain some of the patterns in world trade that are shown in the data.

When you think about the global economy, it should be clear that relative opportunity costs will vary according to the very different balance of conditions around the world, not only in terms of climate (which may be important in agricultural production), but also in terms of the relative balance of factors of production (labour, capital, land, entrepreneurship, etc.) and the skills of the workforce. This helps to explain why MNCs may choose to locate capital-intensive parts of their production process in one location and labour-intensive activities elsewhere, reflecting different relative prices in different countries.

It may also help to explain some of the patterns of trade. At first glance, it may seem curious that the UK both exports and imports cars, as initially this may seem to contradict the notion of specialisation. However, if UK and (say) German cars have different characteristics, then each country may choose to specialise in certain segments of the market, taking advantage of the economies of scale that are so crucial in car production. Consumers benefit from this, as they then have a wider range of products to choose from.

To some extent countries may be able to influence their position in world markets, by encouraging improvements in productivity, making labour markets more flexible, reducing unit labour costs and providing incentives for investment by domestic and foreign firms. However, there may be limits to the extent to which a government can affect the country's international competitiveness. It can provide a stable macroeconomic environment, improve the quality of the infrastructure and provide incentives for domestic and foreign firms to undertake investment. However, it is ultimately the efficiency of firms operating in the domestic economy relative to those abroad, and the quality of their products, that determines the competitiveness of domestically produced goods.

The UK both imports and exports cars — different countries specialise in certain segments of the car market

Summary

- Globalisation has taken place as countries and peoples of the world have become more closely integrated.
- Factors contributing to this process have been the rapid advances in the technology of transportation and communications, the reduction of trade barriers and the deregulation of financial markets.
- There are substantial differences in the degree to which countries trade: trade with and within Europe accounts for an appreciable proportion of world trade, whereas Africa shows very little involvement.
- More than three-quarters of UK exports go to Europe and the USA.
- The pattern of goods and services traded between countries reflects comparative advantage, at least to some extent.
- The international competitiveness of a country's goods and services depends upon the macroeconomic environment and upon the relative efficiency of firms operating in the domestic economy.

Case study 16.1

Uganda's trading position

Uganda is a country in East Africa with a population of about 36 million and average income (GDP per capita) of $551 in 2012, placing it within the low-income group of countries. The population has been growing at a rapid rate of about 3.4% per year. On the latest estimates, about 38% of the population live below the UNDP poverty line of $1.25 per person per day. Two-thirds of total employment is in agriculture, although the sector only contributes 26% of GDP by value added.

Uganda relies heavily on coffee as its main export. There were years in the early 1980s when coffee accounted for more than 90% of its exports. It has diversified since then, but coffee continues to account for between 20 and 30% of foreign exchange earnings. The importance of coffee to the economy is evidenced by the fact that

the coffee sector is dependent on about half a million smallholder farmers, and the sector employs more than 3.5 million families through coffee-related activities, according to the Uganda Coffee Development Authority.

The economic life of a coffee tree is about 40 years, and the majority of trees in Uganda were planted more than 50 years ago, so are past their prime producing stage. Coffee as a crop is often intercropped with other produce such as plantains and beans that are needed as food crops for the household. In some areas, the coffee crop has been affected by coffee wilt disease, which has killed many trees.

Figure 16.7 shows that the international price of coffee has been quite volatile over the past 25 years, which may have further affected the incentive for farmers to undertake investment in new coffee trees.

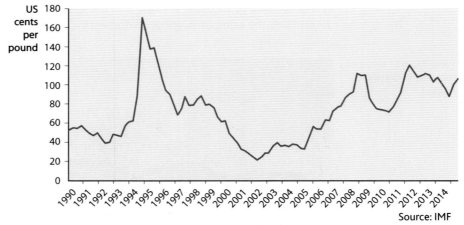

Source: IMF

Figure 16.7 The price of coffee 1990–2014

Follow-up questions

a Discuss why the incentives for investment in new coffee trees may have been weak in spite of the need to improve productivity.

b Given the importance of the coffee crop for the economy, what measures might the government take to encourage improvements in productivity?

c What other measures could be taken to encourage future economic growth?

The balance of payments and the exchange rate

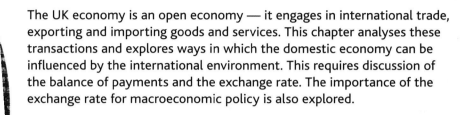

The UK economy is an open economy — it engages in international trade, exporting and importing goods and services. This chapter analyses these transactions and explores ways in which the domestic economy can be influenced by the international environment. This requires discussion of the balance of payments and the exchange rate. The importance of the exchange rate for macroeconomic policy is also explored.

Learning objectives

After studying this chapter, you should:
- be able to outline the structure of the current account of the balance of payments
- be familiar with the role and importance of the balance of payments
- be able to explain how a deficit or surplus on the current account of the balance of payments may arise
- be aware of the consequences of a surplus or deficit on the current account of the balance of payments
- understand how exchange rates are determined
- be aware of how changes in the exchange rate influence the macroeconomy through export and import prices and aggregate demand

The balance of payments

Key term

balance of payments a set of accounts showing the transactions conducted between residents of a country and the rest of the world

The **balance of payments** is a set of accounts that monitors the transactions that take place between UK residents and the rest of the world. For an individual household it is important to monitor incomings and outgoings, as items purchased must be paid for in some way — either by using income or savings, or by borrowing. In a similar way, a country has to pay for goods, services or assets that are bought from other countries. The balance of payments accounts enable the analysis of such international transactions.

As with the household, transactions can be categorised as either incoming or outgoing items. For example, if a car made in the UK is exported (i.e. purchased by a non-resident of the UK), this is an 'incoming' item, as the payment for the car is a credit to the UK. On the other hand, the purchase of a bottle of Italian wine (an import) is a debit item.

Similarly, all other transactions entered into the balance of payments accounts can be identified as credit or debit items, depending upon the

Key terms

current account of the balance of payments account identifying transactions in goods and services between the residents of a country and the rest of the world

financial account of the balance of payments account identifying transactions in financial assets between the residents of a country and the rest of the world

capital account of the balance of payments account identifying transactions in (physical) capital between the residents of a country and the rest of the world

direction of the payment. In other words, when money flows into the country as the result of a transaction, that is a credit; if money flows out, it is a debit. As all items have to be paid for in some way, the overall balance of payments when everything is added together must be zero. However, individual components can be positive or negative.

In line with international standards, the accounts are divided into three categories. The **current account** identifies transactions in goods and services, together with income payments and international transfers. Income payments here include the earnings of UK nationals from employment abroad and payments of investment income. Transfers are mainly transactions between governments — for example, between the UK government and EU institutions — which make up the largest component. Flows of bilateral aid and social security payments abroad are also included here.

The **financial account** measures transactions in financial assets, including investment flows and central government transactions in foreign exchange reserves.

The **capital account** is relatively small. It contains capital transfers, the largest item of which is associated with migrants. When a person changes status from a non-resident to resident of the UK, any assets owned by that person are transferred to being UK-owned.

Figure 17.1 shows the relative size of the main accounts since 1980. Notice that these data are in current prices, so no account has been taken of changing prices during the period. This has the effect of compressing the apparent magnitude of the variables in the early part of the period (when prices were relatively low) and exaggerating the size towards the end of the period. Expressing these nominal values as a percentage of nominal GDP (as in Figure 17.2 for a longer period) provides a less misleading picture.

As the total balance of payments must always be zero, the surplus (positive) components above the line must always exactly match the deficit (negative) items below the line. However, both graphs indicate that the magnitudes of the three major accounts vary through time.

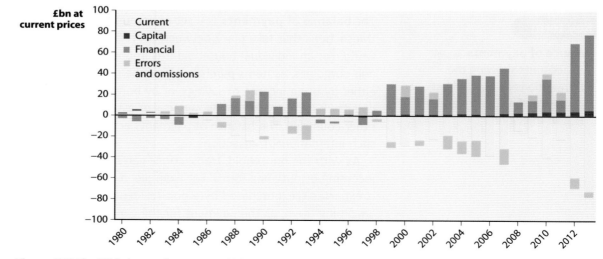

Figure 17.1 The UK balance of payments, 1980–2013

Source: ONS

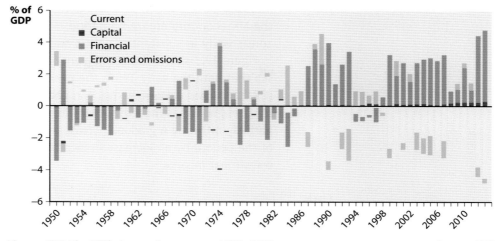

Figure 17.2 The UK balance of payments, 1950–2013   Source: ONS

The current account

Commentators often focus on the current account. Three main items appear on this account. First, there is the balance of trade in goods and services — in other words, the balance between UK exports and imports of such goods and services. If UK residents buy German cars, this is an import and counts as a negative entry on the current account; on the other hand, if a German resident buys a British car, this is an export and constitutes a positive entry. The trade in goods is normally negative overall for the UK. However, this is partly balanced by a normally positive flow in trade in services, where the UK earns strong credits from its financial services.

> **Quantitative skills 17.1**
>
> **Calculate the balance of an item in the balance of payments accounts**
>
> In 2013, the exports of goods amounted to £299.5 billion and imports were £407.4 billion. The balance of trade in goods was thus total exports minus imports: that is, 299.5 − 407.4 = −£107.9 billion.

The second item in the current account is income. Part of this represents employment income from abroad, but the major item of income is made up of profits, dividends and interest receipts arising from UK ownership of overseas assets.

Finally, there are international transfers — either transfers through central government or transfers made or received by private individuals. This item includes transactions with and grants from international organisations or the EU. The current balance combines these items.

The current account has been in deficit every year since 1984. The recorded current account surpluses in 1980–83 were associated with North Sea oil, which was then just coming on stream. There followed a phase in which the deficit grew to record levels, peaking in 1989. During the 1990s, the deficit fell until 1999, at which time the UK economy entered a period in which the current account was consistently in substantial deficit and the financial account in surplus.

Figure 17.3 shows the components of the current account. You can see that until the early 1990s the overall balance on the current account (CBAL) tracked closely the trade in goods. More recently, however, the trade in goods has moved further into deficit, although this has been partially offset by a gradual increase in the trade in services and (for part of the period) by an increase in income — which is made up mainly of investment income.

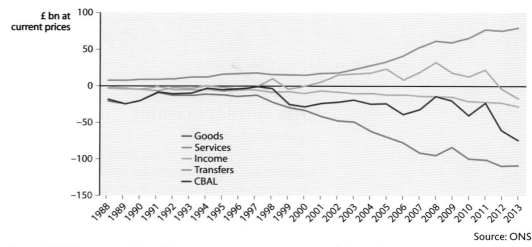

Source: ONS

Figure 17.3 The composition of the current account, 1988–2013 (balances)

Key term

visible trade trade in goods

It is important to realise that the overall balance on the current account arises from combining the balances on all of these items. An overall current account deficit arises when the deficit items outweigh the surplus items in the accounts. Figure 17.3 clearly shows that it is the strong deficit on trade in goods that has resulted in the UK's long-standing overall deficit.

Trade in goods (sometimes known as **visible trade**) has traditionally shown a deficit for the UK — it has shown a surplus in only 6 years since 1950. For a period until 2004, the UK was a net exporter of oil, but as reserves of North Sea oil were run down, the position changed, and the oil balance is now a substantial negative item. Imports of cars and other consumer goods have persistently exceeded exports. A summary for 2013 is presented in Table 17.1, with data for 1996 also provided for comparison. You should be aware that these data are in current prices, so you need to focus on the relative sizes rather than the absolute values. It is interesting to note that in 2013, the only category of goods to show a surplus was chemicals. An important question is whether this needs to be a cause for concern for the UK economy. In order to evaluate this, it is important to consider the extent to which services can be relied upon to help to balance the deficit in trade in goods. In addition, the question of the long-term balance between the current account and the financial account is pertinent, as will be explained later in the chapter.

Table 17.1 UK trade in goods (balances), 1996 and 2013 (£m in current prices)

Item	2013	1996
Food, beverages and tobacco	−18,728	−14,016
Basic materials	−2,343	−2,994
Oil	−15,358	−3,905
Coal, gas and electricity	−7,902	−2,843
Semi-manufactured goods:		
Chemicals	3,423	5,481
Precious stones and silver	−4,299	−1,139
Other	−13,186	−8,786
Finished manufactured goods:		
Motor cars	58	−6,257
Other consumer goods	−27,277	−22,078
Intermediate goods	−12,607	−10,420
Capital goods	−13,351	−14,082
Ships and aircraft	2,384	−1,821
Commodities not classified	483	−771
Total	**−50,793**	**−83,631**

Source: ONS

Key term

invisible trade trade in services

In fact, trade in services has recorded a surplus in every year since 1996. This is sometimes referred to as invisible trade. Table 17.2 shows the component items in 1996 and 2013 — again measured in current prices, so that no allowance has been made for the effects of inflation.

As you can see, apart from travel and government, all items showed a positive balance in 2013. The main reason for the deficit on travel is the increasing number of UK residents travelling abroad. However, this negative item has been more than compensated by the surplus components, especially insurance and financial services, which have grown steadily, as have computer and information services. You can see that 'other business' also makes a significant contribution. This category comprises

Table 17.2 UK trade in services (balances), 1996 and 2013 (£m in current prices)

Item	2013	1996
Transportation	1,025	−2,722
Travel	−9,407	−15,978
Communications	1,526	290
Construction	50	129
Insurance	11,575	2,565
Financial	34,743	22,575
Computer and information	5,130	3,831
Royalties and licence fees	2,670	1,974
Other business	25,447	15,849
Personal, cultural and recreational	2,954	1,285
Government	−1,721	−604
Total	**73,992**	**9,194**

Source: ONS

trade-related services such as merchanting and consultancy services, which include advertising, engineering and legal services and operational leasing.

An important item on the current account is investment income, which represents earnings on past investment abroad. This item experienced some growth between 1999 and about 2005, but then became rather volatile. The largest item in this part of the account is earnings from direct investment, although there is also an element of portfolio investment — earnings from holdings of bonds and other securities. The final category is current transfers. This includes taxes and social contributions received from non-resident workers and businesses, bilateral aid flows and military grants. However, the largest item is transfers with EU institutions, which has been in persistent deficit.

Figure 17.4 shows the size of the current account balance as a percentage of GDP. This is helpful because it removes the effects of prices changes, showing the size of the current account balance relative to GDP. A key question here is whether it is a question of concern to see these persistent deficits being sustained over long periods of time.

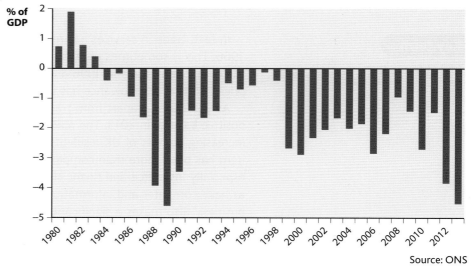

Source: ONS

Figure 17.4 The current account of the UK balance of payments, 1980–2013

One perspective on this is to realise that a deficit on the current account must be balanced by a surplus on the financial and capital accounts. In the short run, it may be possible to finance the trade deficit by selling UK financial assets to foreigners or by borrowing from overseas. However, this might not be regarded as being desirable in the longer term, if this affects the overall ownership pattern of British assets. For this reason, the current account cannot be viewed in isolation from the rest of the balance of payments.

The financial account

The trend towards globalisation means that both inward and outward investment increased substantially during the 1990s, although there was a dip after 2000. However, Figure 17.2 shows that the financial account has been in strong surplus in the early part of the twenty-first century, although it dipped during the financial crisis of the late 2000s.

The surplus on the financial account is in part forced by the deficit on the current account. If an economy runs a current account deficit, it can do so only by running a surplus on the financial account. Effectively, what is happening is that, in order to fund the current account deficit, the UK is selling assets to foreign investors and borrowing abroad.

An important question is whether this practice is sustainable in the long run. Selling assets or borrowing abroad has future implications for the current account, as there will be outflows of investment income and debt repayments in the future following today's financial surplus. It also has implications for interest rate policy. If the authorities hold interest rates high relative to the rest of the world, this will tend to attract inflows of investment, again with future implications for the current account.

The capital account

The capital account is relatively small. The largest item relates to the flows of capital associated with migration. If someone migrates to the UK, that person's status changes from being a non-resident to being a resident. His or her property then becomes part of the UK's assets and a transaction has to be entered in the balance of payments accounts. There are also some items relating to various EU transactions. This account has been in surplus for 20 years.

Summary
- The balance of payments is a set of accounts that contains details of the transactions that take place between the residents of an economy and the rest of the world.
- The accounts are divided into three sections: the current, financial and capital accounts.
- The current account identifies transactions in goods and services, together with some income payments and international transfers.
- The financial account measures transactions in financial assets, including investment flows and central government transactions in foreign reserves.
- The capital account, which is relatively small, contains capital transfers.
- The overall balance of payments must always be zero.
- The current account has been in persistent deficit since 1984, reflecting a deficit in trade in goods that is partly offset by a surplus in invisible trade.
- The financial account has been in strong surplus — as is required to balance the current account deficit.

The exchange rate and international competitiveness

Key term

exchange rate the price of one currency in terms of another

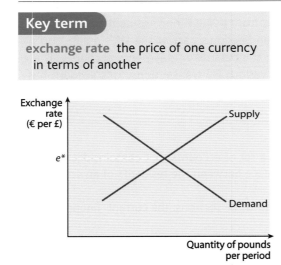

Figure 17.5 The market for pounds sterling

Closely associated with the balance of payments is the **exchange rate** — the price of one currency in terms of another. The exchange rate is important because it influences the prices that domestic consumers must pay for imported goods, services and assets, and also the price that foreigners pay for UK goods, services and assets. Chapter 5 introduced the notion of the demand and supply of foreign currency, shown in Figure 17.5. The demand for pounds arises from overseas residents (e.g. in the USA or the euro area) wanting to purchase UK goods, services or assets, whereas the supply of pounds emanates from domestic residents wanting to purchase overseas goods, services or assets. The connection is that the balance of payments accounts itemise these transactions, which entail the demand for and supply of pounds. Chapter 5 also pointed out that the demand for currency is a *derived demand* — thus pounds are demanded when people holding dollars or other currencies want to buy British. Similarly, pounds are supplied when people holding sterling want to buy foreign goods, services or assets.

In analysing the balance of payments, the relative competitiveness of UK goods and services is an important issue. If the UK persistently shows a deficit on the current account, does that imply that UK goods are uncompetitive in international markets?

The demand for UK exports in world markets depends upon a number of factors. In some ways, it is similar to the demand for a good. In general, the demand for a good depends on its price, on the prices of other goods, and on consumer incomes and preferences. In a similar way, you can think of the demand for UK exports as depending on the price of UK goods, the price of other countries' goods, incomes in the rest of the world and foreigners' preferences for UK goods over those produced elsewhere. However, in the case of international transactions the exchange rate is also relevant, as this determines the purchasing power of UK incomes in the rest of the world. Similarly, the demand for imports into the UK depends upon the relative prices of domestic and foreign goods, incomes in the UK, preferences for foreign and domestically produced goods and the exchange rate. These factors will all come together to determine the balance of demand for exports and imports.

The exchange rate plays a key role in influencing the levels of both imports and exports. Figure 17.6 shows the time path of the US$/£ exchange rate since 1971. It shows some fluctuations between 1971 and the late 1980s, around a declining trend. Since then the exchange rate seems to have remained fairly steady.

International competitiveness

Figure 17.6 shows a fall from a peak of $2.50 to the pound in 1972 to $1.56, 40 years later. Other things being equal, this suggests an improvement in the competitiveness of UK products. In other words, Americans wanting to buy UK goods got more pounds for their dollars in 2012 than in 1972 and thus would have tended to find UK goods more attractive.

However, some care is needed because other things do not remain equal. In particular, remember that the competitiveness of UK goods in the US market depends not only on the exchange rate but also on movements in the prices of goods over time, so this needs to be taken into account — which is why Figure 17.6 refers to the *nominal exchange rate*. In other words, if the prices of UK goods have risen more rapidly than prices in the USA, this will have partly offset the downward movement in the exchange rate.

Figure 17.7 shows the nominal exchange rate again, but also the ratio of UK/US consumer prices (plotted using the right-hand scale).

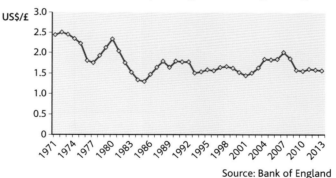

Source: Bank of England

Figure 17.6 The nominal exchange rate, US$/£, 1971–2013

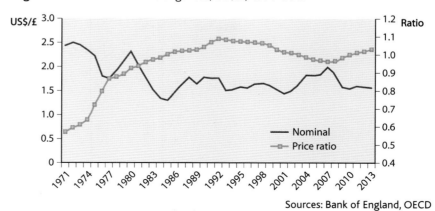

Sources: Bank of England, OECD

Figure 17.7 The nominal exchange rate, US$/£, and the ratio of UK/US prices, 1971–2013

This reveals that between 1971 and 1977 UK prices rose much more steeply than those in the USA and continued to rise relative to the USA until the 1990s. Thus, the early decline in the nominal exchange rate was offset by the movement in relative prices.

In order to assess the overall competitiveness of UK goods compared with the USA, it is necessary to calculate the **real exchange rate**, which is defined as the nominal exchange rate multiplied by the ratio of relative prices.

The real exchange rate is shown in Figure 17.8. The real exchange rate also shows some fluctuations, especially between about 1977 and 1989. However, there does not seem to be any strong trend to the series, although the real rate was higher at the end of the period than at the beginning.

Notice that the series in Figure 17.8 relates only to competitiveness relative to the USA, as it is the real US\$/£ exchange rate. The exchange rate between the currencies of two countries is a *bilateral exchange rate*, and this provides information about the relative competitiveness of goods in the two countries concerned. However, to examine the overall international competitiveness of a country's exports, it is important to recognise that a country like the UK has a variety of trading partners. An alternative measure is the sterling **effective exchange rate**, shown in Figure 17.9. This shows the strength of sterling relative to a weighted average of exchange rates of the UK's trading partners. Notice the rapid fall in this index after 2007, suggesting that the UK lost competitiveness in the financial crisis and its aftermath.

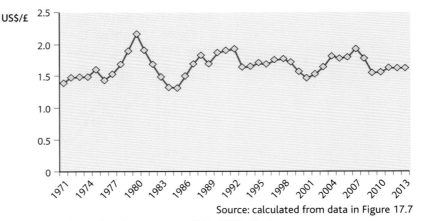

Source: calculated from data in Figure 17.7

Figure 17.8 The real exchange rate, US\$/£, 1971–2013

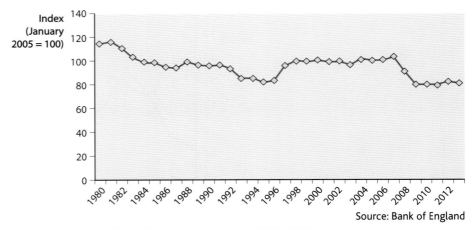

Source: Bank of England

Figure 17.9 The sterling effective exchange rate, 1980–2013

Quantitative skills 17.2

The real exchange rate

Table 17.3 provides data for the €/£ exchange rate, together with the consumer price index for the euro area and for the UK for the period from 2005 to 2013. These data can be used to calculate the real exchange rate.

Table 17.3 Competitiveness of the UK compared to the euro area

	Nominal exchange rate (€/£)	Consumer price index (2005 = 100)	
		UK	Euro area
2005	1.4629	100.0	100.0
2006	1.4670	102.4	102.2
2007	1.4619	104.8	104.4
2008	1.2588	108.6	107.8
2009	1.1233	110.9	108.1
2010	1.1664	114.5	109.9
2011	1.1527	119.7	112.9
2012	1.2337	123.0	115.7
2013	1.1776	126.2	117.3

Sources: based on data from OECD and Bank of England

To calculate the real exchange rate for 2013, the nominal exchange rate must be multiplied by the ratio of prices in the UK to the euro area. This is $1.1776 \times 126.2 \div 117.3 = 1.267$. Thus the real exchange rate had not fallen by as much as the nominal rate, because prices in the UK had risen by more than in the euro area over the period.

Exercise 17.2

Use the data in Table 17.3 to calculate the real exchange rate for each year in the period, plot the results against time and comment on the effect that any movement will have had on the competitiveness of UK goods and services relative to the euro area.

The exchange rate and the financial account

The discussion is still incomplete. The exchange rate is influenced by the demand and supply for sterling relative to other currencies, which reflects the demand from foreigners for UK goods, services and assets, and the supply of pounds from UK residents wanting to buy foreign goods, services and assets. So far the discussion has focused on the current account — in particular, on the demand and supply of goods and services. However, it is also important to be aware that international transactions in financial assets also influence (and are influenced by) the exchange rate.

Suppose that interest rates in the UK are high relative to those that prevail in the USA. American investors looking for a good return may be attracted by the prospect of investing in the UK, so there will thus tend to be an inflow of funds into the UK. This will then lead to an increase in the financial account surplus, helping to fund a current account deficit.

A further twist in the story is that if high interest rates do attract such financial inflows, this means that there is an increase in the demand for pounds, because foreign investors have to buy pounds in order to pay for the British assets that they want to acquire. This will then put upward pressure on the exchange rate, which in turn affects the international competitiveness of UK goods and services. There is therefore a link between movements in the exchange rate and the level of aggregate demand in the economy.

This close interrelationship between the current account, the financial account and the exchange rate is critical in the design of macroeconomic policy. In particular, it will be shown that the way in which the exchange rate is determined has an impact on the macroeconomic policy options open to the monetary authorities.

Summary

- The exchange rate is the price of one currency in terms of another.
- The level of the exchange rate is one influence on the competitiveness of British goods, services and assets in international markets, but this also depends upon relative prices in the UK and the rest of the world.
- The real exchange rate is a measure of the international competitiveness of an economy's goods.
- The effective exchange rate measures the relative strength of sterling compared with a weighted average of the exchange rates of the UK's trading partners.

How is the exchange rate determined?

The exchange rate has been likened to the price of a good, and thus subject to demand and supply. This being so, is the exchange rate always determined by the free interaction of demand and supply? And why does it matter? The rest of this chapter explores these important issues.

A fixed exchange rate system

In the Bretton Woods conference at the end of the Second World War, it was agreed to establish a fixed exchange rate system, under which countries would commit to maintaining the price of their currencies in terms of the US dollar. This system remained in place until the early 1970s. For example, from 1950 until 1967 the sterling exchange rate was set at $2.80, and the British government was committed to making sure that it stayed at this rate. This system became known as the Dollar Standard. Occasional changes in exchange rates were permitted after consultation, if a currency was seen to be substantially out of line — as happened for the UK in 1967.

Figure 17.10 illustrates how this works. Suppose the authorities announce that the exchange rate will be set at e_f. Given that this level is set independently by the government, it cannot be guaranteed to correspond to the market equilibrium, and in Figure 17.10 it is set above the equilibrium level. At this exchange rate the supply of pounds exceeds the demand for pounds. This can be interpreted in terms of the overall balance of payments. If there is an excess supply of pounds, the implication is that UK residents are trying to buy more American goods, services and assets than Americans are trying to buy British: in other words, there is an overall deficit on the balance of payments.

John Maynard Keynes played a leading role in the Bretton Woods conference

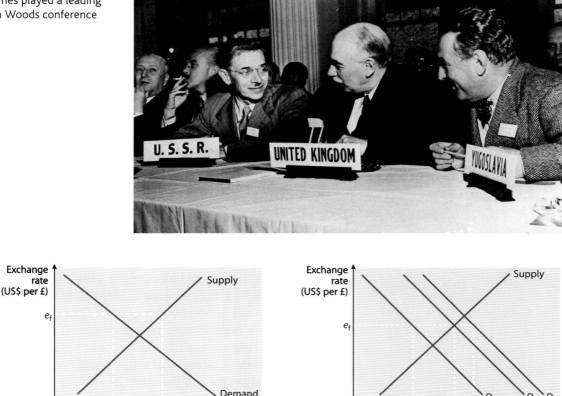

Figure 17.10 Maintaining a fixed exchange rate

Figure 17.11 Maintaining a fixed exchange rate in the face of changing demand for pounds

Key term

foreign exchange reserves stocks of foreign currency and gold owned by the central bank of a country to enable it to meet any mismatch between the demand and supply of the country's currency

In a free market, you would expect the exchange rate to adjust until the demand and supply of pounds came back into equilibrium. With the authorities committed to maintaining the exchange rate at e_f, such adjustment cannot take place. However, the UK owes the USA for the excess goods, services and assets that its residents have purchased, so the authorities then have to sell **foreign exchange reserves** in order to make the books balance.

In terms of Figure 17.10, Q_d represents the demand for pounds at e_f and Q_s represents the supply. The difference represents the amount of foreign exchange reserves that the authorities have to sell to preserve the balance of payments. Such transactions are known as 'official financing', and are incorporated into the financial account of the balance of payments.

Notice that the *position* of the demand and supply curves depends on factors other than the exchange rate that can affect the demand for British and American goods, services and assets in the respective countries. It is likely that, through time, these will shift in position. For example, if the preference of Americans for British goods changes through time, this will affect the demand for pounds.

Consider Figure 17.11. For simplicity, suppose that the supply curve remains fixed but demand shifts through time. Let e_f be the value of the exchange rate that the UK monetary authorities have undertaken

215

to maintain. If the demand for pounds is at D_1, the chosen exchange rate corresponds to the market equilibrium, and no action by the authorities is needed. If demand is at D_0, then with the exchange rate at e_f there is an excess supply of pounds (as shown in Figure 17.10). The monetary authorities in the UK need to buy up the excess supply by selling foreign exchange reserves. Conversely, if the demand for pounds is strong, say because Americans have developed a preference for Scotch whisky, then demand could be at D_2. There is now excess demand for pounds, and the British monetary authorities supply additional pounds in return for US dollars. Foreign exchange reserves thus accumulate.

In the long term, the system will operate successfully for the country so long as the chosen exchange rate is close to the average equilibrium value over time, so that the central bank is neither running down its foreign exchange reserves nor accumulating them.

Can disequilibrium be sustained?

A country that tries to hold its currency away from equilibrium indefinitely will find this problematic in the long run. For example, in the early years of the twenty-first century China and some other Asian economies were pegging their currencies against the US dollar at such a low level that they were accumulating foreign exchange. In the case of China, it was accumulating substantial amounts of US government stock. The low exchange rate had the effect of keeping the exports of these countries highly competitive in world markets. However, such a strategy relies on being able to continue to expand domestic production to meet the high demand; otherwise inflationary pressure will begin to build.

'Stop–go'

During the period of the Dollar Standard, the pound was probably set at too high a level, which meant that British exports were relatively uncompetitive, and in 1967 the British government announced a **devaluation** of the pound from $2.80 to $2.40.

During the Dollar Standard period, the British economy went through what became known as a 'stop–go' cycle of growth. When the government tried to stimulate economic growth, the effect was to suck in imports, as the marginal propensity to import was high. The effect of this was to generate a deficit on the current account of the balance of payments, which then needed to be financed by selling foreign exchange reserves.

This process has two effects. First of all, in selling foreign exchange reserves, domestic money supply increases, which then puts upward pressure on prices, threatening inflation. In addition, the Bank of England has finite foreign exchange reserves, and cannot allow them to be run down indefinitely. This meant that the government had to rein in the economy, thereby slowing the rate of growth again; hence the label 'stop–go'.

An important point emerges from this discussion. The fact that intervention to maintain the exchange rate affects domestic money supply means that under a fixed exchange rate regime the monetary authorities are unable to pursue an independent monetary policy. In other words, money supply and the exchange rate cannot be controlled independently of one another. Effectively, the money supply has to be targeted to maintain the value of the currency.

The effects of devaluation

During the stop–go period there were many debates about whether there should be a devaluation. The effect of devaluation is to improve competitiveness. At a lower value of the pound, you would expect an increase in the demand for exports and a fall in the demand for imports, *ceteris paribus*.

However, this does not necessarily mean that there will be an improvement in the current account. One reason for this concerns the elasticity of supply of exports and import substitutes. If domestic producers do not have spare capacity, or if there are time lags before production for export can be increased, then exports will not expand quickly in the short run, and so the impact of this action on exports will be limited. Furthermore, similar arguments apply to producers of goods that are potential substitutes for imported products, which reinforces the sluggishness of adjustment. In the short run, therefore, it may be that the current account will worsen rather than improve, in spite of the change in the competitiveness of domestic firms.

The J-curve effect

This is known as the J-curve effect, and is shown in Figure 17.12. Time is measured on the horizontal axis, and the current account is initially in deficit. A devaluation at time *A* initially pushes the current account further into deficit because of the inelasticity of domestic supply. Only after time *B*, when domestic firms have had time to expand their output to meet the demand for exports, does the current account move into surplus.

A second consideration relates to the elasticity of demand for exports and imports. Again, if competitiveness improves but demand does not respond strongly, there may be a negative impact on the current account. If the demand for exports is price inelastic, a fall in price will lead to a fall in revenue. There is reason to expect that the demand for exports is relatively inelastic in the short run. In many cases, exports may be supplied under contracts that cannot be immediately renegotiated. Furthermore, people and firms may wait to see whether the devaluation is permanent or temporary, and thus not revise their spending plans in the short run.

The Marshall–Lerner condition

The *Marshall–Lerner condition* states that devaluation will have a positive effect on the current account only if the sum of the elasticities of demand for exports and imports is negative and numerically greater than 1. If there is a devaluation, there will be a quantity effect and a price effect. At the new exchange rate, the quantity effect on the trade balance will be positive because exports tend to increase and imports to decrease. However, there is also a negative price effect, because export prices in terms of foreign currency have fallen and import prices in domestic currency have risen. The trade balance (measured in revenue terms) will improve only if the quantity effect fully offsets the price effect — in other words, if the Marshall–Lerner condition holds true.

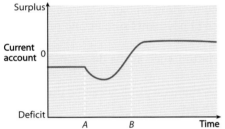

Figure 17.12 The J-curve effect of a devaluation

The end of the Dollar Standard

The Bretton Woods Dollar Standard broke down in the early 1970s. Part of the reason for this was that such a system depends critically on the stability of the base currency (i.e. the US dollar). During the 1960s the USA's need to finance the Vietnam War meant that the supply of dollar currency began to expand, one result of which was accelerating inflation in the countries that were fixing their currency in terms of the US dollar. It then became increasingly difficult to sustain exchange rates at fixed levels. The UK withdrew from the Dollar Standard in June 1972.

Summary

- After the Bretton Woods conference at the end of the Second World War, the Dollar Standard was established, under which countries agreed to maintain the value of their currencies in terms of US dollars.
- In order to achieve this, the monetary authorities engaged in foreign currency transactions to ensure that the exchange rate was maintained at the agreed level, accumulating foreign exchange reserves to accommodate a balance of payments surplus and running down the reserves to fund a deficit.
- Occasional realignments were permitted, such as the devaluation of sterling in 1967.
- Under a fixed exchange rate system, monetary policy can be used only to achieve the exchange rate target.
- A devaluation has the effect of improving international competitiveness, but the effect on the current account depends upon the elasticity of demand for exports and imports.
- The current account may deteriorate in the short run if the supply response is sluggish.
- The Bretton Woods system broke down in the early 1970s.

Exercise 17.3

A firm wants to purchase a machine tool which is obtainable in the UK for a price of £125,000, or from a US supplier for $300,000. Suppose that the exchange rate is fixed at £1 = $3.

a What is the sterling price of the machine tool if the firm chooses to buy in the USA?

b From which supplier would the firm be likely to purchase?

c Suppose that, between ordering the machine tool and its delivery, the UK government announces a devaluation of sterling, so that when the time comes for the firm to pay up the exchange rate is £1 = $2. What is the sterling price of the machine tool bought from the USA?

d Comment on how the competitiveness of British goods has been affected.

e Discuss the effects that the devaluation is likely to have on the economy as a whole.

Floating exchange rates

Under a floating exchange rate system, the value of the currency is allowed to find its own way to equilibrium. This means that the overall balance of payments is automatically assured, and the monetary authorities do not need to intervene to make sure it happens. In practice, however, governments have tended to be wary of leaving the exchange rate entirely to market forces, and there have been occasional periods in which intervention has been used to affect the market rate.

An example of this was the **Exchange Rate Mechanism (ERM)**, which was set up by a group of European countries in 1979 with the objective of keeping member countries' currencies relatively stable against each other. This was part of the European Monetary System (EMS). Each member nation agreed to keep its currency within 2.25% of a weighted average of the members' currencies, known as the European Currency Unit (ECU). This was an *adjustable peg* system. Eleven realignments were permitted between 1979 and 1987.

The UK opted not to join the ERM when it was first set up, but started shadowing the Deutschmark in the mid-1980s, aiming to keep the rate at around DM3 to the pound, as you can see in Figure 17.13. The UK finally decided to become a full member of the ERM in September 1990. However, the rate at which sterling had been set against the Deutschmark was relatively high, and the situation was worsened by the effects of German reunification, which led to substantial capital flows into Germany, reinforcing the overvaluation of sterling. Once it became apparent that sterling was overvalued, speculative attacks began, and the Bank of England's foreign exchange reserves were depleted; in 1992 the pound left the ERM. You can see in Figure 17.13 that the value of the pound fell rapidly after exit.

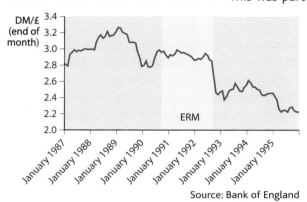

Source: Bank of England

Figure 17.13 The nominal DM/£ exchange rate, 1987–1995

What factors affect exchange rates?

If the foreign exchange market is left free to find its own way to equilibrium, it becomes important to consider what factors will influence the level of the exchange rate. In particular, will the exchange rate resulting from market equilibrium be consistent with the government's domestic policy objectives?

Extension material

Exchange rate equilibrium also implies a zero overall balance of payments. If the exchange rate always adjusts to the level that ensures this, it might be argued that the long-run state of the economy is one in which the competitiveness of domestic firms remains constant over time. In other words, you would expect the exchange rate to adjust through time to offset any differences in inflation rates between countries. The **purchasing power parity theory of exchange rates** argues that this is exactly what should be expected in the long run. The nominal exchange rate should adjust in such a way as to offset changes in relative prices between countries.

In financial markets, 'hot money' moves swiftly around the world in search of the best return

Key term

hot money stocks of funds that are moved around the world from country to country in search of the best return

In the short run the exchange rate may diverge from its long-run equilibrium. An important influence on the exchange rate in the short run is speculation. So far, the discussion of the exchange rate has stressed mainly the current account of the balance of payments. However, the financial account is also significant, especially since regulation of the movement of financial capital was removed. Some of these capital movements are associated with direct investment, but sometimes there are also substantial movements of what has come to be known as **hot money**: that is, stocks of funds that are moved around the globe from country to country in search of the best return. The size of the stocks of hot money is enormous, and can significantly affect exchange rates in the short run. Changes in the domestic real interest rate can have a significant effect on these flows.

Such movements can influence the exchange rate in the short run. The returns to be gained from such capital flows depend on the relative interest rate in the country targeted, and on the expected exchange rate in the future, which in turn may depend on expectations about inflation.

Suppose you are an investor holding assets denominated in US dollars, and the UK interest rate is 2% higher than that in the USA. You may be tempted to shift the funds into the UK in order to take advantage of the higher interest rate. However, if you believe that the exchange rate is above its long-run equilibrium, and therefore is likely to fall, this will affect your expected return on holding a British asset. Indeed, if investors holding British assets expect the exchange rate to fall, they are likely to shift their funds out of the country as soon as possible — which may then have the effect of pushing down the exchange rate. In other words, this may be a self-fulfilling prophecy. However, speculators may also react to news in an unpredictable way, so not all speculative capital movements act to influence the exchange rate towards its long-run equilibrium value.

Speculation was a key contributing factor in the unfolding of the Asian financial crisis of 1997. Substantial flows of capital had moved into Thailand in search of high returns, and speculators came to believe that the Thai currency (the baht) was overvalued. Outward capital flows put pressure on the exchange rate, and although the Thai central bank tried to resist, it eventually ran down its reserves to the point where it had to devalue. This then sparked off capital flows from other countries in the region, including South Korea.

Summary

- Under a floating exchange rate system, the value of a currency is allowed to find its own way to equilibrium without government intervention.
- This means that an overall balance of payments of zero is automatically achieved.
- The purchasing power parity theory argues that the exchange rate will adjust in the long run to maintain international competitiveness, by offsetting differences in inflation rates between countries.
- In the short run, the exchange rate may diverge from this long-run level, particularly because of speculation.
- The exchange rate is thus influenced by relative interest rates and expected inflation, as well as by news about the economic environment.

Fixed or floating?

In evaluating whether a fixed or a floating regime is to be preferred, there are many factors to be taken into account; this section will consider three of them. First, it is important to examine the extent to which the respective systems can accommodate and adjust to external shocks that push the economy out of equilibrium. Second, it is important to consider the stability of each of the systems. Finally, there is the question of which system best encourages governments to adopt sound macroeconomic policies.

Adjustment to shocks

Every economy has to cope with external shocks that occur for reasons outside the control of the country. A key question in evaluating exchange rate systems is whether there is an effective mechanism that allows the economy to return to equilibrium after an external shock.

Under a floating exchange rate system, much of the burden of adjustment is taken up by changes in the exchange rate. For example, if an economy finds itself experiencing faster inflation than other countries, perhaps because those other countries have introduced policies to reduce inflation, then the exchange rate will adjust automatically to restore competitiveness.

However, if the country is operating a fixed exchange rate system, the authorities are committed to maintaining the exchange rate, and this has to take precedence. Thus, the only way to restore competitiveness is by deflating the economy in order to bring inflation into line with other countries. This is likely to bring with it a transitional cost in terms of higher unemployment and slower economic growth. In other words, the burden of adjustment is on the real economy, rather than on allowing the exchange rate to adjust.

The Bretton Woods system operated for more than 20 years in a period in which many economies enjoyed steady economic growth. However, in the UK the system brought about a stop–go cycle, in which the need to maintain the exchange rate hampered economic growth, because of the tendency for growth to lead to an increase in imports and thus to a current account deficit. The increasing differences between inflation rates in different countries led to the final collapse of the system, suggesting that it was unable to cope with such variation.

Key terms

floating exchange rate a system in which the exchange rate is permitted to find its own level in the market

fixed exchange rate a system in which the government of a country agrees to fix the value of its currency in terms of that of another country

Furthermore, a flexible exchange rate system allows the authorities to utilise monetary policy in order to stabilise the economy — remember that under a fixed exchange rate system, monetary policy has to be devoted to the exchange rate target.

Stability

When it comes to stability, a fixed exchange rate system has much to commend it. After all, if firms know that the government is committed to maintaining the exchange rate at a given level, they can agree future contracts with some confidence. Under a floating exchange rate system, trading takes place in an environment in which the future exchange rate has to be predicted. If the exchange rate moves adversely, firms then face potential losses from trading. This foreign exchange risk is reduced under a fixed rate regime.

Macroeconomic policy

Critics of the flexible exchange rate system argue that it is too flexible for its own good. If governments know that the exchange rate will always adjust to maintain international competitiveness, they may have no incentive to behave responsibly in designing macroeconomic policy. Thus, they may be tempted to adopt an inflationary domestic policy, secure in the knowledge that the exchange rate will bear the burden of adjustment. In other words, a flexible exchange rate system does not impose financial discipline on individual countries.

An example of this was seen in the UK in the early 1970s when the country first moved to a floating exchange rate regime. Money supply was allowed to expand rapidly, and inflation increased to almost 25%, aided by the oil price shock. Other examples are evident in Latin America, where hyperinflation affected many countries during the 1980s and early 1990s. For the country itself, such policies are costly in the long run, as reducing inflation under flexible exchange rates is costly. If interest rates are increased in order to reduce domestic aggregate demand and thus reduce inflationary pressure, the high return on domestic assets encourages an inflow of hot money, thereby putting upward pressure on the exchange rate. This reduces the international competitiveness of domestic goods and services, and deepens the recession.

There may also be spillover effects on other countries. Suppose that two countries have been experiencing rapid inflation, and one of them decides to tackle the problem. It raises interest rates to dampen domestic aggregate demand, which leads to an **appreciation** of its currency. For the other country, the effect is a **depreciation** of the currency. (If one currency appreciates, the other must depreciate.) The other country thus finds that its competitive position has improved, and it faces inflationary pressure in the short run. It may then also choose to tackle inflation, which in turn will affect the other country. These spillover effects could be minimised if the countries were to harmonise their policy action.

Key terms

appreciation a rise in the exchange rate within a floating exchange rate system

depreciation a fall in the exchange rate within a floating exchange rate system

Study tip

Make sure that you can distinguish between a depreciation and a devaluation, and between an appreciation and a revaluation.

The exchange rate and macroeconomic policy

The discussion above has shown that the relationship between the exchange rate and macroeconomic policy is an important one. Under a fixed exchange rate system, the need to maintain the value of the currency is a constraint on macroeconomic policy, and forces the economy to adjust to disequilibrium through the real economy. On the other hand, it does have the benefit of imposing financial discipline on governments.

Under floating exchange rates the relationship with policy is less obvious. With a flexible exchange rate, the authorities can use monetary policy to stabilise the economy, knowing that there will be overall balance on the balance of payments. Nonetheless, the government needs to monitor the structure of the balance of payments. When interest rates are set at a relatively high level compared with other countries, the financial account will tend to be in surplus because of capital inflows, with a corresponding deficit on the current account. This may not be sustainable in the long run.

Some attempts have been made to devise a *hybrid exchange rate system* that captures some of the benefits of both fixed and floating regimes. One example is the *crawling peg* system, by which exchange rates were mainly fixed but could be adjusted occasionally as conditions required. Some countries have pegged their currency to a basket of currencies rather than to a single currency in the hope that this will provide more stability. Another intermediate system is where a country allows its currency to float, but nonetheless intervenes in the exchange market from time to time in order to influence the path of the economy. China is an example of a regime in which the exchange rate was floated, but with intervention by the authorities to maintain the competitiveness of exports, which were seen as the driver of economic growth.

China intervenes in the exchange market to maintain the competitiveness of its exports

Critically evaluate the following statements, and discuss whether you regard fixed or floating exchange rates as the better system.

a A flexible exchange rate regime is better able to cope with external shocks.

b A fixed exchange rate system provides a more stable trading environment and minimises risk.

c Floating exchange rates enable individual countries to follow independent policies.

Summary

- There are strengths and weaknesses with both fixed and floating exchange rate systems. A floating exchange rate system is more robust in enabling economies to adjust following external shocks, but it can lead to volatility and thus discourage international trade.
- The move towards a fixed exchange rate system within the European Union is partly in recognition that international trade is encouraged by stability in trading arrangements.
- Under a floating exchange rate system, much of the burden of adjustment to external shocks is borne by changes in the exchange rate, rather than by variations in the level of economic activity, which may be affected more under a fixed exchange rate system.
- A fixed exchange rate system offers stability, in the sense that firms know the future value of the currency, whereas under a floating rate regime there is more volatility.
- A fixed exchange rate system imposes discipline upon governments, and may facilitate international policy harmonisation.

Case study 17.1

Balancing the balance of payments

There are many ways in which the overall balance of the balance of payments can be achieved — which sometimes becomes controversial.

One way in which the balance of payments is made to balance is through allowing the exchange rate to respond to the relative levels of supply and demand in the foreign exchange market. In other words, if the exchange rate is free to find its market level, it will tend to move to equalise the demand and supply of currency.

However, the balance of payments depends not only on trade in goods and services, but also on transactions in financial assets. The demand for a country's financial assets depends not only on the exchange rate, but also on the relative rate of interest in different countries. If UK interest rates are high compared with those elsewhere in the world, there will tend to be an inflow of financial capital. The resulting financial surplus will tend to cause the exchange rate to appreciate. This in turn affects the competitiveness of domestic goods and services, so the net result may be that the financial account surplus will be offset by a deficit on the current account.

Some countries have chosen to treat the balance of payments in a different way, by fixing the exchange rate in terms of some other currency, such as the US dollar. What this means is that any surplus or deficit

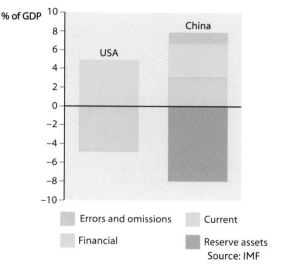

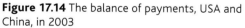

Source: IMF

Figure 17.14 The balance of payments, USA and China, in 2003

on current or financial accounts must be offset by the purchase or sale of reserve assets (that is, financial assets denominated in terms of US dollars) in order to maintain the price of the currency.

The choice between fixing the exchange rate and allowing it to find its market value has a major effect on the structure of the balance of payments. This is illustrated in Figure 17.14, which shows the structure of the balance of payments for the USA and China in 2003.

Case study 17.1 (continued)

In the USA, where the exchange rate is allowed to find its own market value, the accounts reveal a substantial current account deficit (amounting to nearly 5% of GDP), balanced by a financial account surplus. In contrast, China shows surpluses on both the current and the financial account, balanced by substantial transactions in reserve assets, showing that the Chinese authorities have been artificially holding the value of their currency away from its equilibrium value.

Why should they want to do this? One reason is that it has allowed China to maintain rapid growth in exports, by keeping its goods highly competitive in international markets, while at the same time attracting flows of inward foreign direct investment. In order to do this, it has had to purchase US dollar-denominated assets — such as US Treasury Bills. In turn, this has allowed the USA to maintain its current account deficit, funded partly by the sale of Treasury Bills.

Follow-up questions
a Discuss this from the perspective of China. What are the benefits of this strategy — and what are the risks?
b Now view the strategy from the USA's viewpoint. Why do you think that the USA has been trying to persuade China to revalue its currency?

Macroeconomics key terms

absolute advantage a country's ability to produce a good using less resources than another country

aggregate demand (*AD*) curve the relationship between the level of aggregate demand and the overall price level; it shows planned expenditure at any given possible overall price level

appreciation a rise in the exchange rate within a floating exchange rate system

automatic stabilisers effects by which government expenditure adjusts to offset the effects of recession and boom without the need for active intervention

average propensity to consume the proportion of income that households devote to consumer expenditure

balance of payments a set of accounts showing the transactions conducted between residents of a country and the rest of the world

bank rate the interest rate that is set by the Monetary Policy Committee of the Bank of England in order to influence inflation

Canons of Taxation four maxims devised by Adam Smith, setting out the characteristics of a good tax

capital account of the balance of payments account identifying transactions in (physical) capital between the residents of a country and the rest of the world

capital productivity measure of output per unit of capital

claimant count of unemployment the number of people claiming the Jobseeker's Allowance each month

comparative advantage a country's ability to produce a good *relatively* more efficiently (i.e. at lower opportunity cost) than another country

consumer price index (CPI) a measure of the general level of prices in the UK, adopted as the government's inflation target since December 2003

consumption function the relationship between consumer expenditure and disposable income; its position depends upon the other factors that affect how much households spend on consumer expenditure

cost-push inflation inflation initiated by an increase in the costs faced by firms, arising on the supply side of the economy

current account of the balance of payments account identifying transactions in goods and services between the residents of a country and the rest of the world

cyclical unemployment unemployment that arises during the downturn of the economic cycle, such as a recession

deflation a situation in which the average level of prices is falling — this is negative inflation

demand-deficient unemployment unemployment that arises because of a deficiency of aggregate demand in the economy, so that the equilibrium level of output is below full employment

demand-pull inflation inflation initiated by an increase in aggregate demand

depreciation a fall in the exchange rate within a floating exchange rate system; a fall in value of physical capital equipment over time as it is subject to wear and tear

devaluation process whereby a government reduces the price of its currency relative to an agreed rate in terms of foreign currency

discouraged workers people who have been unable to find employment and who are no longer looking for work

disposable income the income that households have to devote to consumption and saving, taking into account payments of direct taxes and transfer payments

economically inactive those people of working age who are not looking for work, for a variety of reasons

effective exchange rate the exchange rate for a country relative to a weighted average of currencies of its trading partners

exchange rate the price of one currency in terms of another

Exchange Rate Mechanism (ERM) a system that was set up by a group of European countries in 1979 with the objective of keeping member countries' currencies relatively stable against each other

financial account of the balance of payments account identifying transactions in financial assets between the residents of a country and the rest of the world

fiscal policy decisions made by the government on its expenditure, taxation and borrowing

fixed exchange rate a system in which the government of a country agrees to fix the value of its currency in terms of that of another country

flat-rate tax system a system of income tax in which each taxpayer pays the same rate of tax on income

floating exchange rate a system in which the exchange rate is permitted to find its own level in the market

foreign exchange reserves stocks of foreign currency and gold owned by the central bank of a country to enable it to meet any mismatch between the demand and supply of the country's currency

frictional unemployment unemployment associated with job search: that is, people who are between jobs

full employment a situation where people who are economically active in the workforce and are willing and able to work (at going wage rates) are able to find employment

GDP per capita the average level of GDP per head of population

General Agreement on Tariffs and Trade (GATT) the precursor of the WTO, which organised a series of 'rounds' of tariff reductions

globalisation a process by which the world's economies are becoming more closely integrated

government budget deficit (surplus) the balance between government expenditure and revenue

hot money stocks of funds that are moved around the world from country to country in search of the best return

human capital the stock of skills and expertise that contribute to a worker's productivity; can be increased through education and training

ILO unemployment rate measure of the percentage of the workforce who are without jobs, but are available for work, willing to work and looking for work

in employment people who are either working for firms or other organisations, or are self-employed

index number a device for comparing the value of a variable in one period or location with a base observation (e.g. the retail price index measures the average level of prices relative to a base period)

inflation the rate of change of the average price level: for example, the percentage annual rate of change of the CPI

inflation targeting an approach to macroeconomic policy whereby the central bank is charged with meeting a target for inflation

investment expenditure undertaken by firms to add to the capital stock

invisible trade trade in services

involuntary unemployment situation arising when an individual who would like to accept a job at the going wage rate is unable to find employment

Keynesian School a group of economists who believed that the macroeconomy could settle at an equilibrium that was below full employment

labour productivity measure of output per worker, or output per hour worked

law of comparative advantage a theory arguing that there may be gains from trade arising when countries specialise in the production of goods or services in which they have a comparative advantage

long-run economic growth the expansion of the productive capacity of an economy

macroeconomics the study of the interrelationships between economic variables at an aggregate (macroeconomic) level

marginal propensity to consume the proportion of additional income devoted to consumer expenditure

marginal propensity to import the proportion of additional income that is spent on imports of goods and services

marginal propensity to save the proportion of additional income that is saved by households

marginal propensity to tax the proportion of additional income that is taxed

marginal propensity to withdraw the proportion of additional income that is withdrawn from the circular flow — the sum of the marginal propensities to save, import and tax

Monetarist School a group of economists who believed that the macroeconomy always adjusts rapidly to the full employment level of output

monetary policy the decisions made by government regarding monetary variables such as the money supply and the interest rate

Monetary Policy Committee body within the Bank of England responsible for the conduct of monetary policy

money stock the quantity of money in the economy

multinational corporation (MNC) a company whose production activities are carried out in more than one country

multiplier the ratio of a change in equilibrium real income to the autonomous change that brought it about; it is defined as 1 divided by the marginal propensity to withdraw

natural rate of output the long-run equilibrium level of output to which monetarists believe the macroeconomy will always tend; corresponds to full employment

net investment gross investment *minus* depreciation

nominal value value of an economic variable based on current prices, taking no account of changing prices through time

productivity measure of the efficiency of a factor of production

purchasing power parity theory of exchange rates theory stating that in the long run exchange rates (in a floating rate system) are determined by relative inflation rates in different countries

quantitative easing a process by which the central bank purchases assets such as government and corporate bonds in order to release additional money into the financial system

real exchange rate the nominal exchange rate adjusted for differences in relative inflation rates between countries

real value value of an economic variable, taking account of changing prices through time

recession occurs when GDP falls for two or more consecutive quarters

retail price index (RPI) a measure of the average level of prices in the UK

revaluation process whereby a government raises the price of domestic currency in terms of foreign currency

seasonal unemployment unemployment that arises in seasons of the year when demand is relatively low

short-run aggregate supply curve a curve showing how much output firms would be prepared to supply in the short run at any given overall price level

short-run economic growth an increase in actual GDP

structural unemployment unemployment arising because of changes in the pattern of economic activity within an economy

supply-side policies range of measures intended to have a direct impact on aggregate supply — and specifically the potential capacity output of the economy

sustainable development 'development that meets the needs of the present without compromising the ability of future generations to meet their own needs' (Brundtland Commission, 1987)

terms of trade the relative prices at which exchange takes place; the ratio of export prices to import prices

total factor productivity the average productivity of all factors, measured as the total output divided by the total amount of inputs used

trading possibilities curve shows the consumption possibilities under conditions of free trade

unemployed people who are economically active but not in employment

visible trade trade in goods

voluntary unemployment situation arising when an individual chooses not to accept a job at the going wage rate

workforce people who are economically active — either in employment or unemployed

World Trade Organization (WTO) a multilateral body now responsible for overseeing the conduct of international trade

Macroeconomics practice questions

Part 4: Economic policy objectives and indicators of macroeconomic performance

1 Explain the difference between nominal and real GDP.

2 **a** 'China's rate of economic growth fell from 9.2% in 2011 to 7.8% in 2012.'
   With reference to the above statement, explain what happened to China's output between 2011 and 2012.

   b 'Brazil's rate of inflation fell from 6.5% in 2011 to 5.5% in 2012.'
   With reference to the above statement, explain what happened to the level of prices in Brazil between 2011 and 2012.

3 Using a production possibility diagram, show the impact of economic growth.

4 Explain how the consumer price index measure of inflation is constructed.

5 Outline **three** differences between the claimant count and ILO measures of unemployment.

6 The UK's rate of inflation was 5.2% in September 2011 but by December 2012 it had fallen to 2.7% as measured by the consumer price index (CPI).

   a Why do the weights used in the CPI have to be changed each year?

   b Explain **two** consequences of a fall in the rate of inflation.

7 In February 2008, the claimant count measure of unemployment was 710,000 but by December 2012 it was 1.56 million. During the same period, ILO unemployment rose from 1.62 million to 2.49 million.

   a Explain how unemployment is measured using the claimant count method and the ILO method.

   b Explain **two** costs of the increase in unemployment.

Part 5: Aggregate demand and aggregate supply

1 Aggregate demand

At the time of the economic crisis in 2008 and 2009, the savings ratio increased significantly from just over 2% to nearly 9%. Consumer expenditure fell, following falling real incomes, even though interest rates were reduced to just 0.5%. Investment has remained low since 2009 because confidence has been low — partly because of the crisis in the euro zone, which has resulted in slow growth in those countries. Despite a 25% fall in the value of sterling, the UK's trade balance remained in deficit and between 2011 and 2012 the deficit increased from £23bn to £37bn.

Although house prices fell sharply in 2009 and again slightly in 2011, there is an expectation that they will increase from 2013.

   a With reference to the information provided, outline the components of aggregate demand.

   b Discuss **two** factors which influence consumer expenditure.

c Explain the impact on aggregate demand of the change in the UK's trade deficit between 2011 and 2012.

d Examine the likely effect of a fall in the rate of interest on investment.

e Apart from the rate of interest, explain **two** factors which influence the level of investment.

f Analyse how the increase in the savings ratio in 2008–09 will affect the value of the multiplier.

g Assess the likely effects of an increase in house prices on aggregate demand.

2 Aggregate supply

Since the 1980s, economic policy in many countries has focused on measures to increase aggregate supply. Despite the success of some of these measures, supply-side shocks such as increases in oil prices have often had the reverse effect. More recently, many governments have been trying to reduce their budget deficits by making steep cuts in public expenditure which, in the case of the UK, have fallen heavily on capital expenditure.

a Explain the meaning of 'aggregate supply'.

b With the aid of an aggregate demand and aggregate supply diagram, assess the likely effects on real output and the price level of a sharp increase in oil prices.

c Analyse the effect of a decrease in public expenditure on real output and the price level. Refer to the multiplier in your answer.

d Productivity has increased more rapidly in the USA than in the UK. Illustrating your answer with an aggregate demand and aggregate supply diagram, analyse the effect of this increase in US productivity.

Part 6: The application of policy instruments

1 Analyse the likely effect of increasing public expenditure on interest rates and private sector investment.

2 Explain how expansionary fiscal policy in the form of higher expenditure on infrastructure might have an impact on aggregate demand and aggregate supply. Illustrate your answer with an appropriate diagram.

3 To what extent might an increase in the size of public expenditure as a proportion of GDP be likely to increase the rate of economic growth?

4 Assess the effect of a reduction in interest rates and an increase in the quantity of money on unemployment and the rate of inflation.

5 Evaluate the effect of expansionary monetary policy on the value of the pound, real output and the rate of inflation.

6 Fiscal and monetary policy

Following the financial crisis in 2008, many governments and central banks used monetary and fiscal policy in order to prevent a depression. In the UK the Bank of England slashed the base interest rate to 0.5% and embarked on a policy of quantitative easing. Increased public expenditure and tax cuts resulted in an increase in the fiscal deficit. As a result of these policies and the perceived weakness of the UK economy, the value of the pound depreciated by about 25%. Some economists have suggested that new supply-side policies need to be adopted to improve long-term growth and living standards.

a Distinguish between fiscal and monetary policy.

b Explain what is meant by 'an increase in the fiscal deficit'.

c Illustrating your answer with an aggregate demand and aggregate supply diagram, evaluate the likely effect of an increase in the budget deficit on the level of real output and on the price level. Refer to the multiplier in your answer.

d Assess the effectiveness of supply-side policies as a means of decreasing the level of unemployment.

e Evaluate policies which a government might use to raise living standards.

Part 7: The global context

1 How will each of the following affect the exchange rate of the pound sterling?

   a A fall in demand for UK goods and services

   b A decrease in the demand for foreign imports

2 A current account deficit

Despite the 25% depreciation in the value of sterling in 2008, the UK's current account has remained in deficit. This deficit was estimated to be £56 billion in 2012, while the trade in goods deficit was over £100 billion. The continued problems in the euro zone combined with low productivity and its depleted manufacturing base have made it difficult for the UK to increase exports.

Some economists argue that a current account deficit is not significant for economic management if it can be financed by inflows into the financial account. However, others consider that such imbalances cannot be sustained in the long run and that measures should be taken to eliminate them.

   a Explain the difference between a trade in goods deficit and a current account deficit.

   b Analyse the likely impact of a depreciation in the external value of a currency on the balance of payments deficit on current account.

   c Apart from the impact on the current account of the balance of payments, examine **two** possible effects of a sharp fall in the external value of the pound.

   d Assess **two** factors which might explain the reasons for the continuation of the UK's current account deficit despite the depreciation in the value of sterling.

   e Evaluate whether a deficit on the current account of the balance payments should be a primary concern to the UK government.

3 Examine the reasons why the exchange rate of a country's currency might appreciate against that of another currency.

4 'The UK has experienced a persistent deficit on its trade balance.'

   a Assess the likely causes of the UK's trade balance deficit.

   b Evaluate measures by which the UK could reduce this deficit.

Index

Page numbers in **bold** refer to **key term definitions**.

M